THE HISTORY
OF LIBYA

THE HISTORY
OF LIBYA

Bukola A. Oyeniyi

The Greenwood Histories of the Modern Nations
Frank W. Thackeray and John E. Findling, Series Editors

An Imprint of ABC-CLIO, LLC
Santa Barbara, California • Denver, Colorado

Library of Congress Cataloging-in-Publication Data

Names: Oyeniyi, Bukola Adeyemi, author.
Title: The History of Libya / Bukola A. Oyeniyi.
Description: Santa Barbara, CA : Greenwood, an imprint of ABC-CLIO, LLC, 2019. | Series: Greenwood Histories of the Modern Nations | Includes bibliographical references and index.
Identifiers: LCCN 2018051064 (print) | LCCN 2018055847 (ebook) | ISBN 9781440856075 (ebook) | ISBN 9781440856068 (hard copy : alk. paper)
Subjects: LCSH: Libya—History.
Classification: LCC DT215 (ebook) | LCC DT215 .O94 2019 (print) | DDC 961.2—dc23
LC record available at https://lccn.loc.gov/2018051064

ISBN: 978-1-4408-5606-8 (print)
       978-1-4408-5607-5 (ebook)

23 22 21 20 19   1 2 3 4 5

This book is also available as an eBook.

Greenwood
An Imprint of ABC-CLIO, LLC

ABC-CLIO, LLC
147 Castilian Drive
Santa Barbara, California 93117
www.abc-clio.com

This book is printed on acid-free paper ∞

Manufactured in the United States of America

To Dodzi, for January 1, 2002; October 16, 2005; August 8, 2007; and February 20, 2018.

Contents

Series Foreword

The Greenwood Histories of the Modern Nations series is intended to provide students and interested laypeople with up-to-date, concise, and analytical histories of many of the nations of the contemporary world. Not since the 1960s has there been a systematic attempt to publish a series of national histories, and as series editors, we believe that this series will prove to be a valuable contribution to our understanding of other countries in our increasingly interdependent world.

At the end of the 1960s, the Cold War was an accepted reality of global politics. The process of decolonization was still in progress, the idea of a unified Europe with a single currency was unheard of, the United States was mired in a war in Vietnam, and the economic boom in Asia was still years in the future. Richard Nixon was president of the United States, Mao Tse-tung (not yet Mao Zedong) ruled China, Leonid Brezhnev guided the Soviet Union, and Harold Wilson was prime minister of the United Kingdom. Authoritarian dictators still controlled most of Latin America, the Middle East was reeling in the wake of the Six-Day War, and Shah Mohammad Reza Pahlavi was at the height of his power in Iran.

Since then, the Cold War has ended, the Soviet Union has vanished, leaving 15 independent republics in its wake, the advent of the computer age has radically transformed global communications, the rising demand for oil makes the Middle East still a dangerous flashpoint, and the rise of new economic powers like the People's Republic of China and India threatens to bring about a new world order. All of these developments have had a dramatic impact on the recent history of every nation of the world.

For this series, which was launched in 1998, we first selected nations whose political, economic, and sociocultural affairs marked them as among the most important of our time. For each nation, we found an author who was recognized as a specialist in the history of that nation. These authors worked cooperatively with us and with Greenwood Press to produce volumes that reflected current research on their nations and that are interesting and informative to their readers. In the first decade of the series, close to 50 volumes were published, and some have now moved into second editions.

The success of the series has encouraged us to broaden our scope to include additional nations, whose histories have had significant effects on their regions, if not on the entire world. In addition, geopolitical changes have elevated other nations into positions of greater importance in world affairs, and, so we have chosen to include them in this series as well. The importance of a series such as this cannot be underestimated. As a superpower whose influence is felt all over the world, the United States can claim a "special" relationship with almost every other nation. Yet many Americans know very little about the histories of nations with which the United States relates. How did they get to be the way they are? What kind of political systems have evolved there? What kind of influence do they have on their own regions? What are the dominant political, religious, and cultural forces that move their leaders? These and many other questions are answered in the volumes of this series.

The authors who contribute to this series write comprehensive histories of their nations, dating back, in some instances, to prehistoric times. Each of them, however, has devoted a significant portion of their book to events of the past 40 years because the modern era has contributed the most to contemporary issues that have an impact on U.S. policy. Authors make every effort to be as up-to-date as possible so that readers can benefit from discussion and analysis of recent events.

In addition to the historical narrative, each volume contains an introductory chapter giving an overview of that country's geography, political institutions, economic structure, and cultural attributes. This is meant to give readers a snapshot of the nation as it exists in the contemporary world. Each history also includes supplementary information following the narrative, which may include a timeline that represents a succinct chronology of the nation's historical evolution, biographical sketches of the nation's most important historical figures, and a glossary of important terms or concepts that are usually expressed in a foreign language. Finally, each author prepares a comprehensive bibliography for readers who wish to pursue the subject further.

Readers of these volumes will find them fascinating and well written. More importantly, they will come away with a better understanding of the contemporary world and the nations that comprise it. As series editors, we hope that this series will contribute to a heightened sense of global understanding as we move through the early years of the 21st century.

Frank W. Thackeray and John E. Findling
Indiana University Southeast

Preface

Like the history of sub-Saharan Africa in general, most literature on the history of Libya traced the history of the different African peoples who are indigenous to areas—from the fringes of the Sahara Desert to the shores of the Mediterranean Sea—to periods of foreign invasions. Susan Raven, in *Rome in Africa*, asserted that "much of the history of north-west Africa is the history of foreigners." Anthony Thwaite, in *The Desert of Hesperides*, explained Libyan history and culture as "the material leftovers of receding cultures." Dirk Vandewalle described it as "an extraordinary odyssey from Ottoman backwater to Italian colony," while John Oakes never stopped short of arrogating developments of (and in) Cyrene, Sabratha, Oea (Tripoli), and Leptis Magna to the ancient Greeks, the Phoenicians, and the Romans. John Wright, writing in 2012, described Libya as both a cultural and a historical void until the coming of invaders. He described what existed and was captured in rock art and cave paintings as mere paperweight and that Libya's real history began with invaders. These descriptions not only skewed the history of Libya as the histories and cultures of other peoples but also presented Libyan history and culture as recent. More importantly, it also denied ancient Libyans of any contribution, no matter how small, to their own history, culture, and development.

These descriptions are not only wrong but also fail to stand up to available evidence. To reduce the history and culture of Libya to mainly or exclusively the activities and cultures of invaders and colonialists— beginning with the Phoenicians in the 12th century to December 1951 when the United Nations General Assembly handed over power to King Idris al-Sanussi—is to ignore historical facts that are available in oral accounts, cave paintings, and rock art, which are found in different parts of Libya and the Sahara Desert. Besides oral traditions, cave paintings, rock art, and other material artifacts found in different parts of Libya attested to human existence, human activities, and human organization in different parts of Libya from as early as the Neolithic period— about 8000 BCE.

Although Libya is a new country, born only in 1951, the name Libya is an old one. While we might never know what the ancient people of the areas called themselves, Ancient Egyptians called the land west of Egypt Libue and inhabitants of this desert wasteland Libyans. To the early Greeks, all Africans except Egyptians were Libyans, while for the Romans, "Libyans" described all Africans living on Carthaginian territory (modern-day Tunisia).

Bordered in the north by the Mediterranean Sea, in the east by Egypt and Sudan, and in the south by Chad and Niger, while Algeria and Tunisia lay to the West, Libya's strategic location made it a gateway to three worlds—Arab, African, and Mediterranean. Libya, throughout recorded history, has consistently linked sub-Saharan Africa with socioeconomic, political, and cultural developments in Europe and Asia. Given this role, Libya has a unique identity that is African, Arabic, and Mediterranean.

Notwithstanding this unique identity, Libya is originally African. From as early as 8000 BCE, Libya's coastal plain was inhabited by Neolithic peoples. These were the Afroasiatic ancestors of the Berber people who asserted control over the areas by the Late Bronze Age. From the rock art and cave paintings that these Neolithic inhabitants left behind, we now know that the areas from the Mediterranean Sea to the West African Sahel were lush and green, filled with rivers, aquatic life, and wildlife of different kinds. The Afro-Asiatic ancestors of the Berber people not only made these areas home but also developed a complex sociocultural, economic, and political organizations that lasted for many years. Climate change, especially increasing aridity and desertification, however, caused them to flee—some to North Africa, others to West Africa.

Who were these peoples, and where are they today? Besides the Berbers, the earliest known names of such peoples include the Garamantes, who were based in Germa, the Tebous (black Africans), Harratins, and Tuaregs. These peoples can be found in different parts of Libya today. Although the largest population in Libya today is the Arabs, Arabs were originally invaders who arrived and settled in the areas only in the seventh century. They live predominantly in Tripolitania and Cyrenaica. The Berbers are the second largest population in Libya. During the Arab invasion, many Berbers escaped from the city centers into the remote areas, mountains, and the deserts in order to escape conversion to Islam. The Tuaregs, a nomadic people, live around oases and are therefore in scattered communities and towns in and around Ghat and Ghadamis. The Tebou live in well populated border communities along northern Chad, Sudan, and Niger Republic.

Except for the Berbers, most ancient Libyans lived far away from the three main regions of Fezzan, Tripolitania, and Cyrenaica. While this might explain why they have been denied their rightful places as owners of Libya in most literature, it ensured that their cultures, although greatly influenced both by the Mediterranean and Arabic cultures, remain essentially African.

An impregnable sea, a series of land barriers, and the Sahara Desert divided Libya into three distinct regions. In the east is Cyrenaica, Tripolitania is in the west. and in the southwest is Fezzan. These divisions play important roles in the socioeconomic and cultural developments of Libya. While Cyrenaica looks eastward to the eastern Islamic world, Tripolitania looks westward to the western Islamic world. Fezzan, which looks toward the south across the Sahara Desert, shared socioeconomic and cultural developments with central and western Africa. For thousands of years, the different areas of contemporary Libya were invaded by the Greeks in Cyrenaica in 632 BCE, the Romans in Tripolitania in 146 BCE, the Arabs in Cyrenaica, Tripolitania, and Fezzan between 644 CE and 663 CE, and Italy between 1911 and 1922 CE. Until 1922 under the Italian occupation, Cyrenaica, Tripolitania, and Fezzan were independent of one another. Notwithstanding the Italian unification of Libya, contemporary Libya is today comparable only to a bowl of salad where various ingredients are mixed but retain their unique flavors. Libya today is a mixture of African, Mediterranean, and Arabic peoples and cultures.

In general, this book surveys the history of Libya. It specifically traces the history of the various peoples who today claim Libya as their home from ancient times, where evidence is available, to the contemporary period. Among other things, the book aims at equipping students of history with verifiable historical facts about Libya. The book is also important to students of history whether in high school or college, professors or journalists, members of the diplomatic corps or any other interested men and women who desire to learn and know more about Libya, especially since the Arab Spring, the removal of Muammar Gaddafi, and the terrorist attack on the U.S. Embassy at Benghazi.

Unlike many others, this book situates Libya and Libyans—from ancient times to contemporary periods—within their own history, without denying the influences of outsiders—invaders and colonialists—in Libyans' developments and culture. Starting with the geography of Libya, the book shows the importance of geography in human existence and, in the case of Libya, how Libyan history and culture are shaped by the country's peculiar geography. Foreign invasion and colonialism also shaped Libyan history and culture. Who were these invaders? And what was their impact on Libyan history and culture?

Since its independence in 1951, the history of Libya has revolved around its erstwhile leader: Muammar Gaddafi. Who was Gaddafi, and how did he come to power? What was the nature of Gaddafi's rule in Libya? Before him, Libya had been in the international limelight. At independence in 1951, no one gave Libya a chance of survival, especially given its absolute lack of resources. However, upon the discovery of crude oil, Libya became a major player in international affairs, playing crucial roles in Africa, the Arab world, and globally.

Within Africa, Gaddafi was not just a leader of Libya; he played significant roles in African independence and in ending apartheid in South Africa. He also advocated for a United States of Africa. At the Organization of Africa Unity, a pan-African body, he also advocated for a uniform currency for the African continent. The geopolitics of the Cold War pitched Gaddafi and Libya against the United States and its allies. At the height of this geopolitical intransigence, Gaddafi and Libya were accused of a couple of state-sponsored bombings and explosions. Notable examples include the Pan Am flight over Lockerbie, Scotland; the French airliner UTA 772 over Niger; and a series of other (terrorist) bombings across the world. The resultant impasses led to a series of UN-backed sanctions against Libya and the U.S. downing of Libyan aircraft over the Gulf of Sirte—which made Libya's engagements with the wider world significant in the 1980s and 1990s.

Intermittent protests and conflicts have always occurred in Libya; however, the racial violence of September 2000 was instructive, as it showed that not all was well internally in Libya. So it took no one by surprise when on February 16, 2011, Libyans trooped out in their thousands to demand that Gaddafi, Libya's second and longest serving ruler, should abdicate.

The assassination of Gaddafi and the subsequent collapse of the Libyan state spewed military-grade ordinance, light weapons, and small arms into West Africa, much of which has found its way into the hands of terrorist groups like Nigeria's Boko Haram and Ansar Dine in Mali.

This volume explores Libya's most distant history and recent past, examining how the country came to be and the events that have shaped the country as it is today.

Acknowledgments

This work is a product of a pleasant "accident." In 2011, I was in Leiden, the Netherlands, when I got a call from Professor Toyin Falola, asking whether I would like to join his two-person team to write a book on the culture and customs of Libya. I obliged, as I had just gotten a fellowship at the Institute of Advanced Study, New Europe College, in Bucharest, Romania. I reckoned that a project of that nature would occupy my time in a new land about which I knew nothing. Perhaps Kaitlin Ciarmiello of ABC-CLIO was convinced of my ability based on the 2011 project that, in 2016, she approached me to undertake the writing of this book. As writers and authors will affirm, writing is like pregnancy. While delivery is usually expected in nine months, it could occur either early or late. Even after I failed to complete the first draft at the agreed date, not only did Kaitlin, Erin, and the editors keep their faith in me, they also continued to encourage me until the project was completed. This printed copy is not simply my effort but also theirs as well. While I did the writing, these marvelous people successfully smoothed the rough edges.

I would have wasted the efforts of Kaitlin, Erin, and the editors if not for the immense assistance of my wife and unpaid in-house editor, Doyin Oyeniyi—who painstakingly read the entire draft and remains my encourager-in-chief. Dr. Oluwafolaranmi Sodade provided me with a safe haven at his flat in Joplin where I wrote some parts of the draft, devouring his food, and gulping down his beer. My colleagues, Professors David Gutzke and John Chuchiak, cultivated the habit of coming by my office to see how "it is shaping out," their own way of saying "never give up, no matter the odds." Oluwasegun Samuel Adegoke, Sheffiq Akinwole Ariwoola, and Babatunde Adeyemi Oyebode—my buddies from the *"alalumole"* days—continued to push and encourage me from across the Atlantic. Rasheedat Egunjobi and Carolyne Moss cultivated the habit of asking for a weekly update on the book. Gals, thank you very much, the last update is simple and straightforward: The job is done.

Missouri State University provided me with the enabling environment that allowed the completion of this book. I used some portion of the book in teaching students in my spring 2018 Global Terrorism class. My students' feedback and comments enriched my thoughts on Gaddafi's role in the phenomenon of global terrorism. Finally, I thank the people of Libya, who allowed me to tell their stories and to put on record their unparalleled courage in the face of adversity. While their lives and the contributions of the aforementioned peoples and institutions played decisive roles in the making of this book, I accept sole responsibility for any shortcomings or errors in the book.

Thank you.

OBA
Springfield, Missouri

Acronyms and Abbreviations

AD	Ansar Dine
ANC	African National Congress
AQIM	Al-Qaeda in the Islamic Maghreb
ASU	Arab Socialist Union
ATC	Air Traffic Controller
AU	African Union
BMA	British Military Administration
BPC	Basic People's Congress
CIA	Central Intelligence Agency
ELNRM	Eastern Libya Native Resistance Movement
ERC	Executive Revolutionary Committee
EU	European Union
FAR	Federation of Arab Republics
FMA	French Military Administration
FOM	Free Officer Movement

FROLINAT	Front for the National Liberation of Chad
GDP	Gross Domestic Product
GNA	Government of National Accord
GNC	General National Congress
GPC	General People's Committee
HoR	House of Representatives
ICC	International Criminal Court
IED	Improvised Explosive Device
IMF	International Monetary Fund
IRA	Irish Republican Army
ISIL	Islamic State of Iraq and the Levant
ISIS	Islamic State of Iraq and Syria
IYSC	Islamic Youth Shura Council
JSO	Jamahiriya Security Organization
JSOC	Joint Special Operations Command
LIFG	Libyan Islamic Fighting Group
LROR	Libyan Revolutionary Operation Room
MOJWA	Movement for Oneness and Jihad in West Africa
MPC	Municipal People's Congress
NAC	National Association of Cyrenaica
NATO	North Atlantic Treaty Organization
NCP	National Congress Party
NSG	National Salvation Government
NTC	National Transition Council
OAPEC	Organization of Arab Petroleum Exporting Countries
OAU	Organization of African Unity
OPEC	Organization of Petroleum Exporting Countries
PFLP-GC	Popular Front for the Liberation of Palestine—General Command

PLO	Palestine Liberation Organization
RARDE	Royal Armament Research and Development Establishment
RCC	Revolutionary Command Council
SAS	Special Air Service
TAB	Technical Assistance Board
TFSL	Tebou Front for the Salvation of Libya
UNO	United Nations Organization
USA	United States of America
USSR	Union of Soviet Socialist Republics
WHO	World Health Organization
WRC	World Revolutionary Center

Timeline of Historical Events

7th century BCE	Phoenicians settle in Tripolitania, western Libya.
6th century BCE	Carthage conquers Tripolitania.
4th century BCE	Greeks colonize Cyrenaica, giving it the name of "Libya."
74 BCE	Romans conquer Libya.
643 CE	Under Amr Ibn al-As, Arabs conquer Libya as they spread Islam.
16th century	The provinces of Tripolitania, Tripoli, Cyrenaica, and Fezzan are joined into one regency, Libya, which becomes part of the Ottoman Empire.
1785	Civil war begins in Tripolitania.
1793	The civil war ends, reestablishing independence in Tripolitania.
1819	Mahmud II, the Ottoman sultan, sends troops to Libya, thereby restoring Ottoman rule in Tripolitania.
1911	Following the Italian-Turkish War, Italy defeats the Ottomans and seizes Libya.

1912   Omar al-Mukhtar begins a 20-year insurgency against Italian rule.

1920s   The Sanussi dynasty joins the al-Mukhtar campaign, leading to increasing resistance to Ottoman rule in Libya.

1931   Italy captures al-Mukhtar, breaking his resistance and sending many Libyans to concentration camps. Al-Mukhtar is executed.

1934   Italy unites all Libyan provinces, beginning the Italian colonization of Libya. Mass migration of Italians into Libya begins.

1940   Italy joins World War II, turning Libya into a home base for Italy's North African campaign.

1942   Allied forces expel the Italians from Libya and divide the country in two; the French occupies and administers Fezzan, while the British occupies and controls Cyrenaica and Tripolitania.

1947   Following a peace treaty with the Allies, Italy relinquishes all claims to Libya.

1951   Libya declares independence as the United Kingdom of Libya, with King Idris al-Sanussi as the first leader of independent Libya.

1956   Libya concedes 14 million acres of land to two American oil companies.

1961   King Idris opens a pipeline that is 104 miles long, linking the oil fields of interior Libya to the Mediterranean Sea, a development that aids in the export of Libyan oil.

1969   Col. Muammar Gaddafi and other members of the Free Officers Movement depose King Idris in a military coup.

1970   Libya begins to pursue pan-Arabism more vigorously, introducing socialism, nationalizing economic activity and property belonging to Italian settlers, including the oil industry, and seeks a merger with other Arab countries. Libya orders the closure of a British air base in Tobruk, as well as Wheelus, a U.S. Air Force base in Tripoli.

1971   Libya, Egypt, and Syria form the Federation of Arab Republics (FAR).

1973   Gaddafi declares the cultural revolution and establishes people's committees in schools, hospitals, universities, workplaces, and administrative districts. In northern Chad, Libya occupies the Aozou Strip.

1977   Gaddafi changes the country's official name from the Libyan Arab Republic to the Great Socialist People's Libyan Arab Jamahiriyah, stating he is a symbolic figure head and passing power to the General People's Committees.

1980   Libyan troops intervene in the civil war in northern Chad.

1981   Libya challenges U.S. war planes flying over the Gulf of Sirte, which Libya claimed as territorial water. In retribution, the United States shoots down two Libyan aircrafts.

1984   The UK ends diplomatic relations with Libya after a British policewoman is fatally shot during an anti-Gaddafi protest outside the Libyan embassy in London.

1986   The United States bombs Libyan military facilities, as well as residential areas in Tripoli and Benghazi, in response to alleged Libyan involvement in the bombing of a Berlin disco frequented by U.S. military personnel. One hundred and one people, including Gaddafi's adopted daughter, are killed.

1988   A Pan Am aircraft blows up in a terrorist attack over the Scottish town of Lockerbie. Two Libyans are alleged to have brought the aircraft down.

1989   Libya, Algeria, Morocco, Mauritania, and Tunisia form the Arab Maghreb Union.

1992   In its effort to force Libya to hand over two Libyans suspected of involvement in the Lockerbie bombing for trial, the UN imposes economic, diplomatic, and other sanctions on Libya.

1994   Libya restores the Aozou Strip to Chad.

1995   To protest Israel's attacks on the Palestine Liberation Organization, Gaddafi expels about 30,000 Palestinians from Libya.

1999   Gaddafi hands over the two Libyans suspected of carrying out the Lockerbie bombing to be tried in the Netherlands under Scottish law. The UN suspends sanctions, as the UK restores diplomatic relations with Libya.

2000	Libyan mobs, angry at the huge number of African labor migrants in Libya, kill dozens of African immigrants in the west of Libya.
2001	Abdelbaset Ali Mohamed al-Megrahi, one of the two Libyans accused of the Lockerbie bombing, is found guilty by the Special Scottish court in the Netherlands and sentenced to life imprisonment. Al-Amin Khalifa Fahimah, Megrahi's coaccused, is freed.
2001	Libyan troops assists President Ange-Felix Patasse of the Central African Republic to avert a coup d'état.
2002	After years of hostility over Libya's alleged sponsorship of terrorism, Libya and the United States mend relations.
2002	Abdelbaset Ali Mohmed al-Megrahi loses appeal against his conviction in the Lockerbie bombing and begins serving his life sentence.
2003	Despite opposition from the United States and human rights groups, Libya is elected chairman of the UN Human Rights Commission.
2003	In a letter to the UN Security Council, Libya takes responsibility for the Lockerbie bombing and signs a $2.7 billion deal to compensate families of the victims.
2003	UN Security Council votes to lift sanctions on Libya.
2003	Libya promises to abandon its weapons of mass destruction program.
2004	Libya accepts responsibility for the bombing of a French passenger airplane over the Sahara that occurred in 1989, agreeing to compensate the families of victims.
2004	Tony Blair, British prime minister, visits Libya, the first such visit since 1943.
2004	Five nurses from Bulgaria and a Palestinian doctor are sentenced to death in Libya after being accused of purposely infecting 400 children with HIV. The European Union eventually strikes a deal to have them released.
2004	Libya accepts responsibility for the bombing of a Berlin nightclub in 1986 and agrees to pay $35 million to compensate victims and their families.
2005	Libya's first auction of oil and gas exploration licenses brings U.S. energy companies back to Libya after more than 20 years.

2006	After a Danish newspaper depicts the Prophet Muhammad in a cartoon, protests break out in Benghazi, leading to the killing of 10 Libyans.
2006	The United States restores full diplomatic ties with Libya.
2008	After decades as an outsider of the West, Libya takes over the one-month rotating presidency of the UN Security Council.
2008	Condoleezza Rice, U.S. secretary of state, makes a historic visit to Libya.
2008	Libya and the United States sign agreement to compensate all victims of bombing attacks that occur on each other's civilians.
2008	Gaddafi assumes the honorific title of King of Kings of Africa.
2009	Presidents and heads of government of member states of the African Union elect Gaddafi as chairman at a meeting in Ethiopia.
2009	Gaddafi visits Italy, Libya's main trading partner. This is the first state visit that made to the former colonizing ruler.
2009	Abdelbaset Ali al-Megrahi is released from Scottish prison on compassionate grounds. His release causes outcry across the world.
2010	Russia and Libya sign a weapon deal worth $1.8 billion.
2010	WikiLeaks reveals that Gaddafi threatened to cut trade with Britain should Abdelbaset Ali al-Megrahi die in prison. Many accuse British Petroleum of lobbying for al-Megrahi's release.
2010	Libya expels the United Nations High Commissioner for Refugees (UNHCR) from the country.
2010	European Union and Libya sign agreement to slow illegal migration.
2011	Arab Spring protests break out in Benghazi, Tripoli, and other cities. The protests are believed to have been inspired by similar protests in Egypt and Tunisia. Police and security forces kill anti-Gaddafi protesters and rebels. NATO launches air strikes to protect civilians.
2011	The National Transitional Council (NTC), a coalition of rebel forces, was formed to act as an opposition government to Gaddafi. The international Contact Group on Libya formally recognizes the NTC as the legitimate government of Libya.

2011	Gaddafi flees his fortress compound in Tripoli, as rebels take control of Tripoli.
2011	African Union joins 60 countries in recognizing the NTC as the new Libyan authority.
2011	Rebel forces capture and kill Gaddafi in his hometown of Sirte. NTC declares Libya officially "liberated," with elections to occur eight months later.
2012	Rebel forces disagree with the NTC, and clashes erupt in Benghazi.
2012	Interim government hands over power to the newly elected General National Congress (GNC).
2012	Ansar al-Sharia storm the U.S. consulate in Benghazi, killing the ambassador and three other Americans.
2012	Al-Baghdadi al-Mahmoudi, Libya's former prime minister, went on trial in Tripoli on charges of "acts that led to the unjust killing of Libyans" and funneling public funds to aid Gaddafi loyalists.
2013	Following growing security concerns in Libya, British Foreign Office withdraws embassy staff.
2013	Libya approves a bill prohibiting anyone who worked for the Gaddafi-led government from holding public office.
2013	Armed militia kidnap Prime Minister Ali Zeidan at a hotel in Tripoli.
2013	Militias blockade petroleum facilities and oil export terminals.
2014	Ali Zeidan is removed from office as prime minister after a tanker filled with oil breaks through a Libyan naval blockade. The General National Congress elects Ahmed Maiteg as the new prime minister.
2014	General Khalifa Haftar, head of the Libyan National Army, a rebel group, launches air strikes against militant Islamist groups in Benghazi.
2014	General Khalifa Haftar accuses Prime Minister Ahmed Maiteg of being under the control of radical Islamist groups.
2014	The Supreme Court rules Maiteg's appointment as prime minister illegal. Maiteg resigns.

2014	As the security situation in Libya deteriorates, the United Nations pulls out its staff. Many embassies shut down, and foreigners evacuate.
2014	Ban Ki-moon, the UN secretary-general, visits Libya to facilitate discussion between Tobruk's new parliament and government and Islamist Libya Dawn militias holding Tripoli.
2015	After UN-backed talks in Geneva, the Libyan army and Tripoli-based militia declare a partial cease-fire.
2015	The Islamic State releases a video of the beheading of 21 Egyptian Christians. A day later, Egyptian security forces bomb Islamic State targets in Derna.
2015	Saif al-Islam, one of Gaddafi's sons, and eight other former officials are sentenced to death by a Tripoli court for the crimes they committed during the 2011 uprising. An armed group loyal to Gaddafi frees Saif al-Islam before his execution.
2016	The United Nations announces a new, Tunisia-based interim government for Libya. Neither the Tobruk-based parliament nor the Tripoli-based one recognizes the authority of this new government.
2016	After two years, UN staff return to Tripoli.
2016	General Khalifa Haftar's Libyan National Army seizes control of oil export terminals in eastern Libya.
2016	Forces loyal to the government of Libya defeat and expel Islamic State militants from Sirte.
2017	Forces loyal to the government of Libya defeats and expels Islamic State militants from Benghazi after three years of fighting.
2018	General Khalifa Haftar's Libyan National Army claims full control of Derna, the last Islamic State stronghold in Libya.
2018	Backed by the UN, Libya declares a state of emergency in Tripoli after militia clashes kill dozens.

AFRICA

1

An Overview of Geography, Earliest Peoples, States, and Societies to the Seventh Century BCE

INTRODUCTION

Although the earliest indigenous Berber settlers of the areas now known as Libya left no written records behind, they did leave a huge number of rock artworks and cave paintings, engravings, and other archaeological evidence in Wadi Teshuinant, Wadi Mattendush, El Awrer, Wadi Tiksatin, Messak Settafet, and Messak Mellet, many of which have shown that ancient Libya was a home to rivers, grassy plateaus, and abundant wildlife. As radiocarbon dating of these material artifacts has shown, some of these rock artworks and cave paintings have been in existence since early 8000 BCE. Today, a region that was once characterized by rivers and waterways, grassy plateaus, and its inhabitants like giraffes, elephants, and crocodiles has yielded place to an arid desert. Besides concrete evidence of grassy vegetation captured in the paintings, we also have evidence that the ancient Berber inhabitants practiced a Neolithic agriculture. They cultivated crops and reared animals, especially cattle, practices that were common to the Mediterranean littoral. In other words, while some Berbers were farmers, others were nomadic herders who roamed the well watered areas with their animals and hunted game.

As of January 2017, Libya's total population stood at about 7 million. Tripoli (in Tripolitania), with about 1 million inhabitants, is the largest city in the country. Benghazi, with about half a million inhabitants, is the second largest city. The history of Libya is a long story of human development and invasions, of migrations and admixture of peoples, and of the impact of these on customs and practices, beliefs and attitudes, institutions and social organizations of the various peoples who inhabit the areas now known as Libya. Without a geographical background, this story would, like a dead carcass, lack life and motion. Given its relationships to human culture, to our way of life, and to social and political institutions, the history of Libya cannot be told without a knowledge of Libya's geography. To this end, this chapter focuses on the physical and human geography of Libya. In addition, it examines the place of geography in the evolution, spread, and development of sociocultural, economic, and political institutions in Libya.

PHYSICAL GEOGRAPHY

With an area of 679,358 square miles (1,759,530 million square kilometers), Libya is more than twice the size of Texas and almost eight times bigger than Great Britain and Northern Ireland. It is the fourth largest country in Africa and the 16th largest country on earth. It lies across 16 full degrees of longitude (9°–25°) and more than 14 full degrees of latitude (18°, 45°, and 33°).

Although with a generally low-lying landform and with two northern upland areas, most of Libya's land is semidesert. In the north, the Mediterranean Sea separates Libya from Europe. Also in the north, especially northern Tripolitania, a fertile coastal strip about seven miles wide merges with the Gefara Plain. This fertile strip rises no higher than 3,000 feet before it curves round to meet the sea at Homs. In the south, the land rises to form the Tibesti and Uweinat Mountains, which form a natural barrier between Libya and Central Africa. In the south, the Sahara Desert separates Libya from West Africa. Bordering countries include Algeria and Tunisia to the west, Egypt and Sudan to the east, and Niger and Chad to the south.

A relatively well wooded and fertile land, however, exists in northern Cyrenaica. This fertile land, called Gebel Akhdar (Green Mountain), rises in two narrow steps from the coast to a 2,000-foot-high plateau, which stretches eastward toward Egypt. Closer to Egypt, the land turns stony and slopes into the Libyan Desert. Herodotus, surprised at Libya's vast semidesert land, described it as "a tract which is wholly sand." As the German explorer, Gustav Nachtigal, who set out in 1869 from Tripoli to Fezzan, noted, "only 1 percent of Libya's total landmass is suitable for agriculture," a condition that remains today.

Libya lacks permanent flowing rivers except for water courses (*wadis*), which flow mainly during the rainy seasons. Approximately 200 miles (322 kilometers) to the south, there are also three oasis systems in western Fezzan—the *Wadis Shatti* and *Ajal* and the *Murzuk* Depression, where water tables lie only a few feet below the surface. Climate and the availability of water restricted settled farming to the coastal strips and the hill ranges of northern Tripolitania and Cyrenaica and to some inland oases and wells, especially Giarabub, Gialo, and Kufra.

The temperature in Libya differs from region to region. On average, temperatures in Tripoli, for instance, range between 46° and 61° Fahrenheit (8° and 16° Celsius) in January, whereas it reaches between 72° and 86° Fahrenheit (22° and 30° Celsius) in August. In general, Libya has two climatic zones: the Mediterranean climate in the coastal areas of the north and the tropical climate in the south. Between October and March, cold winters abound along the Mediterranean, and precipitation can be as low as 24 inches (600 millimeters). Between April and June, the hot southern wind, which Libyans call *Ghibli*, brings sand and dust from southern Algeria. During this time, the temperature along the Libyan coast can rise to between 30 ° and 40° Fahrenheit (–1.1° and +4.4° Celsius). Summer in Libya is intensely hot, and humidity along the coast rises to about 90 percent in August. However, on average, the climate is usually comfortable in Tripoli.

The tropical climate of the south is hot and dry. Occasionally, rainfall, which seldom exceeds 19 inches (500 mm), punctuates this hot and dry southern climate. Wind blows between May and October from north to east and from north to west between November and April. Besides sprinkling layers of fine dust, these two wind systems also destroy growing crops.

In addition to natural resources such as crude oil, geography also plays an important role in the socioeconomic, cultural, and political lives of Libyans. For instance, because between 93 and 95 percent of Libya's total landmass is either semidesert or in the heart of the Sahara

Desert itself, patterns of human settlements favored the Mediterranean coast over everywhere else. Hence, Tripoli emerges as the most populated city in Libya.

In addition to severe limitations imposed by the harsh climatic conditions on patterns of human settlements, geography also impacts socioeconomic and political organization. For instance, whereas grassland encourages movement, ease of communication, and the creation of larger and complex state systems, living in a semidesert or in the desert itself can create nomadic lifestyles, which, in turn, affects Libyans' attitudes toward rules of inheritance, as well as socioeconomic and political institutions. As seen in other parts of Africa, living in the forests, swamps, and mountainous regions also restricts movement and encourages the establishment of small-scale political organizations.

From the Neolithic period to modern times, occupational distribution in Libya favors agriculture. A great majority of Libyans are engaged either in animal husbandry or in crop cultivation. Libya's harsh climatic condition has a role in this. Geography, in Libya, as in the rest of the world, has implications not only for patterns of human settlements but also for socioeconomic and political organization, occupational distribution, and human existence.

HUMAN GEOGRAPHY

Contemporary Libya is a mosaic of indigenous peoples and settler populations. The indigenous peoples of Libya are comprised of the Berbers, Garamantes, Tebous, Harratins, and Tuaregs. While the Berbers were the Neolithic Afro-Asiatic ancestors of hunter-gatherer population that occupied the area eons ago, the Garamantes and Tebous, Harratins and Tuaregs began living in Libya in the late Bronze Age period. The Phoenicians, Romans, and Greeks, like the Arabs and the Italians and others from different parts of Africa, were later settlers.

Unlike the indigenous populations who were highly homogeneous, the settler population was a hodge-podge of different peoples. Egyptians were the first to explore Libya. Phoenician traders, exploring for merchandise of all kinds, followed them. The Greeks and Romans later invaded, occupied, and ruled Libya in succession. The Ottoman Arabs followed and were later deposed by the Italians. Italian colonialism, besides sweeping away Arab political control of Libya, left behind an influx of people from Croatia, Malta, Tunisia, Armenia, and others from different parts of Africa. The United Nations' mandate succeeded Italian rule in Libya after World War II.

While most literature on Libya has traced the history of the country to periods of foreign invasions, conquests, and colonialism, this book, in the remaining part of this chapter, focuses on the indigenous populations to show that Libya and Libyans have a history before foreign invasion and colonialism.

BERBERS

Early Greeks, Romans, and Phoenicians described as Berbers the different peoples inhabiting the lands from the Mediterranean Sea to the Niger River and from the Atlantic Ocean to the Siwa Oasis in Egypt. This broad classification masks the true picture of human geography of the areas, as peoples other than the Berbers also exist there. Notwithstanding the inaccurate nature of the classification, Berbers were among the earliest inhabitants of the area. Berbers, like the Tebou, Harattin, Numidians, and Garamantes, were the descendants of hunter-gatherer populations who settled in the areas before the Egyptians and Phoenicians, Greeks and Romans, Arabs and Europeans.

Berber, as a name, is Greek in origin. It derives from *barbaros*—a derogatory name given to all non-Greek speakers. The Latin equivalent is *barbarus* or *barbaria*. The origin of the term is evidence that the name was imposed on the people by outsiders. The Arabs called them *Mauri*, as cited in *Chronicle 754*. The Berbers called themselves Amazighen or Amazigh, which translates loosely to mean "free people." Berbers were reputed for their strength and bravery, courage and independence. Numbering about 40 million people today, these indigenous peoples can be found between northwest Egypt and the Atlantic Ocean in varying numbers. While they are the dominant ethnic group in Libya, Algeria, and Morocco, there are also significant Berber populations in Tunisia and Egypt, Mali and Mauritania, Niger and Burkina Faso. Today, in addition to those in Africa, about 4 million Berbers live in Europe and North America, especially Belgium and the Netherlands, France and Spain, Canada and Germany.

From the early history until now, most Berbers in Libya and other African countries were animal rearers and farmers. Where arable land existed, they cultivated plants. In other places, they sought pasture and water for their animals. Cave paintings and rock artwork from Tadrart Acacus in the Libyan Desert and from the Tassili n'Ajjer region in Algeria, both of which have been dated to 12 millennia ago, show that the Berbers domesticated animals and practiced subsistence agriculture from between 6,000 and 2,000 BCE, at the least.

The early proto-Berbers were believed to have emerged between the Late Bronze Age and Early Iron Age periods. They were the makers of the Iberomaurusian and Caspian cultures, who must have been around since 5,000 BC. Through uniparental DNA analysis, we now know that Libyan Berbers are related to other Afro-Asiatic peoples in North Africa, as they all belonged to the E1b1b paternal haplogroup—a major human Y-chromosome DNA haplogroup that links from father to son back to a common male line ancestor. DNA analysis of skeletons found in Taforalt and Afalou in 2013 also proved that ancient inhabitants of the Maghreb shared maternal clades with either North Africa or the Mediterranean littoral.

Originally, there were three subgroups of Berbers. These are the Mauri, Numidians, and Gaetulians. These three subgroups occupied from the northwest to northeast of Africa. The colonial creation of nation-states inadvertently led to the division of these three subgroups into smaller groups, parceling them away in different nation-states. For instance, the Mauri are now divided among Mauritania, Morocco, and Algeria.

The Mauri and Numidians, unlike the Gaetulians, were predominantly sedentary farmers, cultivating dates and grains. The Gaetulians were pastoralists who tended their livestock on the margins of the Sahara and who oftentimes accompanied them on a circuit of seasonal pastures. As sedentary farmers, the Mauri and Numidians lived in permanent dwellings and had a complex sociopolitical and economic system. With increasing desertification, livestock rearing imposed on the Gaetulians pastoralists a life of constant movement from one location to another.

Berber society is a close-knit society, with socioeconomic and political lives revolving around both the family and the clan. An individual's identity is subsumed in those of the family and the clan. Group identity among the Berbers is subordinated and it becomes important when relating with non-Berbers. Like in all agrarian societies, land ownership is of utmost importance among the Berbers. In addition, Berbers recognize private property.

Three social classes existed in Berber society. The landowners, who owned all lands, water holes, oases, and the like, was the first. The second social class was the poor, who worked for wages on the lands of the rich. Then came the slaves. Notwithstanding these social classifications, Berber society was remarkably egalitarian.

Over many years, centralized administration emerged among the Berbers, as the Numidians successfully built an elaborate kingdom. The Mauri—Moors in Spanish—took Islam into Europe, founding

A mosque in the ancient Berber oasis of Ghadames, Libya. (iStockPhoto)

universities and establishing public libraries, as well as introducing many fields of study, including tailoring, fashion designing, and so on, everywhere they went in Europe. Owing to their constant movement, the Gaetulians pastoralists did not evolve a centralized administration like that of the Mauris and the Numidians.

In antiquity, Berbers were adherents of traditional religion, which was characterized by ancestor worship, polytheism, and animism. The introduction of foreign religious beliefs, such as Judaism, Iberian mythology, Hellenistic religion, Christianity, and Islam, has altered the religious universe of the Berbers. Although traditional religious worshippers still abound among the Berbers, the influence of Islam remains dominant, shaping religion, popular culture, and tradition.

Egyptian records from between 2700 and 2200 BCE showed that the Berbers, who were called *Lebu* or Libyans by the Egyptians, were constantly raiding the Nile Delta. At about 950 BCE, Berbers took control of Egypt and established Libyan dynasties. Shishonk I was the first Berber pharaoh. A small group of Berbers remain in Egypt to this date. In general, the Berbers lived primarily in remote areas, ostensibly to escape conversion to Islam.

THE TEBOU

Another native inhabitant of Libya is the Tebou. The Tebou are a group of mountain-dwelling nomads who live in southern Libya. They can also be found in northern Chad and Niger, as well as around eastern Niger and northwestern Sudan—all of which surrounds the Tibesti Mountains. In fact, the name Tebou means "Rock People." The Arabs called them Gourane. In general, there are two Tebou subethnic groups—the Teda and the Dazagra. Both share a common origin and speak two dialects of a single language. The two dialects (Teda Tebou and Dazaga Tebou) belong to the Nilo-Saharan language family.

Not much is known about the ancient history of the Tebou. While Egyptian sources are few and far between concerning them, Herodotus noted in 430 BCE that the Garamantes were persecuting the Tebou. There were also passing references to the Tebou in Islamic literature. Notable examples include Ibn Qutaybah, an eighth-century Arabic scholar, who made passing references to the Tebou and the Zaghawa peoples. Additionally, al-Kuwarizmi, a ninth-century Arabic scholar, also made a passing reference to the Tebou. In a number of works of classical literature, references were also made to the Tebou, especially in their relationship with the Garamantes.

Besides sharing the Tibesti Mountains, this group of mountain-dwelling herders and nomads also cultivated plants, especially near the oases and along a few tracks on the mountains.

Essentially, Tebou life revolved around the raising and herding of goats and sheep, donkeys and dromedaries, as well as cattle. The more livestock a person had, the more influence and power he or she wielded in Tebou society. Wealth was also measured by the number of livestock a person has; hence, rearing and herding livestock were of utmost importance. Dowries and bride wealth were paid in livestock, a pervasive culture across West and Southern Africa. Besides raising livestock and farming, livestock trading was another major source of employment, as animal trading made the Tebou important players in linking North Africa with West Africa.

A small number of Tebou cultivated dates, grains, and legumes along mountain passes and near scattered oases, water holes, and wells. Another common occupation among the Tebou was mining. Rock salt and natron were mined in a number of places. Natron is a salt-like substance that is predominant in almost all of Tebou's food and medicines. It is believed to have medicinal value; hence, it is mixed with tobacco, food, and even soap. In addition, it is used in tanning, in textile making, and in treating diseases in livestock.

As noted in this chapter, nomadic and pastoral life facilitates easy communication; hence, settled living was not a common feature of Tebou. As nomadic pastoralists, Tebou were usually on the move. Those who cultivated plants around oases, water holes, and wells also lived in scattered locations. Owing to this geography-imposed lifestyle, the Tebou society was built around the clan, and allegiance was to the clan, not to any community. Belonging to a clan fostered closer ties and communal security.

Whether Tebou live a pastoralist and nomadic life or a settled life, they evolved a patrilineal social system, where the oldest male is the head of the family/lineage. In general, Tebou society could be divided into two segments: the family, as the first and basic social and political unit, and the clan. There is no doubt that the system evolved over many years of living in Libya's unfriendly desert.

Tebou society was stratified into freemen, the artisanal class, and slaves. All property was owned by the freemen. The artisanal class consists of metal workers, leather workers, salt miners, well diggers, date farmers, pottery makers, and tailors. Slaves, *agarah* in Tebou, were a group of non-natives who were captured during raids and wars. As property, they owed their existence to their masters, and their position was held for life. Children of slaves were also slaves, and interclass marriages were forbidden. Tebou society was endogamous. Although the majority of Tebou are Muslims, Tebou culture prohibits marriages between first cousins. However, as in Islam, Tebou culture supports marrying multiple wives.

Among the Tebou, as in the rest of Africa, ownership of land was highly important, as was ownership of livestock. Given its importance, ownership, or more appropriately control, of the oases was as fundamental as ownership of livestock and land. Although oases and water-holes were owned by different clans, clan members recognized and respected each family's rights to oases, water holes, and plots of land under a family's control or ownership. A clan might rent out portions of land, as well as access to and the use of oases and water holes for a part of the harvest or for livestock. A similar system applied to date palm and livestock.

As Herodotus claimed, the Garamantes despised and persecuted the Tebou. A cursory look at Libyan history shows that the hatred for and persecution of the Tebou are not limited to the Garamantes, as the Tebou were persecuted during the Gaddafi years so much that there was a state-led effort to denationalize them. Gaddafi argued that they were Chadians in spite of the fact that they were indigenous to the areas from along southeastern Libya to as far as the oasis town of Kufra. Under

Gaddafi, especially in 2009, the Tebou endured forced eviction from Libya, as the Gaddafi government demolished their homes. While many fled and became homeless, some protested and were subsequently arrested.

Years of persecution have failed to dampen the spirits of the Tebou. In 2008, the Tebou Front for the Salvation of Libya (TFSL), an armed group formed by Tebou, rose against the Libyan government in a five-day standoff. The standoff was effectively crushed by the Libyan army. During the Libyan Arab Spring, the Tebou, ostensibly borne out of many years of persecution, joined forces with the rebel forces to oust Gaddafi.

HARATIN

A small group of oases dwellers called the Haratins also abound in Libya. Across North Africa, most especially Libya, Mauritania, Morocco, and Western Sahara, this group of oasis-dwelling workers were socially distinct from others. Besides having darker skin, they emerged from slavery, especially from Berber's enslavement. It could be argued that the Haratin were not a distinct ethnic group, as it was composed of a hodge-podge of enslaved people from different parts of North and West Africa. The name Haratin was believed to have originated from two words—*ahardan*, a Berber word meaning "dark color" and *haratine*, Arabic for "plowmen"; a Haratin could be anybody other than a Berber or a Tebou. *Ahardan* undoubtedly referred to the skin color of "other'" people, as distinct from the Berbers, whereas *haratine* pointed to the occupation that most Haratin engaged in. Both words point to a social construct that emphasized lowliness and to servile and demeaning status in which this group of people were kept.

Inasmuch as the Berbers and Tebous could not have enslaved their own people but rather their Bambara, Soninke, and other neighbors, it could be argued that as a socially distinct class of workers, the Haratin was a low-status, socially isolated endogamous group of slaves and their descendants. In Libya, they depended on other groups, especially the Berbers, who utilized them on their farms and in rearing livestock. In general, the Haratins were mostly products of raids and conquests; hence they ended up as agricultural serfs, herders, and subservient workers.

They must have originated from either the Sahel or the West African subregion and were brought across the Sahara as slaves. They and their descendants have cultivated lands and reared livestock around the oases for many years. As a social group, they adopted the culture of their masters in dress, language, popular culture, and, in most cases, religion. Hence, most of them speak either Berber dialects or Arabic. Owing to this, many have erroneously classified them as either Berbers or Arabs. Despite the derogatory connotations surrounding the group, members who now number nearly 1.5 million, have developed a sense of separate ethnic identity.

As a socially segregated class, Haratin could not own land and also lack any property rights. The inability to own land or any property rights ensured the continual existence of a patron–client relationship between the Haratins and the Berbers. Many Haratins have lived their lives either as domestic servants or as sharecroppers. In any endogamous and socially segregated society, cross-class marriages are discouraged; hence, slave status and family occupation were passed down from parent to children.

TUAREG

Technically, Tuaregs are a Berber subgroup that evolved a unique and separate identity from other Berbers. Other Tuareg groups include the Lemta and Zarawa. As a people, they abound in different parts of North and West Africa, with a large concentration in Libya, Algeria, Niger, Mali, and Burkina Faso. A small group of Tuareg can also be found in northern Nigeria. In Libya, Tuaregs are indigenous to Fezzan. The Tuaregs call themselves Kel Tamasheq (speakers of Tamasheq) and Kel Tagelmust (the veiled people). Kel Tagelmust is an allusion to the traditional veiled garment worn by Tuareg men. This traditional veiled garment, dyed in indigo, usually leaves blue color on the wearer, a development that gave the Tuareg the appellation—the blue people.

According to Tuareg tradition, between the fourth and fifth centuries, Tin Hinane, a queen, led some descendants of the Berber autochthones from the Maghrib. Takamata, Tin's servant, also followed her queen, who was fleeing to escape punishment for a bad deed. Both the queen and her servant were pregnant. In the middle of the desert and with no food and water, the queen and her entourage faced certain death. Takamata, desirous to save the queen, scouted around for whatever she could find. After a long search, she found an anthill wherein the ants stored grains and other edible things. She scooped out these grains and hurriedly returned to her queen.

Not long after this, they arrived at Abalissa, near Tamanrasset, where both the queen and her servant delivered. The queen had a daughter, while Takamata gave birth to twins—all females. These three females were the ancestors of Tuareg. Tin Hinane's tomb is now a tourist center in Abalissa, in the Hoggar Mountains of southern Algeria. On the walls of Tin Hinane's sepulcher can be found various inscriptions written in Tifinagh, traditional Libyan Berber writing script.

From the 10th to 16th centuries, different writers have called the Tuaregs by different names. For instance, Ibn Hawkal and al-Bakri, writing in the 10th and 11th centuries, called them Tuaregs Mulatthamin, which means "the veiled ones." A similar description can be found in al-Idrisi (12th century), Ibn Batutah (14th century), and Leo Africanus (16th century). The English called them the Blue People. The Tuaregs are also called Imuhagh or Imushagh, which is another name or a variant of Amazighen, the Berbers' true name as previously discussed.

While there are many dialects of the Tuareg language, the main language of the Tuareg is called Tamasheq, which, like those of the Berbers, also belongs to the Afro-Asiatic family of languages.

Traditionally, Tuaregs were nomadic pastoralists whose main occupation was to tend livestock and occasionally to cultivate a few crops along water holes and oases. With the advent of trans-Saharan trade, a trading system that brought goods from Asia, the Middle East, and Europe into Africa with North Africa acting as a gateway, the occupational structure of the Tuareg society changed. While the trade lasted, the Tuaregs were the masters of long-distance trading, exchanging Asian and European manufacture with gold, salt, peppers, and leathers from West Africa. They controlled several trans-Saharan trade routes and superintended who took what goods across the deserts. This brought them not only enormous wealth but also considerable power and influence. It was through them, acting in this intermediary role, that Islam got to different parts of North and West Africa.

Traditional Tuareg society was hierarchical, with the nobles, *imajaghan* (the proud and free), at the top of the hierarchy. These aristocratic nobles owned all lands, oases, water holes, and so on. They held considerable power and influence, with which they controlled society. They reserved the rights to bear arms and to own camels. They were the warriors of the Tuareg regions. Below the nobles were the vassal-herders, the *imghad*. Although the vassal-herders could not own camels, they were free to own donkeys and goats, sheep and oxen. Besides pasturing and tending their herds, they also pastured and tended those owned by the nobles. To enjoy the privilege of being vassal-herders, they had to pay a tribute (*tiwse*) to the nobles.

With the advent of Islam came a third category who were seminoble. This category was composed of mainly religious clerics and the marabouts. The marabouts served as judges (*qadi*) in the Tuareg society.

The artisanal class, *inadan*, included the blacksmith, jewelry makers, woodworkers, and leather workers who were skilled in making and repairing saddles, household items, and the like. Members of the artisanal class were salt and natron miners, livestock traders, supervisors, and so on. The artisans were clients of the nobles and the vassals, who served them as patrons. The artisanal class was important because they included praise singers, musicians, and storytellers—the very sinew of Tuareg oral history. The storyteller (*agguta*) performed and retold oral histories during wedding, funeral, and other ceremonies. Slaves, locally called *ikelan* (or *iklan*, *eklan*), were either kidnapped from neighboring communities or made prisoners of wars from regular raids on neighbors. Children of slaves also inherited the status. Descendants of slaves are known as *irewelen*. Interclass marriages were disallowed. Members of the different classes retained their memberships or statuses for life.

Among the Tuaregs, the family and clan were the most important. At the head of every Tuareg family was a family head, usually the oldest male member of the family. Members of a clan (*tawshet*) traced their origins to an eponymous ancestor; hence, each Tuareg belonged to a clan, and each clan was led by a clan head (*amghar*), whose position was hereditary through a matrilineal principle. The clan head was assisted by clan elders, called *imegharan* (wise men). Until the colonial period, the Tuaregs had no king, as each clan had its own head. At the turn of the 19th century, Tuareg society was organized into confederations, each ruled by an appointed supreme chief (*amenokal*). There were, in all, seven major confederations in Tuareg history. These confederations were the coming together of many different clans. Although the heads of the confederations were colonially created, they were assisted by a traditional Council of Elders composed of the different segments of the society. Together with the wise men and heads of clans, the Council acted in an advisory capacity to the heads of the confederations.

Recent studies have shown connections between the Tuareg and early ancient Egyptian civilization. Even if this claim awaits further evidence, there is no doubt in the fact that the Tuaregs played fundamental roles in the spread of Islam and the sustaining of Islamic and Arabic legacies in both North Africa and the Sahel region. Prior to Islam, the Tuaregs were animists; however, a large number of Tuaregs are today Muslims. Rituals of different kind abound in Tuareg society. For instance, in 1926, an archaeological excavation of a prehistoric tomb in the Maghreb yielded ochre-painted skeletal remains, which were believed to have been part of a ritual practice.

The medieval period witnessed the introduction and adoption of Islam, especially with the arrival of the Umayyad caliphate in the seventh century. Initially, the Umayyad were unable to covert the Tuaregs. While many Tuaregs openly rejected Islam, some fled into the Libyan Desert. Tuaregs general reactions to Islam, however, began to change as the Umayyad allowed few Tuaregs converts to incorporate their traditional religious beliefs with Islam. As studies have shown, these initial converts to Islam were relaxed in their observance of Islamic tenets and practices. They incorporated pre-Islamic cosmology and rituals into Islam. They also brought their traditional respect for matrilineal spirits, fertility, menstruation, earth worship, and belief in ancestors and ancestresses into Islam.

Many scholars have argued that this religious syncretism derived from Sufi Muslim preachers' influences on the Tuaregs. Whatever its source, it must be noted that these changes encouraged more and more Tuaregs to accept and convert to Islam. As traders and through their example, the Tuareg invariably brought Islamic religion, education, law, and philosophy into Western Sudan. Today, the establishment of the Maliki school of the Sunni sect across the Western Sudan can be traced to the Tuaregs.

Notable achievements of the Tuaregs, as far as Islamization and Arabization of Africa were concerned, was the Maghsharan Tuareg founding of the Islamic center in Timbuktu, Mali, at the start of the 12th century. As an important Islamic center famed for its *ulama* (religious teachers), Timbuktu emerged as an iconic center of Islamic religion, education, and philosophy that drew scholars and students not only from the African continents but also from the Middle East. In addition, it emerged as a great center of the trans-Saharan trade system.

At its height of fame and influence, Timbuktu flourished under the protection of a Tuareg confederation, which in 1449, was headed by a Tuareg ruling house, the Tenere Sultanate of Air (Sultanate of Agadez). Notable Islamic scholars of this period include Jibril ibn 'Umar, the 18th-century Tuareg Islamic scholar, and Ibn 'Umar, Usman dan Fodio, the founder of the Sokoto Caliphate.

Among the Berbers, the Tuaregs, with their broadswords, were dogged in resisting the French colonial invasion of Central Sahara in the 19th century. They recorded a landmark victory over the French in 1881. The Tuareg, however, succumbed to superior French firepower between 1905 and 1917. The French subsequently took over Tuareg territories, creating different nation-states of what used to be a bloc of people stretching from southern Morocco and Algeria to Libya and eastern Egypt to as far as Chad and northeastern Nigeria.

Following independence from European colonialism, the traditional Tuareg territory was divided and shared among Algeria, Burkina Faso,

Libya, Mali, and Niger. While colonial rule lasted, different ethnic groups were brought under direct control of the colonial administrators under either the direct rule or the indirect rule system. When a group proved unamenable to the colonial twin projects of sourcing for cheap or free raw materials and markets for European finished goods, that group was either brought under control forcefully or had its neighbors provisioned against it. In this way, the Tuaregs, who were essentially pastoralists, found tight restrictions placed on nomadization, a step that eroded their wealth and consequently their power and influence.

Desertification exacerbated the colonial experience, as increasing population meant increasing pressure and exploitation of resources, such as firewood for use in the newly established and ever growing cities. Consequently, many Tuareg dumped pastoralism and experimented with sedentary agriculture. Others sought employment in towns and cities, abandoning traditional herding of livestock.

GARAMANTES

The Garamantes are another group of people found in Libya. They were an indigenous Berber subgroup who, like the Tuaregs, developed a unique identity for themselves. As noted by Herodotus, the Garamantes inhabited the land between the Mediterranean littoral and the waterless desert of sand, stretching from Thebes in Egypt to the Stelai of Herakles. As Herodotus noted, "in addition to the ridge of sand were lumps of salt . . . in columns, at the top of which sprang cool water." The Garamantes, like the Ammonioi and the Audjila, the Atarantes and the Atlantes, lived in this curious landscape. While the Garamantes lived in the Fezzan region, both the Ammonioi and the Audjila lived around the Oasis of Siwa and the Oasis of Djalo, respectively.

Although the Garamantes had writing (proto-Tifaniq), many of their writings are yet to be deciphered. They are believed to have ruled southwestern Libya since 1000 BCE; however, they became a powerful force in the area between 500 BCE and 700 CE. While many have pointed to the Greek origin of the name, Garamantes could have derived from the Berber word for cities—*igherman*. Another Berber word that could serve as origin for the name, Garamantes, is *igerramen*—which means "saints," "holy" or "sacred people."

Since the 1960s, excavation work has been ongoing in Germa (or Gamma), the capital of Garamantes society. Recent archaeological research has shown that no fewer than eight major towns existed—all occupied by the Garamantes. Germa, the capital, had a population of between 4,000 and 6,000 inhabitants living in villages.

Unlike the Tuaregs and other Berber subgroups, the Garamantes were essentially farmers and traders. As sedentary farmers, they cultivated grapes and figs, wheat and barley. The Garamantes of Fezzan and the Pharusii of Western Sahara were the pioneer trans-Saharan traders. The wheels of their carts and chariots, as captured in cave paintings and rock art of the Sahara Desert, punctuated the arid desert, as the Garamantes exchanged wheat and barley, salt and slaves for imported wine and olive oil, oil lamps and Roman tableware, as well as other manufactured products from Asia, Europe, and the Middle East.

Like all sedentary people across Africa, the Garamantes also evolved a centralized political administrative system. At its height around 150 CE, the Garamantian kingdom in Fezzan covered about 180,000 square kilometers. However, the kingdom, whose decline has been attributed to increasing desertification, collapsed at about 600 CE.

THE ARABS

"Arabs" or "North African Arabs" describes the Arab-speaking inhabitants of the North African Maghreb region. To qualify as an Arab, the individual either self-identifies as an Arab or his or her native language is a dialect of Arabic language. Arabs in Libya, like their counterparts in other parts of Africa, were settlers. The Arab conquest of North Africa during the Arab-Byzantine wars led not only to the spread of Islam but also to the Arabization of Africa. Following military defeat, the mass migration of Arabs to North Africa began, especially in the 11th century.

Many historic Arabic and Islamic dynasties rose and fell, as North Africa became a critical part of the Islamic world. Such dynasties include the Umayyad, Idrissid, Nasrid, Hammudid, Abbasid, and Fatimid. While these historic dynasties rose and fell, different indigenous African groups and subgroups adopted Islam and Arab cultures and traditions.

Today, the descendants of these original Arab settlers, who continue to speak Arabic as a first language, constitute the largest population group in Libya. While some traditional and indigenous culture and customs still abound, perhaps the most long-lasting impact of Islam on Libya is the successful imposition on the area of Islamic and Arabic culture and religion, laws and education.

CONCLUSION

If history is the totality of the human experiences, events, ways of life, and interactions within a group or between one group and outsiders, whether these outsiders are foreign traders, invaders, or colonizers, then it is simplistic, disingenuous, and absurd to situate and discuss the history of Libya as a history of foreigners. Libya and Libyans had a history before contacts with foreign traders, invaders, and colonizers. Not only were the different Libyan indigenous groups interacting, trading, and intermarrying, but they were also engaging in warfare and long-distance trading before contacts either with the Egyptians from Africa or with hordes of foreigners from Europe and the Middle East. Evidence of their histories abounds in rock art, cave paintings, oral traditions, and archaeological remains, many of which have been subjected to various scientific methods of validation.

The Arabs, like the Italians and other Europeans, might have lived for years in Libya, but they were nevertheless settlers. Only the Berbers, Tuaregs, Bedouins, Harratins, Garamantes, and Tebous are indigenous to Libya. To disregard the various events and interactions that characterized the daily lives of these indigenous peoples before contacts with foreigners as no history is to reduce history and historical scholarship to mere absurdity.

LIBYA: PROVINCES AND ADMINISTRATIVE DISTRICTS

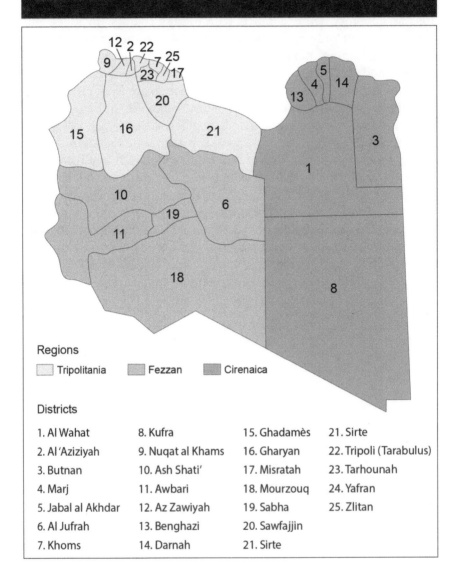

Regions

Tripolitania   Fezzan   Cirenaica

Districts

1. Al Wahat	8. Kufra	15. Ghadamès	21. Sirte
2. Al 'Aziziyah	9. Nuqat al Khams	16. Gharyan	22. Tripoli (Tarabulus)
3. Butnan	10. Ash Shati'	17. Misratah	23. Tarhounah
4. Marj	11. Awbari	18. Mourzouq	24. Yafran
5. Jabal al Akhdar	12. Az Zawiyah	19. Sabha	25. Zlitan
6. Al Jufrah	13. Benghazi	20. Sawfajjin	
7. Khoms	14. Darnah	21. Sirte	

2

Traders, Merchants, and Invaders, Seventh Century BCE–16th Century CE

INTRODUCTION

As demonstrated in Chapter 1, different indigenous peoples inhabited the area now known as Libya before the arrival of the first settler population. These indigenous peoples had their respective histories and cultures, which were different and sometimes similar. Although they existed independently of one another, they nevertheless traded, intermarried, and waged war against one another. Italian colonial rule, as shall be shown in the next chapter, altered not only these relationships but also their independence.

This chapter focuses on the precolonial Libyan states and societies. As the chapter shows, Libya is a gateway to West Africa and Europe. On account of this, it was constantly on the cusp of major socioeconomic, political, and cultural changes throughout its precolonial and colonial histories. For analytical purposes, the history of Libya can be divided into six distinct periods: ancient Libya, the Roman era, the

Islamic era, Ottoman rule, Italian rule, and the modern period. This chapter will focus on Libyans' contact with the Phoenicians, Greeks, Romans, Muslims, and Ottomans. This corresponded to the fifth century BCE, when Phoenician traders settled in Tripolitania, in western Libya, and entered into trading alliances with the Berbers. It extended to 642 CE, when Arab horsemen under Amir Ibn al-As crossed into Cyrenaica and subsequently conquered Libya, spreading Islam. A distinguishing feature of this period is that the different indigenous groups were yet to be ruled as one nation.

PHOENICIANS IN TRIPOLITANIA

The Phoenicians, or the Punics, an eastern Mediterranean people from contemporary Syria, Lebanon, and northern Israel, were the first foreigners to establish commercial outposts in Libya. Before the 12th century BCE, these highly skilled navigators and merchants created numerous trading and commercial outposts in North Africa. When these professional merchants arrived in Libya, they established a series of commercial alliances with the Berber groups, the cornerstones of which were raw materials extraction and markets for their imported goods.

Before arriving in Libya, the Phoenicians had established a trading outpost along the Mediterranean coast of Carthage, in contemporary Tunisia. Efforts at widening trade interests along the west coast of North Africa brought them to Tripolitania. Other commercial outposts established by the Phoenicians in Libya were Oea (now Tripoli), where a line of rocks and shoals extended from a peninsula and formed a defensible anchorage, especially from land attack, and Libdah (now Leptis Magna), a small well protected estuary to the east, 200 miles to Sirte, which was originally thought of as a temporary location but which eventually grew to be one of the most permanent of Phoenician trading outposts in Libya. Another temporary outpost that later became permanent was established in Sabratha. In most literature on Libya, these three places were said to have been founded by the Phoenicians. This is untrue and misleading. The three places had been in existence before the arrival of the Phoenicians. Owing to their nearness to the Mediterranean coasts, Phoenician traders realized the strategic importance of these locations and entered into trade alliances with the Berber inhabitants that enabled them to settle in these areas. The three cities—Oea, Libdah, and Sabratha, which were later called Tripolis—meaning "Three Cities," grew up rapidly owing to Phoenician trading activities. Tripoli is today the capital of Libya.

From Carthage, the Phoenicians controlled their trading enterprises in Tripolitania and other commercial outposts in Libya. Unlike later settlers, the Phoenicians were traders, not invaders and colonizers. Besides establishing commercial outposts, they also cultivated friendly relationships with the different Berber groups—trading with them and learning Berber culture and traditions. The Berbers adopted many of the Phoenician customs, including language. However, the commercial and friendly relations established by the Phoenicians did not affect the Berbers' autonomy and control of their territories. The Phoenicians introduced the olive, vine, peach, fig, and other Asiatic crops into Libya. Of these crops, the olive was most successful, as the light soil of both Carthage and Tripolitania supported it. The Phoenicians recognized and respected the Berbers' authority, and the Berbers, in turn, recognized and respected the overarching importance of Phoenician trade in the success of their cities. Owing to this friendly relationship and amity, the various Berbers groups joined with the Phoenicians during the First Punic War (264–241 BCE) and the Second Punic War (218–202 BCE).

The Phoenicians' loss of Carthage in 530 BCE to the Greeks had tremendous implications for Libya, as the invading Greek armies not only sacked it but also attacked and occupied Cyrenaica, from which they went on to occupy Barce (Al Marj), Eusperides (later Berenice but now Benghazi), Teuchira (later Arsinoe but now Tukrah), and Apollonia (later Susa but now the port of Cyrene)—about half of what is now known as Libya. These five cities formed the Pentapolis, a federation of five cities united in trade. At its apogee, the five cities had a common currency and were administered as republics, with democratic institutions.

Unlike the Phoenicians, whose focus was on trade, the Greeks established Cyrene as a great intellectual center, reputable for its arts and philosophy, medical education, and architecture. However, not even the Third Punic War (149–146 BCE) could keep the Carthaginians at bay; the Greeks of the Pentapolis had to fight off not only the ancient Egyptians from the East but also the Carthaginians from the West. However, in 525 BCE, the army of Cambyses II, the Persian king, defeated Cyrenaica, and the Pentapolis came under Persian control. The Greeks regained control only in July of 332 BCE during the time of Alexander the Great. This development ushered in the Ptolemaic Kingdom, the successor kingdom to Alexander in Egypt, under whom the Pentapolis came to be ruled by a king selected from Ptolemy's lineage.

Under the Ptolemaic kingdom, Tripolitania, the Tripolis, and the Pentapolis witnessed a dramatic change, as they became tightly controlled. To maintain trade monopoly, Carthage banned all ships except its own.

The trading outposts were taxed heavily. Notwithstanding these changes, internal control and domestic affairs were left in the hands of the Berbers. Under Ptolemaic trading influences, Tripolitania, Cyrenaica, and other Libyan cities and towns grew, as trade continued to flourish. No effort was made to influence or alter trade relations with other Berbers in other towns and cities, as the Greeks were content with the control of trade along the Mediterranean coast. The Garamantes, Tuaregs, and others dominated the southern trade routes, as they roamed the deserts—going as far as Lake Chad and Nigeria, bringing with them gold dust, animal skins, ivory, salts, ingredients for perfume making, and slaves for exchange with the Greeks.

ROMANS IN LIBYA

Libya was an unfortunate victim of a power tussle between Rome and Carthage. In the third century BCE, Rome fought Carthage for control of the central Mediterranean trading route, which, of course, extended to North Africa. The Third Punic War in 146 BCE saw the rising power of Rome over provinces in Africa, including all areas that were originally under the control of Carthage. Although Rome defeated the Carthaginians, it, however, did not colonize Libya and other parts of North Africa. Rome left Libya and other North Africa Berber territories that Carthage once controlled in the hands of the indigenous Numidian kings. In 74 BCE, Ptolemy Apion, the last Greek ruler, ceded Cyrenaica to the Romans, who turned it and Crete into a Roman province.

The indigenous inhabitants of Cyrenaica were the Berbers. These earliest inhabitants founded and lived in different cities and towns in Cyrenaica. They spoke a dialect of the Berber language that can still be found among the Awjila-Berber around the Awjila oasis.

According to Egyptian records, Libu and Meshwesh were two Berber subgroups in Cyrenaica. In the 13th century BCE under the Ramessides in Egypt, these subgroups of Berbers frequently attacked Egypt. However, the Greeks, led by Aristotle, who later took the Libyan name Battos, invaded and colonized Cyrenaica in the seventh century BCE. Battos, who settled in Cyrene, established the Battaid dynasty in about 631 BCE.

The area was remarkable for the cultivation of barley and wheat, olive oil and wine, figs and apples, wool and sheep, cattle and silphium. Silphium, which was believed to be a medicine and an aphrodisiac, is a plant that is found only in Cyrenaica.

Famous for its medical school, learned academies, and architecture of different kinds, Cyrene emerged to become one of the greatest intellectual and artistic centers of the Greek world. A shrine of Aesculapius, god of medicine, was erected in one of the surrounding hills. Notable philosophers, such as Aristippus, mathematicians like Callimachus, and scientists like Theodorus and Eratosthenes—the geometrician—were from Cyrenaica. It is important to mention that Plato was a student of Eratosthenes.

Cambyses II, the Persian leader, conquered Egypt and Pentapolis in 525 BCE. In 332 BCE, Alexander the Great took over Egypt and part of what later became known as Libya. Under the Persians, Cyrenaica, together with Crete, was organized as one administrative province in 78 BCE and became a Roman senatorial province in 20 BCE.

Fezzan, largely a desert in the southwestern region, was a home to the Garamantian Empire, a state that operated the Trans-Saharan trade routes successively between Carthage and the Roman Empire in North Africa and the Sahelian states of west and central Africa. Fezzan, from the fifth century BCE to the fifth century CE, came under Roman rule and became part of what later became known as Rome's Africa Nova province under Augustus Caesar. While Roman rule lasted, Fezzan was a client state of the Roman Empire. Even during the Roman civil wars, Tripolitania, Cyrenaica, and Fezzan remained independent. This was in spite of the fact that two of the contenders in the civil wars, Pompey and Marcus Antonius regarded these three Libyan regions as the food baskets of the Roman Empire.

Tripolitania on the coastal plain emerged as an important source of olive oil, especially from about 363 BCE to the time of Julius Caesar (100-44 BCE). On its own, Leptis Magna emerged as an important cultural and architectural center. Its own sons, Septimius Severus (ruled 193–211 BCE) and Caracalla (ruled 211–217 BCE), later became Roman emperors. The Berbers, especially the Austuriani, rebuffed increasing Roman political involvement in Libya between 363 and 365 BCE. The attacks, which lasted for a few years, came to a halt following the Vandals' invasion and conquest of Libya. Sabratha, like Leptis Magna and Oea, was also affected by the Roman conquest. It emerged from being a sleepy Carthaginian trading outpost into a thriving Roman city, notable for a magnificent forum and over a hundred columns. However, the Austuriani who were desirous of retaining control, sacked it in the fourth century BCE, as did the Vandals later in the fifth century.

An important development that occurred between the Roman invasion of Tripolitania and the Vandals' invasion and conquest was the advent of Christianity. Cyrenaica was the first to taste Christianity in Libya. Jews had visited, settled, and traded in different parts of North Africa, especially Libya. Simon, from Cyrene, assisted in carrying Jesus

The ancient marketplace of Leptis Magna in Libya. Roman emperor Septimius Severus was born in Leptis, and the city flourished during his reign. (Robert Bamler)

Christ's cross on his way to crucifixion. On the day of the Pentecost, among the numerous Jews who listened to the apostles and heard them preach in their own tongues after the Holy Spirit had descended on them were "inhabitants of parts of Libya about Cyrene."[1] In the stoning of Stephen, the first Christian martyr, were Jews of Cyrene. In addition, a certain Lucius, a Cyrenaican Jew, was with Paul and Barnabas at the beginning of their missionary journey.

How did Christianity get to Libya? One of the three popular local stories in Cyrenaica was that Mark, the apostle and founder of the Alexandrine Church, journeyed unto Cyrenaica, where he domiciled for a time. Another popular narrative among the Muslim Berbers in Gebel Nefusah was that it was Philip the apostle, not Mark, who brought Christianity to Cyrenaica. The third and most probable was that Apostle Paul, who undoubtedly preached in Libya following his shipwreck in Malta, brought Christianity to Cyrenaica. Whichever way Christianity reached Libya, there is no doubt that the most enduring legacy of the Roman invasion and conquests of Libya is the introduction of Christianity.

The earliest Jewish converts, many of whom were at loggerheads with the temples in Cyrene and other cities and towns in Cyrenaica, spread

Christianity to Tripolitania between the reign of Emperor Septimius Severus when Christianity ceased to be regarded as a *religio illicita* and became a popular movement and the reign of Emperor Constantine in 313 CE, when Christianity became the official religion of the Roman Empire. After 313 CE, Christianity grew in leaps and bounds, with native Libyans playing important roles in its growth and spread across North Africa. Archaeus of Leptis was the first Bishop of Tripolitania. Among the Council of Carthage, which St. Cyprian called in 256 CE, were four bishops from Oea, Girba, Leptis Magna, and Sabratha. Three bishops from Libya—Berenice, Teuchira, and Barce—also attended the Council of Nicaea in 325 CE. During the Diocletian persecution of 303 CE, a bishop from Cyrene was among the martyrs.

The spread of Christianity into the interior of Libya turned out to be a double-edged sword, as many native Berbers regarded Christianity as a tool of protest against both Roman Catholicism and Roman rule; hence, many converted to Christianity. These Berber converts allied with the Donatists, a breakaway Roman Catholic group whose teachings differed only to a degree from Roman Catholicism. Together with the Berbers, the Donatists vehemently opposed Roman rule and the Catholic church, a development that threatened Rome's food basket—North Africa, in general. Owing to the impact of Berber-Donatists protests over agriculture and trade, Rome initially passed a law proscribing Donatism and, in 377 CE, outlawed membership of the group. Although the law was successful, the numerous protests had devastating effects on the economies of both Libya and the Roman Empire in general.

Despite Roman conquests, local political administration of most of Libya was under the Numidian kings, and this arrangement lasted for a whole century. As the century wore on, the Romans concentrated mainly on commerce, not colonization. Numidia (*Inumiden*, as Berbers called it) was an ancient Berber kingdom that stretched from what is now Algeria and small portions of both Tunisia and Libya. It was the first Berber state in North Africa. Prior to becoming a kingdom under Massinissa, king of the Massylii, it was divided into Massylii in the east and Masaesyli in the west. Under Massinissa, Numidia controlled most of Algeria and parts of Libya and was desirous of annexing Carthage. Massinissa deployed 4,000 men who fought on the side of Rome during the Second Punic War, and the Roman victory was due largely to Massinissa's intervention. As a compensation, Massinissa was allowed to rule over Carthage and other areas of Massinissa's choice. At about 165 BCE, Massinissa seized Tripolitania, Gefara Plain, and, later, Oea, Leptis, and Sabratha.

When, in 150 BCE, Carthage went to war with Massinissa, Rome intervened, sacking both Carthage and Massinissa's Numidian kingdom. It was in an attempt to bring Massinissa's ambitious project of building a Numidian kingdom, whose capital would be Carthage, under control that Rome gained political control of Tripolitania. Leptis Magna, Oea, and Sabratha became parts of Roman province in Africa owing to Leptis's support for Pompey against Julius Caesar. With Caesar's victory over Pompey in 48 BCE, much of what is now known as Libya came under Rome's effective political and economic control.

After a century of political independence, Tripolitania and Cyrenaica became parts of the Roman state, and, like any other Romans, Libyans in Tripolitania and Cyrenaica spoke the Roman language, adopted Roman laws, and assumed Roman identity. For more than 400 years, Libyans in Tripolitania and Cyrenaica, Leptis Magna, and Sabratha witnessed unprecedented socioeconomic and political development. Social amenities, such as the forum, markets, public entertainments, and baths that characterized Roman cities and towns, were established everywhere in Libya, and Libya became effectively a part of the Roman Empire.

The majority of Berbers remained in agriculture and trade even under Roman rule. For instance, Tripolitania contributed olive oil, ivory, and wild animals, while wines, drugs, and horses continued to pour into the Roman Empire from Cyrenaica. The Garamantes continued to serve as intermediaries, interfacing between Roman merchants and native populations in both North Africa and West Africa.

Customs diffused into Libya, and many Berbers became largely "Romanized" in language and culture. Notwithstanding this, Tripolitania remained essentially Punic in character, while Cyrenaica remained Greek.

Roman rule and political control of Libya ended abruptly with the Vandals' invasion and conquest in the fifth century. Romans' political and social order, like their architectural legacies in Libya and the rest of North Africa, fell into ruin following the Vandals' invasion and conquest. The Vandals were not astute administrators and merchants like the Romans. As a consequence, many Libyans who had been assimilated into Roman culture reverted to their traditional practices.

Under the Vandals, Cyrenaica became a military camp. Byzantine Emperors introduced different categories of taxes and levies to meet the cost of stationing the military in Cyrenaica. Public services such as roads, irrigation, canals, and baths were left unattended as attention shifted toward the building and maintaining of a stronger military. The costs were enormous, and public services collapsed in towns and cities. Berber nomads, taking advantage of the chaotic situation, rebelled again and again in the seventh century.

A brief respite came in the sixth century, when Emperor Justinian not only reconquered much of the Roman world from the Vandals but also made concerted efforts to rebuild the old cities. His efforts were, however, inadequate, and the chaotic situation that followed the Vandals' rule deprived the Libyans of any vigorous efforts to defend Libya against the Arab/Muslim invasion of the seventh century.

THE VANDALS IN LIBYA

In 429 CE, a group of Germanic warriors—the Vandals—entered North Africa, having been invited from Spain by Count Boniface. The Vandals' king, Geneseric, led 3,000 soldiers and 50,000 men and women into Morocco. After a few months, the Vandals defeated the Romans. Rather than returning to Spain, the Vandals ran riot across North Africa, destroying and pillaging city after city. After ten years, Geneseric captured Carthage. In 455 CE, Geneseric captured Tripolitania and, later, Rome. The great walls of Leptis and Sabratha were destroyed.

Except for the Donatists, Jews and Roman Catholics in North Africa suffered greatly under the Vandals, who confiscated their possessions, ransacked their homes, and destroyed their temples and public buildings. In 484 CE, many Roman Catholics were executed, including six Berber bishops from Tripolitania. While the coming of the Vandals spelled a great doom for the Romans, it, however, aided the cause of the Libyan Berbers, many of whom had been fighting the Romans for political and economic control of their lands for many years.

By the late fifth century, many Berber subgroups had not only asserted their independence but had also reverted to their traditional practices. The Vandals made no effort to curb these Berber insurgencies. Rather, the frontiers were left undefended, and as soon as they conquered the Romans, Libyan Berbers regained control of their lands. With nothing hindering Berber nationalism, many Berber subgroups came together as a federation called Zenata. Zenata was reputable for its fighting effectiveness and stratagems, coherent organizational structure, and tremendous discipline. In many works of literature on Africa, Eurocentric writers have adduced the sophistry with which the Zenata was administered as deriving from the activities of persecuted Jews. This is untrue.

The Romans made spirited efforts to oust the Vandals but to no avail. Only the Byzantine ruler, Emperor Justinian of Constantinople, successfully defeated the Vandals in 533 CE. Justinian also persecuted the

Berbers, the Donatists, the Jews, and the pagans. Justinian and his successors were as cruel as the Vandals and proved to be in no way like the Romans in nation-building and trade.

The Berbers, who had become too independent to submit willingly to any invader, were placed under burdensome taxations and levies. No sooner had Justinian successfully wiped out the Vandals than insurrections against Greek rule began. In 534 CE, Justinian had to quell an insurrection in Tripolitania. In 544 CE, eight Berber leaders were executed in Leptis Magna alone in order to discourage insurrections. After a century of Byzantine rule, Sabratha and Leptis became deserted, with its public infrastructure—water system, roads, buildings, and the like in great ruin. Most Romans—Jews and Christians—were forced to ally with the Berbers around them for existence.

All efforts to restore Libya proved inadequate, as the Byzantine inadequacies in governance ensured that commerce, nomadism, and the cultivation of crops kept failing year in, year out. To restore Tripolitania, Justinian organized civic and religious programs. In Leptis and Sabratha, new walls were erected but only around small areas of the old city centers. In addition, missionaries were sent into the interior— from Tripolitania through Ghadames to Fezzan—to Christianize the Berbers. No evidence exists attesting to either the success or failure of the missionary enterprise.

The Byzantine's inability to organize Libya and all of North Africa gave impetus to the division into Greek eastern and Latin western halves. It also led to the flowering of Berber nationalism, as the Berbers emerged stronger and more organized, mobile, and daring, as well as becoming far more formidable than anything the Romans had ever met. Cyrenaica, despite belonging to the western Mediterranean, was incorporated into the eastern bloc and was ruled as an imperial province directly from Constantinople. Unlike the western half, the eastern half was a maritime and commercial power. Byzantine concentrated mainly on the coastal cities and their immediate hinterland, as a way on reopening the Mediterranean trade. The rest of Libya was left to the Berbers, and Saharan trade fell as a consequence.

At the beginning of the sixth century, although the city walls at Apollonia and Teuchira were still standing and new ones were erected at Cyrene and Tolemaide, much of Cyrenaica was in ruin and almost deserted. When the aqueduct at Tolemaide broke down and there was no skilled person to repair and restore it, most of its inhabitants deserted the city, escaping into the countryside, where they cultivated the land and reared livestock. Northern Cyrenaica, unlike other parts of Libya, was well defended against the Berbers; hence, many of the cities and towns in the region were prosperous. New fortresses were built at Boreum, Tobruk, and Paraetonium, affording security for the Mediterranean coastal trade. No one is in doubt that, by the end of the sixth century, over ten centuries of Mediterranean incursions and the imposition of settler cultures on Libya and North Africa had come to an end, as the Berbers were taking over their ancestral lands, which had been raped and pillaged for years by the Carthaginians and Romans, Greeks, and Byzantines, and were reversing many years of alien cultures, ranging from those of the Semitic lands to those of the Greeks and Latins. Only the Arab invasion of the seventh century prevented the complete triumph of the Berbers in regaining their ancestral lands.

ARABS IN LIBYA

Following the death of the Prophet Muhammad in 632 CE, his followers, with the Quran in one hand and sword in the other, spread Islam from the Arabian Peninsula into contemporary Iran and North Africa. Led by Amr ibn al-As, they conquered Byzantine Syria in 636 CE, Persia in 637 CE, Alexandria in 643 CE, and Cyrenaica in 644 CE. Abdullah ibn Saad led the Arab army into Tripolitania in 646 CE, while in 663 CE, Uqba bin Nafi and his Arab army took Fezzan. After an initial delay in Tripolitania, where it took about two years to put down Berber resistance, Uqba and his men invaded and took Carthage, modern Tunisia, in 670 CE. When Uqba reached the Atlantic Ocean in 682 CE, he rode his horse into the sea saying: "Oh God! If the sea had not prevented me, I would have coursed on forever like Alexander the Great, upholding your faith and fighting all who disbelieved."[2] The Sahara Desert, which for many years had proved too formidable for other invaders, was never a threat to Uqba and his hordes of Arab warriors—thanks to their camels.

The Arabs were successful where others had failed. By 715, the Arabs had conquered and dominated all empires and kingdoms, towns and cities, big and small, from the Arabian Peninsula throughout North Africa and to the Pyrenees—the very limit of the old Roman Empire.

A number of factors could explain the Arab successes in Libya. Since the Roman invasion, the Berbers had to fight for their ancestral land. Poor administration during the Vandals' invasion completely ruined Libya's economy, and the Byzantines' inability to stem the decline provided the needed opportunities for the resurgence of Berber nationalism. Between Bacra and Tripoli was a 300-mile-long arid desert, called Sirtica, which only a handful of armies had ever crossed. Arab mastery of the use of camels in warfare meant that the Sirtica and the entire

Sahara Desert were never threats. As Gibbon described their passage, the Arabs, attended by their faithful camels, like the troops led by Amr Ibn al-As, "beheld without terror the familiar aspect of the soil and climate."[3]

Arab invasion of North Africa ushered in Islamic religion, along with Arabic culture and language. Far and above every other effect, religion, language, and culture remain the most enduring legacies of the Arabs' invasion of North Africa. Following their conquests, Tripolitania and Cyrenaica, like the rest of Africa, came under the Umayyad Caliphate, whose headquarters were in Damascus. As the caliph (*khalifa*), successor to the Prophet Muhammad and to the secular and religious heads of the Muslim community, the Umayyad governed from North Africa to Spain and southern France from 661 CE to 750 CE. The Umayyad instituted a theocracy, with the caliph as a representative of God (Allah) and the custodian of the *Sharia*, the Islamic legal code that derived from the Quran. The legal system was administered by religious judges, under whom all loyalties were subordinated. The primary goal of administration was the establishment of religious and political unity.

Although Islam was introduced by force, the Arabs recognized local authorities. Like others before them, the Arabs were also confined exclusively to the North African littoral. To avoid conversion to Islam, many Berbers escaped from the cities and towns into the mountains and the deserts, where they eked out a daily living either by animal husbandry or by trade across the Sahara. The spread of Islam was not the work of the Arabs but that of the native Berbers themselves. As many who converted to Islam carried out trading expedition into the mountains and deserts, trading with their fellow Berbers, Islam began to penetrate the inner recesses of the Sahara Desert, and it was through the efforts of these Berber traders that Islam crossed into West Africa. In Islam, religion and culture are bound up; hence, one cannot be a Muslim without adopting the Islamic culture. In other words, the Arabization and Islamization processes were the work of the Berbers, which took a long time to take hold. Over the years, the Arabs came to recognize the authority of the local chiefs and allowed the chiefs to carry on with local administration as long as this was carried on according to the dictates of the Quran.

Between 750 and 1258 CE, the Islamic world was in turmoil, as the Abbasid dynasty overthrew the Umayyads and relocated the headquarters of the caliphate from Damascus to Baghdad. The bone of contention was the issue of succession after the Prophet Muhammad's death. For the Abbasid, only those who are related by blood to the prophet are eligible to be the caliph; hence, they chose Ali, the prophet's cousin and son-in-law. They became known as Shiat-Ali (also Shiah)—the "partisans of Ali." To the Sunnis (Abbasids), however, succession should be on merit, and any pious and devoted Muslim could aspire to the caliphate.

After overthrowing the Umayyads, the Abbasids appointed Ibrahim ibn Aghlab (ruled 786–809 CE) as the *amir*—leader of the faithful—in the areas today known as North Africa. From his base in Kairouan in modern Tunisia, Aghlab ruled Tripolitania. Aghlab and his children proclaimed allegiance to Baghdad and observed the strict Sunni ideology. The Aghlabids, as Aghlab's hereditary dynasty was called, repaired roads, public buildings, irrigation systems, and other structures in Tripolitania and consequently restored the region's economic prosperity.

The question that dominated the Muslim world after the death of the Prophet of who should succeed the Prophet Muhammad eventually fractured the Muslim world in two—Shiites and Sunnis. To the Shiites, only direct descendants of Ali, the fourth caliph and son-in-law of the Prophet Muhammad should ascend to the office of the caliph. The Shiites had a huge followership among non-Arab Muslims in Iran and southern Iraq, Bahrain, and Azerbaijan. Large Shiite communities could also be found in Afghanistan and India, Kuwait and Lebanon, Pakistan and Qatar, as well as in Syria and Turkey, Saudi Arabia, Yemen, and the United Arab Emirates. The rest of the world's Islamic countries are Sunni. The Sunnis believe that the Prophet Muhammad had no rightful heir and made no attempt to appoint one; hence, any member of the Islamic community, chosen through election from the ranks of the *shurfa*, the Prophet's descendants via Fatima, his daughter, could be appointed as caliph. While the Shiites chose the descendants of Ali, the fourth caliph and son-in-law of the prophet, the Sunnis chose Abu Bakr, Prophet Muhammad's close friend and adviser, as the caliph.

In 909 CE, a group of Shiites, the Fatimids, in alliance with the Kutama Berbers of the Kabylie region of Algeria, attacked the Aghlabids, and, after intense fighting, Kairouan, the Aghlabid's capital, fell. In 969 CE, the conquerors, the Fatimids, also took Egypt and moved the capital of their caliphate to Cairo, from which they ruled North Africa. Like others before them, the Fatimids also limited their activities to the coastal areas and major cities. The control of the hinterland was left in the hands of a Berber dynasty, the Zirid, whose control of parts of present-day Algeria, Libya, and Tunisia from the late ninth century to the middle of the 12th century proved disastrous.

Under the Zirid dynasty, the economic base of Libya and other areas under their control collapsed, as little or no attention was paid to agriculture, and public infrastructure was left to decay. In 1049 CE, the Zirid abandoned Shiite Islam and adopted Sunni Islam. In order to restore Libya and other areas under the control of the Zirid dynasty to Shiite Islam, the Fatimids invited Bani Hilal and Bani Salim, two Bedouin ethnic groups from Saudi Arabia, into North Africa, bringing Shiites and Sunnis into an open conflict.

The Hilalians, as the two ethnic groups were called, invaded Cyrenaica, Tripolitania, among other places in North Africa, leaving behind great destruction. The population fell drastically, and sedentary agriculture collapsed, as the Hilalians forced many Berbers into adopting pastoral nomadism. Almost a million Arab migrants poured into Libya and North Africa from Saudi Arabia under the Hilalians. Today, descendants of these Arab immigrants, called Marabtin, claim Libya as their homeland. No sooner had they expelled the Sunnis than a few Berber ethnic groups—the Almoravid, Almohads, and Hafsids—from Morocco also expelled the Fatimids from Libya and other parts of North Africa.

For 200 years, the Almoravid, Almohads, and Hafsids, ruling from Marrakesh, controlled from North Africa to Muslim Spain. Although these groups were themselves Sunnis, they belonged to the Maliki School of Sunni Islam, a militant Sunni Islamic sect. They were renowned for their strict interpretation of the Sharia and incomparable zeal in spreading Islam. Their leader, Abu Abdullah Mohammad Ibn Tumart, instituted a centralized theocratic government. Abd al-Mu'min bin Ali al-Kumi, Tumart's military commander, later deposed his master and set up a dynasty that brought many cities and towns—from Tripoli in Libya to Tinmallal in Morocco and from Islamic Spain to the Western Sahel—under Islamic rule. The new dynasty also brought many cities and towns in Spain, including Cordova and Almeria, under Islam; however, it could not withstand the combination of Spain and Italy in 1492 CE. Despite defeat at the hands of Spain and Italy, the Almohad dynasty still held its North African possessions. While it succeeded in preventing Spain and Italy from taking over these possessions, however, it fractured into three dynasties: the Marinids, who ruled in Morocco between 1244 and 1420 CE, the Zayinids who ruled in Algeria between 1236 and 1318 CE, and the Hafsids who ruled in Tunisia and Tripolitania between 1228 and 1574 CE.

Muhammad ben Abu Hafs, the head of the Hafsid dynasty, controlled Tunisia and Tripolitania between 1207 and 1221 CE. For about the 300 years of Hafsid rule, their control of Tripolitania was limited only to the coastal areas. The hinterlands were left to the indigenous Berbers, who did not recognize the authority of the Hafsids and constantly sought ways of recovering their ancestral lands. Under the Hafsids,

Libya was a mosaic of ethnic states, theocratic republics, and costal trading outposts.

While towns and cities in Tripolitania came under the control of different Maghribi dynasties between the seventh and 12th centuries, Cyrenaica and Fezzan had a totally different experience. As early as in the seventh century, a succession of Mamluk dynasties in Egypt claimed control of Cyrenaica. Although under the Mamluk, both the Berbers and Bedouins in Cyrenaica recognized no other authority over them than their indigenous chiefs, the Mamluk's control was nominal, and the Bedouins asserted their control over trade along the oases—demanding levies and tolls from merchants on all merchandise. In Fezzan, indigenous chiefs, under the headship of Beni Khattab, retained control. Like the Garamantes, they also took control of trading activities and agriculture around the oases.

In 1550, Beni Khattab's control of the Fezzan region ended abruptly, as Muhammad al-Fasi removed the Khattab and began Ottoman rule in Fezzan. Despite Ottoman control, Fezzan was allowed some measure of internal freedom, as the Ottomans limited their involvement in the political administration in order to ensure allegiance to the Ottomans and to preserve trade.

While foreigners and invaders controlled trade along the coastal trading outposts, most of Libya was under either effective or nominal Berber control until 1510 CE, when Spanish forces captured Tripoli. However, Draughut Sinan Pasha, a Turkish admiral, acting on behalf of the Ottoman sultan, invaded Tripoli in 1551 CE, driving away the Knights of St. John of Malta, with whom Emperor Charles V (1500–1558) had entrusted the defense of Tripoli in 1524 CE, and ushering in a period of Ottoman control.

After Pasha's successful defeat of Tripoli, he embarked upon an ambitious project of pacifying the Arab nomads of the hinterland, and, by the end of the 17th century, he had converted a large part of North Africa—from Algeria to Libya and Tunisia—into a series of Ottoman provinces. The new ruler stationed a commander in Benghazi, while making Tripoli the capital.

OTTOMAN LIBYA

By the middle of the 17th century CE, the Ottoman Empire, which started in the 13th century in western Asian Minor, had expanded west and east, conquering erstwhile empires, states, and kingdoms such as the Byzantines and Serbs, the Bulgarians and Anatolia (Asia Minor), as well as others in western Asia, northern Africa, and southeast Europe. After a failed initial attempt in 1529, a second attempt at conquering central Europe in 1683 met with a catastrophic defeat in Hapsburg, Vienna. Despite its defeat, the Ottoman Empire controlled southeast Europe for over 200 years, and for more than 300 years, it controlled contemporary Turkey and Syria, Lebanon and Iraq, Israel and Palestine, Jordan and Saudi Arabia, as well as North Africa.

Libya first came under the Ottomans in 1551, as part of the Sublime Porte—the central government of the Ottoman Empire—in North Africa, which was composed of the three regencies of Algiers, Tunis, and Tripoli. By the 17th century CE, these three regencies had become Ottoman vassal states. The Ottoman sultan in Constantinople (modern Istanbul) imposed a *pasha* (governor) on each of the vassal states. To assist the various *pashas*, the sultan stationed an elite military caste, the *janissaries*, in Libya. By the 18th century, the *janissaries* had evolved into a self-governing military guild with its own laws and subject only to a local council of senior officers, the *divan*. Mutinies and coups d'état were commonplace, and when, in 1611, local chiefs staged a coup, Suleiman Safar—the coup leader, was appointed head of government. Suleiman took the title *dey* (local chief).

The *janissaries* collected taxes and maintained order while the Berber corsairs collected ransoms and booties for the governors. In addition, the corsairs also contributed soldiers to the governor's army in cases of war or external attacks. Under the *janissaries*, Libya was divided into administrative units (*sanjaks*) and districts (*qadas*). The *qada* and *sanjak* were the basic administrative divisions on which administration rested. While each *sanjak* was administered by a *dey*, the *qada* was supervised by a *qaimmaqam*. The *sanjak dey* and *qaimmaqam* were responsible only to the military governor. These officials fixed prices of items and imports, inspected weights and measures, and supervised weighing stations. In addition, they also oversaw local markets.

Like others before the *janissaries*, Ottoman rule was also limited to the coastal areas, major towns, and cities. In the hinterland, Berbers and other indigenous people carried on trade and commerce, animal rearing, and date cultivation unhindered. From 1661, more and more military commanders took control, and the *pasha*'s power declined. Between 1672 and 1711, Ottoman rule in Libya entered into another phase, a phase that was characterized by incessant coups—as no military ruler held power for a year before being removed in another coup. In 1711, Ahmad Karamanli, a khouloughi cavalry officer, overthrew the Ottoman *pasha* and commenced the Karamanli dynasty, which briefly stemmed the tide of the decline.

Under Ahmad Karamanli, Libya witnessed improved foreign relations with Europe, an improved military, and successful coordination
of political authority over Tripolitania, Cyrenaica, and Fezzan. Berber
and Arab rebellions were quashed, and the trans-Saharan trade resumed
in earnest. Following Ahmad Karamanli's death, his son, Muhammad,
became the new leader. He was, however, a weaker leader, and, no
sooner did his father die than decline set in again. Berber and Arab
rebellions resumed after Ahmad's death. Drought, famine, and locust
invasion occurred in quick succession, bringing untold hardship to
Libya. It was under this condition that Ali Benghuli, a Turkish official,
seized power in 1754 and briefly restored Ottoman rule in Libya.

Ottoman control was short-lived, as Yusuf Karamanli, son of Ali, took
control again and ruled until Napoleon Bonaparte's invasion of Egypt
in 1798–1799. Faced with mounting debt, Yusuf hoped to defray some
of the debt by raising taxes and levies. This development was the death
knell that led to his abdication. His son, Ali II (ruled 1832–1835), found
himself at the mercy of Libya's British and French creditors and therefore requested the assistance of the Ottomans. He was, however,
deceived by his Ottoman friends, who deployed an intervention force
in 1835 to save Libya from France. Upon arrival at the port in Tripoli,
Ali II went onto the ship to welcome his allies and was promptly
detained and later deported. The Sultan in Istanbul appointed Mohammad Raif Pasha as governor to rule over Libya.

The Ottoman second invasion and rule differed significantly from
its first. It marked the end of decentralized political authority in Libya.
Raif Pasha and his successors closely aligned Libya with the Ottoman
state, instituting a series of policies and programs that played significant roles in consolidating Ottoman power in different provinces of
Libya. At the beginning of Raif Pasha's rule, he inherited a war-ravaged
Libya, whose inhabitants, especially in Cyrenaica, had fled into the desert to avert conversion to Islam and the devastation of civil wars.

Land reform, which aimed at destroying the power of longtime influ-
ential groups such as the Berbers', was one of the most significant steps
taken immediately upon Raif Pasha's coming to power. The land reform
aimed at making previously nomadic people sedentary. Underlying this
policy was the need to break ethnic loyalty to indigenous chieftains and
the fostering of new relationships between the new rulers and the
citizens.

In the implementation of this policy, indigenous ownership was dismantled, and lands were distributed among individuals who could pay
a small registration fee. The newly redistributed land stayed in the
hands of the farmers, thereby encouraging settled living rather than

nomadism and leading to the loosening of kinship ties. The land reform, in addition to creating wealth for many, undermined ethnic loyalty and redistributed wealth.

In addition to the land reform was administrative reorganization. Administrative and village councils were established, as well as a court system composed of distinct criminal and civil courts. This administrative reorganization led to the emergence of different categories of administrative officials, which, in turn, brought governance down to the local level. Procedures for the collection of taxes and levies were also reorganized to facilitate transparency. In addition, post and telegraphs were introduced, which connected different parts of Libya with one another, as well as connecting Libya with Malta.

Most Libyans witnessed increasing economic growth and therefore became mollified under Ottoman rule, especially with increasing European intrusion and the scramble for Africa. These changes were consolidated in Libya with the emergence of the Young Turks Revolution, which among other things, sought to reform, revamp, and reinvigorate the Istanbul sultanate, modernize Ottoman rule, and ensure equality for its provinces.

In summary, over 360 years of Ottoman rule witnessed the socioeconomic and political transformation of Libya. It also brought about order and control, administrative reorganization, and increased education. Crop cultivation and animal husbandry, which saw a resurgence, combined to weaken long-distance trading and ethnic loyalties—a major problem in the flowering of a Libyan nationalism. The emergence of Libyan nationalism, which followed, aided the Ottoman governors in staving off Italian occupation.

CONCLUSION

From all this, it can be asserted that while many foreigners have conquered and ruled parts of Libya at different times, not one of them was able to rule Libya as a whole or to impose its authority and political control on Libya as a whole. For many of them, trade and trading activities along the coast were enough, while political administration of either the hinterland or even the coastal cities was left to the Libyans themselves.

As shall be seen in the next chapter, Libya later came under Italian colonial conquests, and the Italians remained the only foreign power to rule Libya as a whole. Even at that, conquest came at a great cost in human life (on both sides) and materials.

NOTES

1. Holy Bible, Acts of the Apostle, Chapter 2, verse 10.

2. M. Brett and E. Fentress, *The Berbers* (Oxford: Blackwell, 1998), 82.

3. Edward Gibbon, *The History of the Decline and Fall of the Roman Empire* (London: John Murray, 1862), 343.

3

The Italian Colonial Conquest, 1911–1912

INTRODUCTION

As Chapter 2 showed, since the arrival of the Phoenician traders, Libyans have had to cope with foreign invaders. However, for most of its history, these invaders were unable to establish full political control over Libya. While the invaders controlled trade along the coastal areas, Libyans were in complete control of politics and administration, especially of the hinterland. Out of the different invaders, only the Ottomans, especially during their second invasion, were able to gain partial political control of Libya, a development that was short-lived. While the Ottoman invaders controlled the coastal trade, trade along the Sahara and between North Africa and West Africa was solely in the hands of the Libyans. The Libyans in towns and cities along the coastal areas and the hinterlands left no stone unturned in their defense of their political sovereignty.

This socioeconomic and political situation, however, changed with the Italian conquest of October 1911. Compared to previous invasions, the Italian invasion, like the 19th-century European colonial conquests of Africa, was completely different. Not only did the Italians completely conquer Libya, they also succeeded in establishing complete political control over the entire country. Contemporary Libya, as a nation-state, is the result of this Italian invasion; Libya, effectively, is an Italian colonial creation. What were the underlying reasons for the Italian invasion of Libya? In what ways did the phenomenon of the Industrial Revolution contribute to this development?

The Industrial Revolution was a watershed development in European history. Besides leading to the emergence of factories and the mass production of industrial goods, it also gave rise to two important developments that altered the course of human history. For the Industrial Revolution to be successful, European industries needed cheap raw materials and markets for the products of these industries. In their mad frenzies for cheap, if not free, raw materials and markets for industrial goods, different European powers cultivated spheres of trade interests in different parts of Africa. For instance, while Britain established Egypt, Kenya, Ghana, Nigeria, and a large swath of lands in different parts of Africa, as spheres of trade interests, Italy, having failed in its attempt to establish Ethiopia as a sphere of trade interests, concentrated its efforts on acquiring control of Libya.

Mercantilism, the idea that trade creates wealth and is encouraged by the buildup of profitable balances, undergirded this development. The idea of mercantilism was popular in Europe, so much so that many European powers established colonial enterprises in the Americas, Asia, and Africa. Mercantilism, it must be noted, aimed at consolidating the home economy; hence, colonies were established to produce free or cheap raw materials for European industries. The finished products from these European industries were brought back to these colonies for sale. To foster the system and make it more profitable, colonies were prohibited from trading except with those European mother countries that founded them. Consequent upon this development, colonialism, trade protection, and monopoly trading characterized European intrusions in Africa between the 16th and middle of the 20th centuries.

The Italian invasion of Libya was therefore not only for the twin mercantile objectives but also because the invasion of Libya afforded Italian control of all commercial opportunities and activities along the Mediterranean coasts. In addition, it also served as an outlet for Italy's surplus population. By controlling Libya, Italy hoped to gain a strategic advantage in trade along the Mediterranean and also across North Africa. This strategic advantage was pivotal, as the Mediterranean Sea had become a major node in Europe's mercantile economy. Gaining a foothold in Libya would secure Italy's Great Power ambition; hence, to many Italians, an outright conquest of Libya was a manifest destiny.

It is on account of these factors that the Italian colonization of Libya is treated differently and separately from other foreign intrusions in Libyan history.

ITALY'S INTERESTS IN LIBYA

Before the Italian unification of the 1860s, Italy, like other European powers involved in the Mediterranean trade, nursed a disturbing ambition concerning Libya. Libya's strategic location on the Mediterranean littoral made it an important player in the Mediterranean trading system. Hence, for Italy, as for France, controlling Libya would certainly deliver Mediterranean wealth to the Italians. Therefore, Italy was interested not only in controlling Libya but also in fighting other European powers, including the French, for the control of Libya. As the *Opinione*, a Turin periodical, put it in 1863: "If Egypt, and with it the Suez Canal, falls to the British, if Tunis falls to the French, and if Austria expands from Dalmatia into Albania, etc. we will soon find ourselves without a breathing space in the center of the Mediterranean."[1] Therefore, when Giuseppe Mazzini, the Italian leader, argued that "North Africa must belong to Italy" at the Berlin Conference of the 1870s, he was mainly expressing a popular opinion and a wish that was common to most European powers involved in the Mediterranean trading system. However, for Italy, the control of the Mediterranean trading system depended on controlling that "breathing space," Libya. Standing on the path of Italy's control of the Mediterranean trade were France, Britain, and the Ottomans. Of the three, only the Ottomans were considered a serious threat to Italy's trading and strategic interests in Libya.

Before the Italian invasion and conquest of Libya, the Ottoman rulers nominally controlled Libya's coastal areas. The hinterlands were under the control of the various ethnic groups in Libya. The Ottoman era in Libya dates from 642 CE, when Ottoman Arab troops invaded and conquered the local Berber population of the eastern part of Libya, Cyrenaica. Using their camels, they crossed over 300 miles of open desert separating the coastal regions of Cyrenaica and Tripolitania from Sirtica. The Ottomans also defeated the indigenous Berber people of Tripoli. Between 1050 and 1100 CE, Libya, especially in the coastal areas, had thoroughly accepted Islam and Arab language and culture. The encouragement given to trade made the nomadic way of life popular. Nomadism not only affected agricultural production but also stimulated the growth of the caravan trade, especially between the Mediterranean Sea and West and Central Africa.

Berber traders had been exchanging gold, ivory, and slaves from West and Central Africa for European products, especially textiles, timber, and firearms along the Mediterranean coasts, since the days of the Crusaders. Many Europeans from Venice, Pisa, Sicily, Naples, and elsewhere were smuggling firearms into the Libyan coasts, against the Holy Roman Empire's laws that aimed at preventing arms and ammunitions from reaching the Islamic world, which was engulfed in a series of holy wars against the Crusaders. Many Italian and other European merchants were dependent on this trade; hence, they trooped toward the Libyan coast and toward different oases along the caravan routes. Berbers, like these Italians, profited immensely from this trade.

Having defeated a number of Crusaders, the Ottoman rulers in Turkey, desirous of controlling these coastal areas in the 16th century, invaded and conquered much of North Africa, organizing them into three regencies: Algeria, Tunisia, and Tripoli. The regency of Tripoli, comprised also of Cyrenaica and Fezzan, was administered by the Ottoman-appointed governor—the *pasha*.

Between 1711 and 1836, Ottoman control of Libya was nominal, with concentration mainly on the coastal areas while the Libyan local rulers were left with the administration of the hinterland. The Ottomans were content with control of coastal trade, including piracy on the Mediterranean. Huge numbers of Ottomans, Italians, and Libyans daily traded along the coastal cities. The Ottomans derived wealth from the imposition of a small amount of "tribute" on Italian and other traders for the "privilege" of maintaining warehouses and other property in port cities. None of these sources of wealth compared to firearms, as the sales of firearms gave social, economic, and political control of the different areas to the Ottomans.

With an increasing number of small but prosperous communities of Italian traders along the North African coast, competition for the wealth of Libya became acute. More and more Italians were migrating to Libya, the majority of whom were involved in looting and piracy of ships along the Mediterranean Sea as a means of economic survival. The strategic importance of Libya's coastal cities, not only in trade and piracy but also in relation to the Crusade, was not lost on any of the European powers involved in the maritime trade of the 18th century. Britain, France, Germany, and the United States were all interested in establishing control over Libya.

Having secured the support of Britain and France, Italy initiated a gradualist policy of slow economic penetration of Libya, beginning in the late 19th century. The Italian government resettled thousands of Italians in Libya, encouraging Italian businessmen to buy existing commercial, manufacturing, and shipping firms in different Libyan ports. Within a few years, the Banco di Roma—an Italian bank—opened in 13 locations across Libya. Italians schools emerged, and Italian merchants controlled export trade, especially in ivory, cereals, esparto grass (used in making high-quality paper), sponges, and wool.

France had already taken over Tunisia, while Britain took over Egypt. In 1868, Italy signed a 20-year agreement with the *bey*—the Ottoman's appointed governor of Libya. Under this agreement, Italy commenced a "peaceful penetration" of Libya, which saw the emigration of more than 25,000 Italians into Libya. These Italian immigrants established trading firms, banking operations, and schools to spread the Italian language, businesses, and culture in Libya. For many Italians, peaceful penetration was too much of a palliative; only an outright colonization would do. "To emigrate is servile, but to conquer colonies is a worthy task for a free and noble people," Francesco Crispi, the Italian prime minister of the time, said.[2] However, Benito Mussolini, the Italian leader after Crispi, stated Italy's ambition more aptly: "[F]or others the Mediterranean is just a route, for us it is life itself."

In May 1881, the *bey*, displeased at the growing Italian interests in Libya, unilaterally annulled the 1868 agreement. Italy not only considered the annulment of the 1868 agreement and the *bey*'s sudden romance with France an insult, it also considered it a comfortable excuse to invade Libya. However, before invading Libya, Italy sought and obtained the support of Britain, France, Belgium, Portugal, and Spain. As Francesco Crispi framed it, by joining other Europeans in the so-called Scramble for Africa, "the seas between Sicily and the two Sirtic Gulfs shall become almost an Italian strait."[3] In other words, by joining in the Scramble for Africa, Italy hoped to change its trading influence in Libya into a full-fledged colonial enterprise. Although many Italians justified the invasion and colonization of Libya as an attempt to prevent France's expansion on the Mediterranean, the fact is that Italians, even before the French's colonization of Tunisia, referred to the Mediterranean as *Mare Nostrum*—"Our Sea."

As a part of the resolutions reached at the Berlin Conference of 1884 and 1885, where Africa was carved out, divided, and shared among the various European powers, Italy obtained France's commitment to stay out of Italy's actions in Tripoli. In return, Italy recognized France's claim to Morocco. In the same year, Britain also assured Italy of its claim to Libya. Buoyed by France and Britain, Italy basked in the euphoria that it would easily overrun the Ottomans in Libya. The popular thinking in Italy was that the Libyans, in themselves, were tired of the Ottomans and that the Libyans would gladly accept any Italian intervention, as a way to get rid of the Ottomans. Evidence also abounds to support the fact that Italy clandestinely sent arms and ammunitions to some Berber groups in the hope that these Libyans would fight on Italy's side once a war was declared against the Ottomans. To the Italian's chagrin, rather than supporting Italy against the Ottomans, the Berber groups teamed up with the Ottomans against the Italians. Even when the Ottomans had accepted defeat, the Berbers carried on fighting the Italians. It took Italy the better part of 20 years before it could conquer and effectively colonize Libya.

Another important factor in Italy's invasion of Libya was concern about Germany and the United States of America, as both were also interested in controlling Libya. To stave off any German or American invasion, therefore, Italy invaded Libya before the two powers could make any such attempt.

Italian cavalry on the march, ca. October 1911. In early October, Italy invaded Libya, hoping to expand its territory at the expense of a weakening Ottoman Empire. The Italians took Tripoli from the Turks, but the Italo-Turkish War ended in a stalemate in October 1912, leaving Italy with tenuous control over the regions of Tripolitania, Cyrenaica, and Fezzan. (Hulton Archive/Getty Images)

The Ottomans were not ignorant of Italy's ambitions in Libya; hence, they were against Italy's peaceful penetration of Tripoli and rallied Libyans against Italy. However, when in 1908, two Italians were killed in Libya, Italy argued that the Ottomans were killing Italians and that Italian lives and property were no longer safe in Ottoman-controlled Libya. Only the removal of the Ottomans and the colonization of Libya would resolve the impasse. Having secured a pretext to attack the Ottomans, in October 1911, Italy declared a war on the Ottomans, thereby bringing the 30-year-old Italian "peaceful penetration" to a sudden halt.

In order to avoid another embarrassing defeat like the one suffered at the Battle of Aduwa, Ethiopia, in 1838, Italy deployed a large number of soldiers—comprised of 34,000 armed men and 603 hundred horses, as well as heavy equipment—including four warships—the *Vittorio Emmanuele*, *Regina Elena*, *Roma*, and *Napoli*. On October 2, 1911, more men and 1,050 wagons, 48 field guns, 24 mountain guns, 145 warships, and 114 other vessels also arrived at the shores of Tripoli from Italy.

On October 3, the bombardment of the joint forces of the Ottomans and Libyans commenced. On October 4, Italian forces took Tobruk. Tripoli was taken on October 5. By October 18, Derna had been taken, while Benghazi was taken on October 19. Despite concerted resistance by the Libyan Berbers and the Ottomans at Henni, Sidi, Mesri, and Sharia Shatt, they were eventually overtaken on October 26. On November 1, 1911, as Lieutenant Giulio Gavotti's plane flew over the Gefara Plain, he dropped a hand grenade on Libya, making it the first time an airplane was used in warfare.

Despite its successes, Italian forces could not conquer the combined forces of Ottomans and Libyans. As more men and equipment poured in from Italy, the tide of the war began to change, and the Ottomans eventually gave in to the Italians. The Libyans, despite having rudimentary weapons, continued fighting, as they had always done against foreign domination. Following the Ottomans' acceptance of defeat, the Italians signed the Treaty of Ouchy with the Ottomans and the Libyans. The Treaty gave Tripolitania, Fezzan, and Cyrenaica to Italy.

In the treaty, Italy issued a decree declaring Libya its subject nation. While still under Italian administration, Tripolitania and Cyrenaica were granted full independence. In addition, the Ottoman sultan demanded that a representative be appointed to look after Ottoman investment in both Tripolitania and Cyrenaica. This representative was to be supervised by the Italian authority. The Sultan retained the right to appoint the Grand Quadi of Tripoli. Given all this, it can be argued that while the treaty gave socioeconomic, political, and secular authority to the Italians, the Ottomans held religious authority. Libyan interests were never considered in the treaty.

Given the terms of the treaty, many Libyans felt abandoned by the Ottomans, and factional groups emerged among Libyans. These factions were agitating for different forms of post-Ottoman involvement in the administration of Libya. Under the leadership of Sulaiman Baruni, a 40-year-old Ibadite Berber from the Gebel Nefusha, these factional groups gathered at Azizia to discuss the Libyan position in the administration of Libya. While Sulaiman Baruni's group favored an outright expulsion of the Italians, another group of Libyans, led by Mohammad Farhad of Zavia, advocated a submission to the Italians, believing that the Italians would respect the independence of Tripolitania and Cyrenaica, as stated in the Treaty of Ouchy. Unable to come to a unified position, Baruni and his men retreated into the Gebel mountains, where they declared an independent Berber state under Baruni's leadership.

Initial efforts to rein in Baruni and his men ended in mass casualties for the Italians. The Italians eventually were able to defeat Baruni and his men in the Battle of Asabaa on March 23, 1913. By March, Yefren had fallen to the Italians, and Nalut was taken in April. By the end of April, different Berber ethnic groups from Sirtica to Fezzan and Ghadames had submitted to the Italians. In Qasr Bu Hadi, Ramadan al-Suwayhli and his men, whom the Italian thought were their allies, killed more than 500 Italian soldiers, and a large amount of Italian equipment, supplies, and money was also lost.

The situation in Cyrenaica, where Sayyid Ahmad al-Sharif led members of the Sanussi Order against the Italians, was a bit different. The Sanussi Order was a strongly nationalistic Sunni political and religious group. The Sanussi Order, founded by Omar al-Mukhtar, domiciled around the Jebel Akhdar Mountains in Cyrenaica. Under Sayyid Ahmad al-Sharif, the Order led the Libyan resistance against Italy's attempts to colonize Libya.

Popular opinion in most writings is that members of the Order were more interested in Islam than they were in fighting for their homelands in Libya. This reading of the Sanussi Order's engagement with the Italian invaders fails to take into consideration the many years of long-drawn-out battles that the various Berber groups had fought against different invaders, including the Ottoman Arabs. It stands logic on its head that members of the Order could be fighting the Italians on account of religion, as the Treaty of Ouchy already granted them the right to practice Islam under the banner of the Ottoman Sultan. With the Ottomans' withdrawal, Islam provided members of the Order, many of whom were from different ethnic groups, a common platform upon which they could continue their long-term opposition to foreign rule and colonization. In addition, the Order, under Sayyid Idris al-Sanussi, never made its intention hidden. For example, following the Ottomans' request that members of the Order should attack the British in Egypt, Sayyid Idris al-Sanussi made it clear to the Ottomans that the fight was to save Libya from invaders and not to become a pawn in any of Ottoman's wars in Africa or elsewhere. So, rather than attacking the British, members of the Order adopted guerrilla-style warfare in the fight against the Italians in order to save Libya, their homeland. When Italy could not defeat the Order, it eventually agreed to a peace treaty—the Akrama Agreement of April 1917, which gave Cyrenaica to the Order.

The Order's resistance was highly successful because the Tebu, Tuaregs, and thousands of Berber ethnic groups, especially from Wadi Shatti and the deserts, allied with members of the Order in repelling the Italian attacks. Saif al-Nasr, leading his Fezzan men in 1915, expelled the Italians from Mizda-Nalut. Italy's counterattack that met the Order near Mizda was almost wiped out. Another group of Libyans led by Ramadan Shutaywi triumphed over the Italians in Misurata, where more than 4,000 Italian soldiers perished at the hands of the Libyans in one day. The losses in men paled in comparison to the losses in equipment. Shutaywi, beside killing the Italian soldiers and their Eritrean mercenaries, seized 5,000 rifles, millions of rounds of ammunition, and all the Italian supplies and money in Misurata. By turning Italian guns against the Italians, Shutaywi regained some of the towns and cities already conquered by the Italians except Homs, Misurata-Marina, Tagiura, and Tripoli. By May 1915, Italy's losses stood at an estimated 30 pieces of artillery, 15,000 rifles, and a huge quantity of ammunition. In addition, 3,000 officers and 24,000 men were taken prisoners.

By the close of 1915, the Order had resoundingly defeated the Italians and chased them out of most towns and cities in the Cyrenaican and Tripolitanian areas. Shutaywi, with the support of Sulaiman Baruni, who returned from exile brandishing the title of governor of Tripolitania; Abd-al-Nabi Bilkhayr, chief of the Orfella; Ahmad Marayi of Tarhuna; and many members of the Gebel ethnic groups, also chased the Italians out of Misurata. Shutaywi soon emerged as the most powerful Libyan factional leader in the fight to rid Libya of foreign rule. It took British intervention in January 1916 to break the Order's resolve to fight for their homeland. Rather than succumbing to the British, Sayyid Ahmad, leader of the Order, transferred power to his cousin, Sayyid Mohammad Idris, who, in July 1916, entered into peace talks with the British.

BRITISH INTERVENTION AND ITS IMPACT

The British were concerned about the Order's incursion into Egypt and intervened solely to prevent further encroachment. Under British mediation, Italy and Libya agreed to an armistice, which allowed for a free flow of trade and movement of people and goods between Italy's occupied zones and the Order's occupied zones. The armistice also allowed for the disarming of troops, exchanges of prisoners, and the practice of Islam everywhere in Libya. In turn, the British were able to secure their colony, Egypt. Although Italy was allowed to rule the coastal cities that it occupied, it was unhappy and left no one in doubt that it would stop at nothing but a reconquest of Tripolitania.

As Tripolitanians were declaring an independent republic in 1918, Italy, aided by the British, bombed Misurata. This was followed by a massive reinforcement from Italy, comprised of 70,000 fighting men, tanks, heavy artillery, airplanes, flamethrowers, and other equipment. In March 1919, the Italian forces besieged Tripoli. Successes were, however, few and far between.

Defeated in Libya and also in Europe, the Italian General Giuseppe Tarditi decided to negotiate with the Libyans rather than risking another round of defeats. At a camp near Tripoli, Tarditi met with Ramadan Shutaywi, Sulaiman Baruni, and Abd-al-Rahman Azzam. The latter represented Egypt. Libyans, undeterred by the heavy equipment and hordes of Italian officers and men, left no one in doubt that Italy had to deal with them as equals; hence, they demanded recognition of Tripolitania's independence and promised otherwise to intensify their guerrilla warfare along their strongholds. Italy acquiesced and, in the Fundamental Laws of June 1919 that followed, partially surrendered.

At yet another meeting in October, Tripolitania was granted the right to a separate parliament. In addition, all Tripolitanians were also granted Italian citizenship. On its part, Italy was to oversee governance at the local councils. Marshall Pietro Badoglio, like many other Italians, described the resulting stalemate: "[W]e got ourselves mixed up in some black comedy."[4] Following Badoglio's inability to win any decisive victory over the Libyans, Italy replaced its Libyan governor, Baron Vittorio Menzinger, with Luigi Mercatelli as governor of Italy's occupied territories in Libya.

Despite repeated successes in curbing the Italians, the factional leaders were, however, unable to come to a unified position. Between 1919 and 1922, the different Libyan ethnic groups held a series of meetings with the Italians. In the Al-Zuwaytina negotiation meeting of April 1916, Italy's right to hold onto the coastal areas it had forcefully occupied and ruled since 1911 was recognized. In 1918, at a meeting in Akrama, the Sanussi Order's rights to Tripoli were recognized. While Ramadan al-Suwayhli was recognized as the ruler of Misurata and eastern Tripolitania (up to 1915), Sulayman al-Baruni was recognized as the ruler of western Tripolitania. After 1915, Sheik Suf al-Mahamudi took over western Tripolitania, and Khalifa al-Zawi took over Fezzan between 1916 and 1926. A political conflict between these factional leaders, however, resulted in the death of Ramadan al-Shutaywi.

In general, the ethnic groups were divided in their opinions about Italian rule. While Baruni and some others opposed Italian occupation of Libya and would stop at nothing to expel the invaders, others preferred negotiation with Italy. Underlying the infighting and divisions among these factional leaders was the inordinate and selfish desire of Baruni and his ilk to rule Libya, while, for those seeking negotiation with Italy, it was the only way to end Italy's wanton destruction of Libyans' lives and property.

Under the fascist government, new military leaders—Generals Pietro Badoglio and Rodolfo Graziani—were appointed for Libya. These men, desirous to stem the tide of Italian losses, embarked upon a series of punitive expeditions in Eastern Libya, most especially in Cyrenaica. Under Generals Badoglio and Graziani, the Italian forces committed all kinds of atrocities and war crimes in their attacks on Libya. Following the Libyans' massacres of Italian soldiers at Sciara Sciat and other localities, Italian attacks morphed into campaigns of punitive expedition, which involved the establishment of concentration camps and gas chambers (thousands of Libyans were dispatched to these camps), mass killings of women and children, as well as the wholesale forced migration of populations, as retribution for Libyan attacks on Italian forces.

In Cyrenaica, Omar al-Mukhtar Muhammad bin Farḥat al-Manifi and his followers mounted a fierce defense of their homeland, embarking on a series of guerrilla warfare operations aimed at preventing the Italian conquest. Omar, who was born August 20, 1861 and executed on September 16, 1931, was a Quranic teacher, who was also skilled in the strategies and tactics of desert warfare. His knowledge of local geography was an asset that he deployed in battles against the Italians, who were ignorant about desert warfare. Although small in numbers, Omar's Sanussi fighters were highly skillful. The group was extremely successful in their attacks on the Italians. They cultivated the habit of disappearing into the desert after every attack on Italian outposts, or after ambushing Italian troops, or after cutting Italian lines of supply and communication. Omar and his group were therefore a big embarrassment to the

Italian Royal Army, who were ignorant of guerrilla warfare and who did not know how to deal with this guerrilla group.

Between 1911 and 1931, as the leader of the Eastern Libya Native Resistance Movement and a major leader in the Sanussi Movement, Omar organized and led a series of successful guerrilla attacks. He was such a veritable terror that the Italians named him Matari of the Mnifa - the Lion of the Desert. Omar was a national hero and a symbol of Libya's resistance to foreign invasion not only in Libya but also in Chad against French colonization and in Egypt against British colonization.

Omar—who was famous for his statement, "We are a nation that knows no surrender, we win or we die"—was of a medium height, stout, with white hair, beard and mustache. He was wounded in a battle near Slonta on September 11, 1931, and the Italian army subsequently captured him. In the hope that Libyan resistance would die with him, the Italian court ordered his execution to take place on September 16, 1931. Omar, 73 years of age, was publicly executed in the presence of his followers at the prisoner of war camp at Suluq. In a brutal and bloody act of repression, the Italians also summarily executed thousands of Omar's Sanussi fighters, including innocent people, many of whom were accused of supporting Omar.

While Omar's resistance lasted, Italy constructed a barbed wire fence from the Mediterranean to the oasis of Al-Jaghbub, a measure aimed at curbing resistance by cutting off lines critical to the Libyans. Besides the Frontier Wire, as the barbed wire fence was called, the Italians also commenced a deportation program that was aimed at the wholesale deportation of Libyans from the Jebel Akhdar region to concentration camps. This was a way to deny the various resistance groups the support of this local Libyan population. This program led to a forced migration of more than 100,000 people to Italian concentration camps in Abyar, El-Magrun, El-Agheila, and Suluq. Combined with the squalid conditions of the camp, severe punishments such as electrocution, maiming, and dismemberment led to the deaths of tens of thousands of Libyans in the camps.

A conservative estimate of Libyans who died in the 15 Italian concentration camps across Libya was about 80,000—about one-third of the Cyrenaican population. Other estimates maintained that the number was much higher, especially when those who were killed in combat or mainly through starvation and disease were added. Besides the Cyrenaican population, many sources also estimated that between 1928 and 1932, the Italian army, using starvation and torture, also killed half the Bedouin population. Writing about this in his book, *Cerinaica Today*, Dr. Todesky, who was the director of the Italian Army Health Services in 1931, noted that "from May 1930 to September 1930, more than 80,000

Libyans were forced to leave their land and lived in concentration camps, they were taken 300 at a time, watched by soldiers to make sure that the Libyans go directly to the concentration camps" and "by the end of 1930, all Libyans who live in tents were forced to go and live in the camps. 55 percent of these Libyans died in the camps."[5]

While some Italian authors dispute that the number was high, evidence abounds to support the fact that the Italians realized how successful the concentration camps were, not only in curbing resistance, but also in decimating Libyan population, that Marshal Pietro Badoglio, the Italian governor of Libya from January 1929, proposed to convert these camps into permanent settlements. It was against the backdrop of treatments being meted out to Libyan populations in these camps that many factional leaders argued for cooperation with the Italians.

Although many European authors either denied the Italian atrocities or played down their magnitude, Italy, under Prime Minister Silvio Berlusconi on August 30, 2008, agreed to pay US$5 billion to Libya as compensation for the Italian atrocities in these concentration camps and for Italy's military occupation of Libya.

After two decades, Italian fascism and its use of concentration camps deprived Libyan resistance of help and reinforcements. In addition, Libyans were pursued on the ground by the Italian forces and bombed from above by Italian aircraft. Their hideouts were also spied upon by local informers and collaborators. With increasing acts of repression against the local population, which starved Libyan resistance groups of recruits; with more and more resistance leaders wounded, arrested, and executed; and with many resistance leaders escaping into exile, the resistance waned, and Italy eventually predominated. By the 1930s, the policy of Italian Fascism toward Libya began to change, and, by 1934, under Governor Italo Balbo, Cyrenaica, Tripolitania, and Fezzan were incorporated into Italian Libya—thus bringing the whole of Libya under full Italian political control.

NOTES

1. Geoff Simons, *Libya and the West: From Independence to Lockerbie* (Oxford: Centre for Libyan Studies, 2003), 4.

2. Geoff Simons, *Libya: The Struggle for Survival* (Oxford: Palgrave Macmillan, 2003), 111.

3. Simons, *Libya and the West*, 4.

4. Ronald Bruce St. John, *Libya: From Colony to Revolution* (Oxford: Oneworld Publications, 2008), 64.

5. Anna Baldinetti, *The Origins of the Libyan Nation: Colonial Legacy, Exile and the Emergence of a New Nation-State* (London: Routledge, 2014), 65.

4

Colonial Rule, Anticolonial Struggles, and World War II, 1912–1950

INTRODUCTION

Italian colonial rule in Libya is something of a paradox: On the one hand, it capitalized on the existing ethnic, religious, and political differences among different ethnoreligious groups in the areas now known as Libya. On the other hand, using divide-and-conquer tactics, Italian colonial administrators created new differences, as they played one ethnoreligious group against the other. These differences, which were created by many years of foreign invasions, continue to fuel mutual suspicions and hatred among the different ethnocultural groups in Libya today.

The quest for cheap (sometimes free) raw materials for European industries and the need for markets for finished goods from these industries were the two cardinal objectives behind the European colonization of Africa. In the case of Libya, another important point was the desire to gain prestige among other European powers by establishing a colony along the Mediterranean coast—a development that would make Italy one of the masters in Mediterranean trade. With the brutality with which Italy went about obtaining victory in Libya, what, then, were the nature and characteristic of Italian colonization? How did the Libyans react to Italian colonial rule and the different policies and programs that gave expression to Italian colonization?

As noted in Chapter 3, in the midst of the 1911–1912 Italian-Libyan War, the Ottomans, who ruled coastal Libya before the Italian invasion, withdrew from the war, leaving Libya's ragtag forces to face Italy's superior military power. As disappointed as the Libyans might have felt over this development, they fought tenaciously against Italian foreign invasion, and the war stalemated for months. Eventually, Italy defeated and established Libya as its colony in 1912.

Within the first ten years of its victory and eventual occupation, more than 150,000 Italians were officially relocated from Italy to Libya. Although control and administration were slow, by 1934, the Italians had established their presence in different regions of what is now known as Libya. For the first time in Libyan history, these regions were brought under one government and became officially known as Libya.

Opposition to Italian colonization was met with unprecedented brutality, including the mass deportation of entire populations into concentration camps, the mass extermination or massacres of ethnic groups that were considered recalcitrant, the branding as rebels and terrorists of ethnocultural leaders who were fighting against the imposition of foreign rule, the hunting and forcing into exile of ethnocultural leaders, disappearances and deaths, and other measures. Notwithstanding such inhuman treatment, Libyans fought foreign invasion and imperialism fiercely and tenaciously. Military superiority, coupled with political and technological factors, was, however, an important factor in the inability of Libyans to fend off the Italian imperialist ambitions and eventual military invasion.

This development, which was not limited to Libya, as it was experienced in other parts of Africa during the 19th century, brought profound and even revolutionary changes in the sociocultural, economic, and political history of Libya. As the political control of old Libyan kingdoms and states changed, new socioeconomic and political institutions were introduced. Compare to the precolonial institutions, these newly established institutions worked on different ideological and social premises.

There is no denying the fact that there was a huge technological disparity between Libya and Italy. Italy, a beneficiary of the technical advances of the Industrial Revolution, deployed deadly firearms, machines guns, repeater rifles, artillery guns, aircraft, and armored cars in conquering Libya's ragtag forces. Libya's forces, in general, fought with bows, arrows, spears, swords, locally fabricated rifles, and cavalry. It was therefore an unequal war, and the Libyans' ability to hold out for a year showed that Italy would not have defeated the Libyans had the Libyans been similarly well equipped.

After conquering Libya, Italy established a colonial state system. As in the rest of Africa, the colonial state was an administrative tool for domination, which was aimed at bringing about an effective control of the colonized societies and ensuring the appropriation of their resources. The colonial state, which was administered by military officers and civil servants appointed by the Italian political class, was a product of racist ideology. It was authoritarian, bureaucratic, imposed, and maintained by force of arms. It derived its legitimacy not from the consent of the governed but from the whims and caprices of Italian politicians and military leaders who were based in Italy. To this end, it lacked the effective legitimacy of a normal government.

As Chapter 3 showed, the 1911–1912 Italian-Libyan War led not only to the invasion and colonization of Libya but also to the replacement of the Ottomans with the Italians as the controllers of the different regions that made up today's Libya. Undoubtedly, the Italians' feat was unprecedented. It marked the first time that all regions of what is known today as Libya came completely under foreign administration. Compared to others before it, what were the differences between Italian colonial administration of Libya and others, especially the Ottomans? With the Italians' mass deportation of Libyan populations to concentration camps and the wholesale immigration of Italians to replace these Libyans, how were Libyans able to obtain independence in 1951? What was the role of World War II in Libya's road to independence? These and other questions are answered here.

NATURE OF ITALIAN IMPERIALISM IN LIBYA

Between 1912 and 1934, Italy introduced the indirect rule system in administering its colonial possessions in Libya. Indirect rule is a system of government that allows a conquered people to retain a certain level of administrative control of their communities. While other Europeans have used the indirect rule system, especially in their administration of their colonial dependencies in Africa and Asia, the British Empire was synonymous with the indirect rule system. As a system of government, underlying the indirect rule system was a paucity of administrative staff; hence, the British Empire was forced to rule its colonial dependencies through preexisting local power structures.

Under this system, the newly established government fused all preexisting sociopolitical structures into a national government, regional, and district administrations. At the head of the national government was an appointed colonial governor-general, who was assisted by a retinue of European colonial staff and a few lower-cadre indigenous staff. These indigenous staff—employed essentially as cleaners, gardeners, and the like—played insignificant roles in administration.

At the regional level, the governor-general appointed regional commissioners or resident officers to carry out the day-to-day administration of the regions. A corps of professional-class European surveyors, administrative officers, police officers, accountants, and others assisted these regional heads. While this corps of professionals reported to the regional heads, the regional heads reported to the governor. Like the corps of professionals, the regional heads were predominantly Europeans. They were aided by the native population whose appointments were subject to the whims and caprices of these regional heads.

At the district level, a colonial officer—the district officer—supervised the day-to-day administration of each district. Previously appointed indigenous kings and chiefs aided these district officers. In addition to these, new offices—the police, tax office, road supervision, and the like—were created where the district officers, in conjunction with the indigenous kings and chiefs, appointed indigenous people as officers. Where no king or chief existed, as in noncentralized societies, the colonial administration made kings and chiefs of men who were amenable to colonial control. Where erstwhile kings and chiefs were not amenable to colonial control, such kings and chiefs were deposed and replaced with those who were. In this way, the indigenous kings, chiefs, and these new officers were made integral parts of the colonial system.

The appointed indigenous officials, local kings and chiefs, whether indigenous or colonially created, were the main instruments of district administration. With European colonial officials, these indigenous office holders involved in district administration reported to the district officers. Orders and directives on all issues emanated from the district officers, while complaints or reactions flowed from these native officials—local kings and chiefs and the appointed indigenous officials—through the district officers to the regional commissioners and to the governor-general.

The incorporation of local kings, chiefs, and officers earned the indirect rule system its appellation. Under the indirect rule system, the

European colonial powers controlled external affairs, the military, and tax collection. Every other aspect of life was left to indigenous kings, chiefs, and officers. These kings, chiefs, and officers, many of whom may have collaborated with the colonial power during the wars of conquest, carried out the colonial policies and programs, and it was on them that the effective administration of the system rested.

Underlying this system was the need to provide a careful solution to a situation whereby a tiny group of foreigners had to relate with a huge population that might not be amenable to dealing with an imperial power. Designed in this way, the indirect rule system left the day-to-day administration, which would have ordinarily brought this small group of foreigners into a direct contact with a huge local population, in the hands of indigenous rulers who dealt directly with the local population on behalf of the foreign conqueror. The indirect rule system therefore presented the small group of foreigners as "advisers" rather than as conquerors and therefore enabled a colonially mediated administration to effectively oversee the governance of a large number of people who were spread over extensive areas.

As in all cases of colonial rule in Africa and Asia, the reality was that these traditional rulers not only lost direct control of their territories and citizens but also found their powers eroded under the newly introduced colonial system. In a dramatic twist, the newly appointed officers in charge of taxes, police, and other units gained prestige, wealth, stability, and protection from the new system. With such wealth and empowerment, these individuals soon become well attuned to colonialism.

Although a huge number of Italians had relocated and settled in Libya, in November of 1911, when Tripolitania and Cyrenaica became Italy's two regions in Libya, Italy could not establish a direct rule system, as protests against foreign rule continued in the hinterland. Before the Italians, the Ottomans used the indirect rule system. In Tripolitania and Cyrenaica, Italy resorted to the indirect rule system in administering the coastal and other areas that they occupied since the Italian-Libyan War.

From inception, Italy appointed two separate governor-generals for Tripolitania and Cyrenaica. Vice-Admiral Raffaele Borea Ricci d'Olmo, a naval officer, was the first Italian governor-general of Tripolitania. Although he later assumed control over the entire region, in his earliest days, the spate of violent protests against the Italian occupation limited his rule to only the city of Tripoli. He began his assignment in Tripolitania on October 5, 1911. General Ottavio Briccola, who participated in the Italian-Libyan War, was appointed as the first Italian governor-general of Cyrenaica. Both men adopted the indirect rule system over Tripolitania and Cyrenaica. Altogether, a total of 14 governor-generals were appointed for Tripolitania between 1911 and 1934. In Cyrenaica, however, a total of 11 governor-generals were appointed between 1912 and 1935. Table 4.1 shows the names of these governor-generals and the duration of their administrations.

The indirect rule system allowed these governor-generals to bring a small number of native populations into the socioeconomic and political administration of Libya.

The use of two separate governor-generals for the two regions persisted between 1911 and 1934 for Tripolitania and between 1912 and 1935 for Cyrenaica. These governor-generals were both the overall heads of government and commanders-in-chief in their respective regions.

The governor-general's office was staffed entirely by Italian officials and administrators. All directives emanated from the home office in Italy. The duty of implementing these directives was that of the governor-general who also reserved the rights to make laws and orders for the administration and effective governance of the region under his control. The governor-general controlled all appointments into other divisions of the colonial government. The governor-general had broad powers—ranging from civil to military power. He supervised political and administrative matters, defense and public welfare.

In general, both Tripolitania and Cyrenaica were divided into two distinct zones—the civilian zone, which the governor-general headed, and the military zone, which was headed by an appointed Military Commander who reported directly to the governor-general. The civil zones were composed entirely of districts that had been pacified, while the military zones consisted entirely of districts where pacification was either in progress and therefore incomplete or about to be pacified. This clear distinction between military and civilian zones allowed for a gradual socioeconomic and political transformation of Libya. It also allowed the colonial government to showcase areas of civilian administration as a model for Libyans in the military zones and therefore created a situation whereby the native population found themselves caught up between either continual warfare, with its attendant mass killing and deportation to concentration camps, or peaceful and prosperous existence under the Italian governor-generals in the pacified zones. This had a psychological impact both on recruitment into what should effectively be called Libya's liberation forces, and on Libyans' support for the liberation struggle itself.

Table 4.1 Italian Governor-Generals of Tripolitania and Cyrenaica, 1912–1934

Tripolitania	When	Cyrenaica	When
Vice-Admiral Raffaele Borea Ricci D'Olmo	October 5–11, 1911	General Ottavio Briccola	October 15, 1912– October 1913
General Carlo Caneva	Oct 1911 to September 1912	General Giovanni Ameglio	October 1913– August 5, 918
General Ottavio Ragni	September 2, 1912–June 2, 1913	General Vincenzo Garioni	June 2, 1913– October 1, 1914
General Vincenzo Garioni	June 2, 1913– October 1, 1914	Mr. Giacomo De Martino[i]	August 5, 1919– November 23, 1921
General Giorgio Cigliana	October 2–30, 1914	Mr. Luigi Pintor[ii]	November 23, 1921– October 1922
General Luigi Druetti	November 1, 1914– February 5, 1915	Mr. Eduardo Baccari[iii]	October– December 1922
General Giulio Cesare Tassoni	February 9–July 15, 1915	General Luigi Bongiovanni	December 1922– May 24, 1924
General Giovanni Ameglio	October 1913– 5 August 1918	General Ernesto Mombelli	June 16, 1924– December 2, 1926
General Vincenzo Garioni	June 2, 1913– 1 October 1914	Attilio Teruzzi[iv]	October 31, 1939–July 25, 1943
Mr. Vittorio Menzinger[v]	August 16, 1919–July 10, 1920	General Domenico Siciliani	January 24, 1929– March 1930
Luigi Mercatelli[vi]	July 6, 1920– July 1921	Rodolfo Graziani[vii]	March 17, 1930– May 31, 1934
Giuseppe Volpi[viii]	July 1921–1925	General Guglielmo Nasi	June 1934– April 1935
Major General Emilio De Bono[ix]	1925–1929		
Pietro Badoglio[x]	January 24, 1929– December 31, 1933		

Sources: Compiled by the author from http://www.worldstatesmen.org/Libya.htm.

(*continued*)

Table 4.1   Italian Governor-Generals of Tripolitania and Cyrenaica, 1912–1934 (*continued*)

<hr>

[i] An Italian politician and diplomat. He also served as governor-general of Somaliland between 1910 and 1916.

[ii] An Italian jurist and politician who represented Italy during the negotiation with the Sanussi Order in 1917.

[iii] An Italian politician and diplomat to London and Italian Somaliland.

[iv] An Italian soldier who fought in the Italian-Libyan War. He was awarded the Silver Medal of Military Valor for his role in the capture of Misrata and Nalut in 1911.

[v] The first politician to be appointed as governor of Italian Libya.

[vi] A lawyer and diplomat who had headed Somaliland between 1905 and 1906.

[vii] Later the governor-general of Italian Libya when the different regions were ruled as a single Italian colonial state July 1, 1940–March 25, 1941. Between 1926 and 1930, he was the vice-governor-general of Cyrenaica.

[viii] Italian businessman and politician.

[ix] Later the Italian minister of the colonies between 1929 and 1935 and governor of Eritrea.

[x] 28th Prime minister of Italy, commissary of Tripolitania and Cyrenaica between January 24, 1929 and December 31, 1933.

Notwithstanding the separation of military from civil administration, a large number of residencies were established for military officers where they exercised effective governmental powers. To maintain peace and facilitate a peaceful takeover, troops were stationed in different parts of Libya, especially Tripolitania and Cyrenaica. Overall, the arrangement made the governor-general the chief security officer and commander-in-chief of each of the regions.

Over the years and as peace was gradually restored, the military zones lost their importance. In addition, the two regions also witnessed further delineation and devolution of power, as Regional Councils whose members, composed of both Italians and natives, were appointed by the governor-general. At the head of each Regional Council was a regional commissioner, appointed by the governor-general. The regional commissioner was not only the head of the council but also in charge of the day-to-day administration of the region. The regional commissioners were completely Italians, and they were responsible only to the governor-general. The natives in regional administration were merely advisers, and the regional commissioners reserved the right to either listen to them or not.

Although the commissioners were not bound to take the advice of the natives, many of these commissioners knew that effective administration depended upon securing the cooperation of these natives who had a better understanding of the local situations and populations. As a result, while the Italian commissioners and officials concentrated on leadership and surveillance, the incorporation of native Libyans into regional administration provided for sufficient decentralization that allowed the colonial administration to meet local demands and politics.

The regions were further divided into circuits. Amenable kings and chiefs were made heads of these circuits. A king or chief who became recalcitrant was deposed, and a replacement was appointed to facilitate a smooth colonial administration of the affected circuit. While the circuits were entirely composed of native population and headed by local kings and chiefs, the governor-general also appointed an Italian official to superintend each of the circuits.

Each circuit was further divided into districts. There were two types of districts—urban and rural districts. Urban districts, like the circuits, were composed entirely of the native population and were headed by local chiefs. The governor-general also appointed an Italian official to superintend each of the urban districts. Unlike urban districts, rural districts had no Italian superintendent, but were placed under the direct supervision of the circuits.

Between 1934 and 1943, the two regions came to be administered as one nation—Italian Libya. From this period, Italy appointed only one governor-general for Libya. The first was Italo Balbo, who assumed duty on January 1, 1934 and was replaced on June 28, 1940. Rodolfo Graziani succeeded him on July 1, 1940. His rule was, however, short, as he was replaced on March 25, 1941 by Italo Gariboldi. Ettore Bastico replaced Italo Gariboldi on July 19, 1941 and stayed in office till February 2, 1943 when Giovanni Messe took over. Giovanni Messe ruled until May 13, 1943.

Under this system, the participation of Libyans in the administration of the different levels or layers of government was limited to merely implementing orders and directives from the Italian officials and advising these Italian officials whenever necessary.

With the total subjugation of Libya by 1934, the indirect rule system gave way to a settler administrative system, which bordered on direct administration. During this time, Libya was divided into four provinces (*governatores*) and a military territory. The four provinces were Tripoli, Benghazi, Darnah, and Misurata. The only military territory was the Military Territory of the South. Each of these provinces was headed by a provincial commissioner, who was responsible for the day-to-day administration of the province. Key towns, such as Tripoli, Benghazi, Derna, Misrata, Hun, among others, were ruled as Italian municipalities (*comune*) and governed by an appointed chief magistrate or rector (*podesta*). Each province was further subdivided into wards, which were administered by magistrates.

While colonial indirect rule lasted, a small but amenable number of Libyans participated in government and administration. From 1934 when a settler rule began, the roles of Libyans in the administration of Libya became so insignificant as to be ineffective in making any meaningful impact on politics and administration. Notwithstanding all this, there were a small number of natives at different levels of government—from the governor-general's office to regional commissioner's to circuits and districts under the indirect rule system and from the provincial to municipal system under the direct rule system.

How did the Italian officials go about attaining the classic objectives of the colonial state—the economic exploitation of the colonies? How did the Libyans react to Italian colonial policies and programs? The remaining sections of this chapter provide answers to these questions.

THE COLONIAL ECONOMY

With more and more areas of Libya conquered, colonial authority was reorganized, especially in Cyrenaica. Although indirect rule was instituted in the two traditional provinces of Tripolitania and Cyrenaica since 1912, it was not until between 1919 and 1929 that Tripoli and Cyrenaica were united as a colonial province. With Benito Amilcare Andrea Mussolini as the 27th prime minister of Italy came a new era of Italian engagements with Libya. Mussolini, who began his reign between October 31, 1922 and July 25, 1943, demanded a total pacification of Libya from his Italian governor-generals. As a result of this, military engagement was intensified. The military engagement was so intense that Muhammad Idris bin Muhammad al-Mahdi al-Sanussi, the emir of Cyrenaica, fled to Egypt in 1922. Despite the intensity of the Italian military engagement in Libya, in 1931 and 1932, Italian forces, led by General Badoglio, were unsuccessful in their punitive war against the Libyans. General Rodolfo Graziani, Badoglio's successor, however, promised Mussolini a total defeat of Libyan resistance.

Omar al-Mukhtar, the leader of the Sanussi Order discussed in Chapter 5, however led the Libyans in the continued defense of their homelands, especially in Cyrenaica. Sadly for the Libyans, on September 15, 1931, Omar was captured and executed in Benghazi. While this development weakened Libyan's resistance initially, Sheik Idris emerged as the new emir of Cyrenaica, and limited resistance soon developed around him.

Despite Idris's leadership and renewed Libyan resistance, by 1934, Italian forces successfully pacified Libya, and General Italo Balbo was appointed as the new Italian governor-general of a united Libya. Upon resumption of duty, General Balbo commenced a colonial policy that aimed at integrating Italians with the Libyans. Under Balbo, Fezzan was named Territorio Sahara Libico and administered militarily. Balbo also merged Tripolitania and Cyrenaica as Italian Libya—thereby bringing the two separate administrative regions into one in 1934. Although ruled as one country—Italian Libya—Libya was divided into four administrative provinces: Tripoli, Misrata, Benghazi, and Derna.

Colonial rule in Libya, as in the rest of Africa, was not a singular event. It was a series of interactions and events that lasted a long period. It involved not just Italians and Libyans but other Europeans. As seen in the previous chapters, while it was easier to conquer the coastal areas, the hinterland proved difficult. As in other parts of Africa, European colonial powers found it difficult to colonize stateless societies where no precolonial centralized political administration existed. Pastoralist communities like the Berber and Bedouin of Morocco and Libya, Baoule of Cote d'Ivoire, the Igbo in Nigeria, among others, presented so much resistance to European imperialism and experienced much violence and repression with their attendant losses in lives and property.

Once Italy believed that the so-called Libyan pacification had been achieved, it turned its attention to the main agenda of colonial rule: the development and implementation of a series of complementary and transformative policies and programs aimed at the reorganization of Libyan economies for the Italian economic exploitation. As with other European powers in different parts of Africa, these programs and policies included the introduction of or the expansion of new cash crops, the expansion of export–import trade—with a carefully designed program of excluding African producers and traders from this trading system; the altering and redirection of trade routes to newly established colonial capitals and ports; the construction of new transportation system, especially air, rail, and harbor; the expansion of road transportation to feed and to service air, rail, and harbor transportation systems. These measures, coupled with the rationalization of land ownership, the introduction of direct and indirect taxes and forced labor, ensured that the Libyan economy served Italy's economic interests throughout the colonial period.

None of these policies and programs could function without a corresponding change in Libya's social and political institutions. In other words, the Italian colonization of Libya, as in other European colonies in the rest of Africa, was a huge and multifaceted project that aimed at socioeconomic, cultural, and political changes. So, to create an efficient and effective self-sustaining commodity-producing colony in Africa, Italy invested not only personnel but also time and money.

A number of economic policies and programs embarked upon by Italy in its efforts at expropriating the resources of Libya are discussed in the remaining part of this chapter.

UFFICIO FONDARIO AND MASS EMIGRATION

Prior to the Italian colonization of Libya, land belonged to the family, and family heads held land in trust for and on behalf of the family. In other words, land use, whether for grazing of animals or for farming, was communal. The family head had the duty of apportioning land to each family member based on need, and such apportioned land passed from father to son. Land was not a commodity that could be exchanged. With the Italian colonization, the land tenure system changed dramatically.

In 1913, Italy established the Ufficio Fondario (Land Office), which aimed at providing land to Italian colonists. With the Italian pacification of Libya, the Land Office declared on July 18, 1922, that all uncultivated land in Libya belonged to the public. Through this law, many lands were confiscated as "uncultivated," and their Libyan owners—nomads and farmers—were forced to either settle on poorer land elsewhere or become landless people. While the resistance lasted, a huge number of Libyans who fled their homes for safety in the desert and the mountains lost their lands in this way. Their lands were declared "uncultivated" and subsequently taken over by the Italians.

In 1923, these uncultivated lands were taken over by the Italian colonial state. There were two important factors for the takeover of these uncultivated lands. On the one hand was the need to starve and deny Libyans who were fighting against Italian colonization of any source of economic prosperity—a way of weakening the resolve of these nationalists and their sympathizers. On the other—perhaps the more important reason—was the need to provide hordes of Italian migrants with arable land.

Having secured a large tract of arable land, a huge number of Italian colonists were transported from different parts of Italy to Libya. Under Balbo in October 1938, a single convoy of Italian colonists, numbering about 20,000 people, relocated to Libya aboard the Italian ship, the *Ventimila* (*Twenty Thousand*).

By 1950, the Land Office planned to resettle half a million Italian colonists in Libya. In order to have enough land to distribute to these Italian colonists, the Land Office on July 18, 1922, reversed its earlier land law and declared that all unoccupied and uncultivated land belonged to the state. By ceding more and more land to the colonial state, more and more Libyans were pushed off their land, thereby giving these Libyans more reasons to continue fighting Italian colonial rule.

To make Italian relocation and establishment in Libya easier, Guiseppi Volpi, the governor of Tripolitania, on July 1925, provided financial assistance, credits, and subsidies to the Italian colonists. The Bank of Italy opened branches in different parts of Libya, where these colonists obtained loans to ensure their economic prosperity. Balbo also continued these practices. Given these incentives, more and more Italian colonists emigrated to Libya. For instance, Balbo led another 12,000 Italian migrants to Libya in 1939.

In its bid to maximize its colonial economic gains, the Italian colonial administration in Libya not only settled Italy's landless unemployed and peasants on new lands in Libya but also forbade them from employing Libyans. In order to prevent what was called "the scarce Italian capital being used to pay for Libyan labor,"[1] the Italian settlers (concessionaires) were mandated to settle and employ Italian families rather than utilizing Libyan labor on their farms.

The place of the Land Office in the Italian economic exploitation of Libya cannot be overemphasized. Between 1914 and 1929, the Land Office had taken away over 180,000 acres of arable land from Libyans and distributed them among Italian colonists. Under the Fascist government, a set of more intense, state-sponsored, and highly subsidized incentive programs were instituted to help these Italian colonists settle and cultivate their allotted lands. By 1940, over 225,000 hectares—495,000 acres—were under the control of these Italian colonists, whose number had risen to 110,000.

On these allotted lands, the Italian farmers were self-contained, with each family supplying its own labor. Between 1936 and 1942, Italy spent two-thirds of its investment in Libya on land reclamation, allocation, and agricultural cultivation. Italian peasants, who were poor and landless prior to their emigration from Italy, overnight became aristocratic landowners who were not only employing Libyans, the original landowners, but also controlling the government.

The population of Italians that were relocated to Libya grew from 26,000 in 1927 to 119,139 in 1939. From 1931, Italy had begun to realize some of its colonial objectives—the relocation of excess population in

Italy to Libya. In order to facilitate these objectives, thousands of native populations were forced from Cyrenaica into concentration camps, and their lands were allocated to Italian immigrants. Many of these Italians were settled along Libya's coastal areas, especially from the beginning of the Fascist period.

These Italian immigrants became the core settler population along Libya's Mediterranean coast, in urban centers, and on farmlands around Tripoli. By 1939, they constituted about 41 percent of the population of Tripoli, and they were about 35 percent of the total population in Benghazi. There were so many Italian immigrants in Cyrenaica that by 1938, 27 new villages were founded to accommodate them.

Using the Land Office, Italian colonial rulers successfully established Libya as a settler colony. The colony, which served as an outlet for Italy's population pressures and class contradictions, served Italy in two primary ways. On the one hand, it was a source of raw materials for Italian industrial production. On the other hand, it was a market for Italian industrial production. In both ways, Libya, as Italy's colony, served the colonial interest of Italy. Besides the Land Office, in what other ways did Italy set Libya up to serve its economic interest?

THE VILLAGIZATION POLICY

Italian colonial power in Libya began to build whole villages and farms for Italian peasants in 1934. These large-scale, state-financed mass settlements of Italian peasants in government-built villages in Libya aimed at stabilizing Italy's economic pressures and class contradictions. It is also important to note that the League of Nation, a global body formed at the end of World War I, had orchestrated a global boycott of Italy and Italian products for Italy's invasion of Ethiopia, a development that had serious economic and social impacts on Italy. So, to ameliorate these problems, Italians hoped to make Libya its bread basket—supplying Italy with food, grain, and oil.

By 1937, there were only 1,300 Italian peasant families farming in Libya, most of them as wage laborers on the large concessions. With the approval of the mass settlement scheme in March 1938, Italy relocated about 20,000 colonists in Libya by October. The newly built villages were intended not only to house these Italian poor but also to provide them with a better life and shore up the image of the Italian state.

Using Libyan labor, the newly built colonial villages were provisioned with health care facilities, schools, movie houses, drill wells, and other modern facilities. In addition to providing them with well equipped homes, their farms were already cleared, crops planted, with their

Officer and politician Italo Balbo, acting as governor of Libya, talks to Italian settlers after their arrival in Homs (Khums) in 1939. (Heinrich Hoffmann/ullstein bild via Getty Images)

pantries stocked with, at least, a week's provisions. As small as candles and matches might appeared, they were also provided before the arrival of these Italian immigrants. Each Italian family selected for relocation to Libya was, upon arrival, allocated a home in these villages based on family size and political affinity.

In its bid to secure the best land both for the villages and for farms for these Italians, the Italian colonial rulers of Libya displaced many Libyans. In order to cultivate Libyans' loyalty and to avert a continuing anticolonial war, ten such villages were built for Libyans, and those Libyans who collaborated with the Italian colonialist were allocated homes in these 10 villages. Although built to curry the loyalty of the Libyans, the Libyans' 10 settlements were not as well provisioned as those of the Italian settlers. Called Muslim Italians, the Libyans who were allocated these 10 villages in 1939 were, however, provided with mosques, schools, sport grounds, cinemas, a small hospital, and other social centers. Although elementary schools were built in the 10 villages for the Libyans, the educational policies prohibited Libyans from going beyond elementary school. Whereas the Italian villages had higher educational facilities, Muslim Italians were prohibited from attending Italian schools. As the Italians argued, Libyans' "requirements are less."

Many Libyans who relocated to these newly established and provisioned villages were members of the *Savaris* (a Libyan cavalry regiment)
and *Spahi* (mounted police that were established since the 1920s). Members of these colonial troop not only cooperated with the Italians in the
pacification of Libya but also played roles in Italy's invasion of Ethiopia. Also found among them were Eritreans and Somalis, who fought
for and on behalf of Italy against Libya, Eritrea Somalia, and Ethiopia.

Royal Decree No. 70 of January 9, 1939 granted these Libyans—
Muslim Italians—Italian citizenship, which allowed them to rise in the
military and civil administration. The incorporation of Muslim Italians
into the Italian Army gave Italy better opportunity to recruit many of
these Libyans into military service. On March 1, 1940, these Libyans
formed the 1st and 2nd Libyan Infantry Divisions. These divisions were
organized along the lines of the Italian infantry division. As a colonial
formation, the divisions were entirely composed of Libyans. Both divisions had Italian commanding officers, with the highest-ranking Libyans being noncommissioned officers.

In term of training and battle readiness, these Libyan formations
were on an equal footing with the regular Italian formations in North
Africa. Given their professionalism and esprit de corps, these Libyans
were not only awarded the Gold Medal of Honor for their performance
in battle but were also incorporated into political and administrative
positions. They constituted the main population of Libyans who were
allocated the 10 government-built villages in Libya. Table 4.2 presents
the names of these 10 villages.

Table 4.2 Italian-Created Arab and Berber Villages in Libya

S/N	Libyan Names	Italian Names	English Names
1	El Fager	Alba	Dawn
2	Nahima	Deliziosa	Delicious
3	Azizia	Profumata	Perfumed
4	Nahiba	Risorta	Risen
5	Mansura	Vittoriosa	Victorious
6	Chadra	Verde	Green
7	Zahara	Fiorita	Blossomed
8	Gedina	Nuova	New
9	Mamhura	Fiorente	Flourished
10	El Beida	La Bianca	White

Sources: Compiled by the author from different sources.

In addition to these Muslim Italians, the Italians granted privileged positions in the government and administration of Libya to two other groups: the more than 22,000 Libyan Jews in Cyrenaica and the German Afrika Korps, another class of native colonial division. In order to accommodate these two classes, a number of Libyans were relocated to internment camps in the summer of 1941.

As from 1936, the economy of Libya revolved around these Italian immigrant settlers. While about 31 percent of them were engaged in the construction industry, 30 percent were in government and administration. They also dominated in agriculture, with about 30 percent in plant cultivation and 17 percent in aquaculture and fishing. More than 17 percent were engaged in trade and commerce, while about 11 percent were in the transportation sector. Other areas where they dominated include the legal profession, teaching, banking, and insurance.

Because lands were taken away from the Libyans and the settlers were prohibited from employing Libyans, many Libyans migrated into the coastal cities and towns in search of manual and menial jobs. Even in the towns and villages, Libyans were prohibited from holding any position or practicing a profession that could be filled or practiced by an Italian. In this way, both the Land Office and Villagization policies severely limited Libyans' economic and social mobility.

Above all other things, these policies led to the first substantial rural–urban migration in Libya. In cities and towns, Libyans were limited to casual jobs in construction and in commercial and manufacturing firms. They were prohibited from seeking placement in the administrative offices, as they were prohibited from seeking education beyond elementary school. The result of all these developments was the emergence of a large informal sector of workers, most of whom were involved in hawking, small shop keeping, and artisanship.

Owing to their state, Libyans' participation in politics was limited, as the Italian settlers disbanded and replaced the different councils with Italian-appointed leaders. This massive injection of Italian investment in Libya developed the economy for the benefit of Italy and Italian settlers. In addition to providing jobs for Italy's surplus population and therefore saving Italy from internal crisis, the huge investment of Italian resources in Libya secured Libya as Italy's strategic Fourth Shore on the Mediterranean Sea, thereby making Italy a major player in Mediterranean trade. Not only did the Italian colonizers drive Libyans to the marginal land in the interior, they also settled along the coast and on the most fertile lands in Libya. This gave Italy exclusive control of Mediterranean trade and allowed Italians to exploit the resources from the hinterland.

The new socioeconomic and political system did little to improve the quality of life of Libyans, many of whom had been uprooted and relocated to internment camps. For instance, little or no effort was made to improve education among Libyans. Between 1939 and 1940, 81 elementary schools were established in Italian-occupied areas—catering for just 10 percent of the total population. 97 such schools existed in other parts of Libya throughout the Italian colonization. Until 1940, only three secondary schools were established in Libya—with two in Tripoli and one in Benghazi—serving 85 percent of the total population.

TRANSPORTATION AND INFRASTRUCTURAL DEVELOPMENT

Transportation is important to colonialism in many ways. The main forms of transportation that played a significant role in the Italian colonial exploitation of Libya were roads, rails, and harbors. Before the Italian colonization, Libya had different categories of roads. In addition to roads constructed by the indigenous Libyan people, a network of roads was one of the legacies of Roman rule. These roads served in local and long-distance trading systems. With the resettlement of Italian colonists in different locations in Libya, the existing roads became inadequate given the economic and political growth of Italian Libya. While the road networks served in bringing resources from different places of production, they were inadequate in bringing bulk products down to the coastal areas for haulage to Italy.

As colonial history in Africa and Asia has shown, the need to discourage other European powers from meddling in the affairs of another European power in areas where it had established its trade interest was one of the reasons for railway construction. In Libya, railway construction was strategic to the Italian colonial enterprise. While roads served in assembling agricultural products and mineral resources from different centers of production, they were, however, inadequate in moving bulk products; hence, railways were constructed as arteries of trade. Roads served as a means to bring products to the arteries—the train terminuses. From these terminuses, trains moved bulk products from different parts of the colony to the coast where the products were shipped across the Mediterranean Sea to Italy.

In this simple way, roads, railway, and harbors became intertwined in the Italian colonial economic exploitation of Libya. So, when Mussolini described Italy's construction of public works, roads, railway lines, and other infrastructure as Fascism's attempts at creating a "Western civilization in general and Fascist civilization in particular"[2] in

Libya, it was sheer propaganda that masked the true economic intent of the projects.

Between 1932 and 1942, Balbo built hundreds of kilometers of new roads, expanded old ones, and constructed railways to connect one part of Libya to the other. In March 1937, Mussolini made a state visit to Libya, where he declared the Via Balbia, an east–west coastal route connecting Tripoli in western Italian Tripolitania to Tobruk in eastern Italian Cyrenaica, opened. The Via Balbia was a military highway constructed by Balbo to link the entire colony. Balbo also built the *strada litoranea* (coastal highway), which connected Libya from the borders of Tunisia to the frontier with Egypt. This gigantic road project was strategic to Italy's European power ambition, as it became the main road of invasion during World War II. On the one hand, Italian and the German allies moved their soldiers to Egypt on this road between 1940 and 1942, while the British, on the other hand, used the same road between 1940 and 1943.

Altogether, by 1939, the Italians had built 2,500 miles (4,000 kilometers) of new roads in Libya. The Via Balbia and other roads constructed in Libya played a dramatic role in Italy's economic exploitation of Libya. Through these arteries of railways and veins of roads, one major center in the interior was linked to the other, and products from different parts of Libya's hinterland were transferred to the railway stations, where the accumulations of wealth were brought down to the coastal cities by train before they were shipped across the Mediterranean Sea to Italy.

Benito Mussolini took the decision to build an extensive railway system in Libya. Underlying this decision, on the one hand, was the need to widen the trade network. On the other hand was the need to transport troops to the frontier during the war with the British in Egypt. So, in the spring of 1941, the Italian government started the construction of the rail line between Tripoli and Benghazi. The outbreak of World War II (September 1, 1939–September 2, 1945) brought rail construction in Libya to a halt. Notwithstanding this development, Italy successfully constructed 250 miles (400 kilometers) of new railway lines in Libya.

In total, there were five railways in Libya during the colonial period. The first was from Tripoli to Zuara, which covered a distance of 118 kilometers. The Tripoli–Zuara rail line had 13 terminuses and one station at Tripoli. The terminuses were at Gurgi, Gargaresc, Janzur, Saliad, Lemaia, EtTuebiaGarg, EzZauia, EsSabria BuIsa, Sorman, Sabratha Vulpia, Zungael Agelat, Mellita, and Zuara. The second railway line—from Benghazi to Barce—covered a total of 108 kilometers, with the main station at Benghazi. This rail line had 11 terminuses at Lete, Benina,

Regima, GabreGira, BuMariam, el-Abiar, SidiMaius, Sferi, Sleaia, Sidi-Gibrin, and Barce.

The third railway was from Tripoli to Garian. This rail line covered a total of 56 miles (90 kilometers) and had its central station in Tripoli, and terminuses were located in Gurgi, Gargaresc, El-Misciasta, En-Ngila, Suani Ben-Adem, Bir El-Miamin, Ummel Adem, El-Azizia, Henscir El-Abiat and Vertice. The fourth linked from Benghazi to Soluch, with the Benghazi station serving as the central station. Other terminuses were located at Benghazi-Porto, Berca, Guarscia, Guarscia Ben, Nauaghia, Giardina, Giardina, Soluch. Both Nauaghia and Soluch had two terminuses. The last railway line was from Tripoli to Tagiura. With Tripoli as the central station, it covered a total of 13 miles (21 kilometers) and had terminuses at Tripoli-Riccardo, Cavalleria, Sidi-Messri, Fornaci, Ain-Zara, Sghedeida, El-Mellaha and two terminuses at Tagiura.

Given this, it could be deducted that the Tripoli Central Station, which covered western Libya, and Benghazi Central Station, which was located in downtown Benghazi, were the two primary stations, while the stations at Barce, Zuara, Garian, Soluch, and Tagiura were secondary stations.

In most coastal cities and towns, Italians revamped existing harbors while new ones were also built. Although the importance of railways and harbors cannot be overemphasized, the Via Balbia was the most important and largest highway project that Italy built in Libya. All of these road, rail, and harbor projects were initiated and completed between 1934 and 1940, when General Italo Balbo was the governor-general of Italian Libya. The railway line connecting Tripoli to Benghazi would have overshadowed the Via Balbo, but only eight miles were completed when World War II began, and the defeat of Italy in the war meant that the railway line connecting Tripoli to Benghazi was not completed.

AGRICULTURE

Although the outbreak of World War II hindered the development in the transportation sector and, to a large extent, brought Italy's economic exploitation of Libya to a halt, it must, however, be noted that Libyan economy grew significantly in the late 1930s. This growth cannot be dissociated from the development in the agricultural sector. During this period, significant growth was also recorded in building construction and manufacturing, especially the food-processing industry.

OTHER INDUSTRIAL DEVELOPMENTS

Other areas of Italian economic interests include explosives manufacture, automobiles, electrical engineering, ironwork, water plants, agricultural machinery factories, breweries, distilleries, biscuit factories, a tobacco factory, tanneries, bakeries, lime, brick, and cement works, the esparto grass industry, mechanical sawmills, and petroleum. Irrespective of products and minerals, Italy's colonial enterprise aimed at taking advantage of the colony for the benefit of Italy.

WORLD WAR II AND THE ENDING OF THE ITALIAN COLONIZATION OF LIBYA

During World War II, many Muslim Libyans enlisted in the Italian Army. They, like the *Savari* and *Spahi*, fought on the Italian side and won a decisive victory for Italy in the North African Campaign. They also participated in the Italian invasion of Egypt of September 1940. Using its Eighth Army, the British pushed the Italian forces and their Libyan troops back in December of 1940 in Operation Compass.

Fearing defeat in Egypt and a subsequent loss of Libya to Britain, the Italians appealed to the Germans and the Axis powers for support. With German and the Axis powers' support, Italy regained control of parts of Libya that the British had taken over during Operation Sonnenblume. During Operation Brevity, Italian, German, and the Axis powers forced the defeated British troops back into Egypt. At the Battle of Gazala in 1942, Italy, ably supported by Germany and the Axis troops finally conquered Egypt. However, in February 1943, Italy and the Axis forces were defeated during the Second Battle of El-Alamein in Egypt. This defeat not only ended the Western Desert Campaign but also led the Italian forces to abandon Cyrenaica, Tripolitania, and other parts of Libya, thus ending Italian colonization of Libya.

Thirty years of Italian rule had considerable impact on Libya. Besides developments in roads, rail, harbor, industrial complexes, and other economic impacts, Italian colonial policies left Libyans largely uneducated, politically less developed, and far removed from the nation's economy. The ethnocultural differences fostered by Italian colonialism hardened existing precolonial differences, with important implications for future nation-building and national cohesion in Libya.

For the most part, Libyans were more loyal to pan-Islamic identity than to any pan-Libyan nationalistic feelings. While Italy's racist physical and cultural war of extermination polarized Libyans and reduced their culture to primitivism, Italy embraced and appropriated Libya's economic wealth and used it to benefit Italians in Italy and Italian colonists in Libya.

NOTES

1. Ruth First, *Libya: The Elusive Revolution* (London: Penguin African Library, 1974), 4.

2. Siegbert Uhlig, Maria Bulakh, Denis Nosnitsin, and Thomas Rave, *Proceedings of the XVth International Conference of Ethiopian Studies* (Wiesbaden: Harrassowitz Verlag, 2006), 332.

5

Independence and Nation-Building, 1951–1968

INTRODUCTION

Libya's independence cannot be dissociated from the circumstances of World War II. On the one hand, Italy and the Axis powers lost the war, a development that led to the Allied powers' takeover of Italy's African possessions. On the other hand, the geopolitics of the Cold War compelled the Allied powers to submit to Libyans' demands for independence rather than accepting the trusteeship that Britain and France proposed after the war.

What happened and how did Libyans negotiate independence in the midst of contending interests of both the Allied and Axis powers? Given that the Italians fostered a system that discouraged Libyan participation in the economic and political administration of Libya during the Italian colonization, what form of political agitation emerged in Libya after Italy's defeat? What was the nature of the postcolonial Libyan state? These and many related questions are answered in this chapter.

POST–WORLD WAR II DELIBERATIONS AND LIBYAN INDEPENDENCE

At the beginning of World War II, Germany appeared invincible. The alliance between Italy and Germany ensured Italy's initial defeat of the British in Egypt. The euphoria of victory was, however, short-lived, as Italy and its allies were defeated after the second battle of El Alamein in late 1942. This defeat led to the expulsion of Italy and Germany not only from Britain-held Egypt but also from everywhere else in Africa, including Libya. It also set in motion a frenzied and hurried return migration of Italians to Italy. It was by far more distasteful for Italy compared to its loss at the Battle of Adwa of March 1, 1896, which led to Italy's defeat in Ethiopia.

Prior to the war, the different ethnocultural groups in Libya entered into alliances with either the French or the British. For instance, a delegation of about 60 Libyan exiles, representing northern Libya, met in Alexandria in 1939 to discuss what option Libya should take in view of the impending clash between the Allied and Axis powers. Sayyid Idris, speaking for Cyrenaica, advocated that Libyans should support Britain and the Allied powers. His argument was premised on the fact that should Britain win, Libya could negotiate independence and that, in case the Axis powers won, Libya shall inevitably return to the *status quo ante*. At yet another meeting of these Libyan delegates in Cairo in August 1940, both Tripolitania and Cyrenaica agreed to ally with the British and the Allied powers. In return for joining forces with the British and the Allied powers, Britain promised Tripolitania and Cyrenaica independence after the war. After securing British and the Allied powers' commitment, Tripolitania and Cyrenaica established the Libyan Arab Force, a five-infantry-battalion unit of volunteers who joined forces with the British. As Anthony Eden, the British foreign secretary, noted in January 1942, the British would ensure that Cyrenaica did not return to the Italians whatever the outcome of World War II. Although many in Tripolitania recognized that the arrangement would put the Sanussi leadership and Cyrenaica in a primal position, they would rather stay under a free Sanussi-led state than return to being under Italian colonial rule.

In 1943, the British established a British Military Administration (BMA) over Tripolitania and Cyrenaica. In the same year, the French also established a French Military Administration (FMA) over Fezzan. In 1949, under the BMA, Britain yielded control of Cyrenaica and Tripolitania to the Libyan leaders. It was not until 1951, when Libya became independent, that the FMA returned control of Fezzan to their Fezzan political leaders.

World War II left Libya in a bad state: Much of the infrastructure and industries established by the Italians were destroyed during the war. Cyrenaica and Benghazi were the most affected. Benghazi, for instance, endured more than 1,500 air raids. Given its loss, Italy hurriedly evacuated its citizens between November and December of 1942. Their homes were destroyed in the numerous air raids. As millions of Bedouins who had fled into the mountains and deserts during the Italian occupation returned, their animals devastated the farms that the Italians abandoned so hurriedly.

At the end of the war, Cyrenaica and Tripolitania were granted a "care and maintenance" status, as stipulated in the 1907 Hague Convention. Owing to this special status, political activities began earlier in Cyrenaica and Tripolitania than in Fezzan. In Cyrenaica, the Sanussi enjoyed the respect and trust not just of the British but of so many natives too. As early as 1946, the Sanussi, using their newly founded National Congress Party (NCP), began to canvass for self-government. Another major political party was the National Association of Cyrenaica (NAC). It developed from a club originally founded by Omar al-Mukhtar. While not in any way against the Sanussi, the NAC advocated for inclusive politics that would unite the different ethnocultural groups in Libya.

Politics was more intense in Tripolitania than in Cyrenaica. A number of reasons could be offered to explain this. In the first instance, Tripolitania was more urbane and civilized than other parts of Libya, even under the Italians. In addition, a huge number of exiles who had spent many years in various Arab nations returned to Tripolitania following Italy's loss of Libya. These exiles greatly enhanced the sociocultural and political plurality of Tripolitania. It must also be remembered that Tripolitania was at a time an independent republic; hence, remnants of its past resurfaced again under the BMA's control.

By 1947, more than six political parties had emerged in Tripolitania. Although each of these parties had its respective agenda, they were united in the desire for Libyan independence. Unlike other provinces, Tripolitania had a pan-Arab nationalism at heart and therefore wanted independence for the whole of Libya rather for a part.

The geopolitics of the Cold War between the United States and the Union of Soviet Socialist Republics (USSR) also played an important role in the emergence of Libya as an independent state. After World War II, Italy attempted to assert its claims over Libya; however, Britain,

France, the United States, and the USSR mandated Italy to relinquish its colonial sovereignty over Libya. With Italy out of the way, the three powers were unable to decide on the fate of Libya. France wanted to hold on to Fezzan, while Britain desired to continue its control of Cyrenaica and Tripolitania. In Cyrenaica, although the National Congress party had successfully arrogated popular views around independence, it, however, would not join Tripolitania in an independent Libya unless under the Sanussi leadership.

This deadlock lasted for three years. In order to resolve it, Britain and France submitted a proposal—the Bevin-Sforza Plan—that sought to place Cyrenaica under Britain's trusteeship, Tripolitania under Italy's trusteeship, and Fezzan under France's trusteeship for 10 years. Libyans in Cyrenaica and Tripolitania took to the streets, protesting this arrangement. Both the Soviet Union and the Arab states supported the Libyans' position. Fearing the Soviets' interest, members of the United Nations General Assembly, at its meeting of September 15, 1948, opposed the Bevin-Sforza Plan. In the fall of 1949, the United Nations granted independence to Cyrenaica, and Sayyid Idris was granted leadership of the independent Cyrenaica. After an initial tardiness, France set up a transitional government in Fezzan in February 1950. Shortly after this, a Representative Assembly was also set up by France.

At its meeting of November 21, 1950, the United Nations General Assembly passed a resolution, calling for the independence of Libya not later than January 1, 1952. In addition to this, the General Assembly, on December 10, 1949, appointed Dr. Adrian Pelt, assistant secretary-general of the UN, as the United Nations' commissioner for Libya. His mandates included supervising Libya's successful transition to independence.

On January 18, 1950, Pelt arrived in Tripoli and visited Cyrenaica, Tripolitania, and Fezzan. He outlined his mission as including "consultation with the administrating powers, the members of the Council, and the leaders and representatives of the political parties in Libya, to appoint the representatives of Libya in the Council."[1] After consultation with Idris al-Sanussi, the emir of Cyrenaica, and other principal leaders of political parties in the three provinces, Pelt requested the different political leaders to nominate the four representatives who will represent the three provinces in the Advisory Council that the UN General Assembly mandated him to set up.

Political leaders in Cyrenaica and Tripolitania were bogged down with concerns over the modalities for the selection of these representatives. They therefore failed to come to any conclusion on who would represent the two provinces. Fezzan, on the other hand, submitted a name. It was after its meeting of March 28, 1950 that Cyrenaica submitted eight names to Pelt, asking him to choose from the list. As in Cyrenaica, the political parties in Tripolitania could also not come to a unified position on who should represent them. They also submitted seven names, asking Pelt to choose four out of the seven. In addition to the seven names submitted to Pelt, another four names were submitted to represent the minorities in Tripolitania.

The following Libyans were finally appointed to the Advisory Council as representatives of the three regions: Ali al-Jerbi, who was later replaced by Ali al-Unaizi, represented Cyrenaica; Mustafa Maizran represented Tripolitania; Ahmed al-Hajj al-Sanousi, who was later replaced by Mohammed Ben Uthman, represented Fezzan. Giacomo Marchino represented the minorities.

In constituting a National Constituent Assembly to write Libya's constitution, Pelt also set up a Preparatory Committee on which each of the provinces had seven representatives. To appoint representatives to the Preparatory Committee, Pelt constituted a 10-man committee that was mandated to:

  (i) organize elections into local assemblies in Cyrenaica and Tripolitania by June 1950;
 (ii) select members of a Preparatory Committee of the National Assembly who will determine the most appropriate method of election into the Libyan National Assembly—the Committee was mandated to submit its report not later than July 1950;
(iii) elect members of the Libya National Assembly and convene the meeting of the Libya National Assembly during the fall of 1950;
(iv) establish a provisional Libyan government in early 1951;
 (v) adopt a form of government and a constitution for Libya by 1951;
(vi) proclaim the independence of Libya and form a substantive Libyan government before January 1, 1952.

As much as Libyans were ecstatic about this development, political leaders in Tripolitania expressed serious concern over the establishment of an elected Preparatory Committee under the British Military Administration. As they argued, such an election will ensure that only representatives that were sympathetic to the whims and caprices of Britain would be elected. They therefore demanded that, rather than conduct any election, the party leadership be allowed to appoint representatives to the committee. After an initial rejection, Pelt agreed to the arrangement, and political leaders in Tripolitania handpicked party men who served as representatives of Tripolitania on the committee.

After its meeting of June 14, 1950, the committee submitted a draft resolution, which reads, in part:

(i) that the Commissioner should request the emir of Cyrenaica to submit names of seven people to represent Cyrenaica;

(ii) that the Commissioner should consult with the political leadership in Tripolitania to obtain names of seven personalities to join the Representatives for Cyrenaica;

(iii) that the Commissioner should request the Chief of the Territory of Fezzan to nominate seven representatives for Fezzan who would consult with other representatives from Cyrenaica and Tripolitania;

(iv) that the representatives of the inhabitants of Cyrenaica, Tripolitania, and Fezzan should meet in a National Assembly in Tripoli not later than July 1, 1950, to fulfill the purposes stated in paragraph 3 of the resolution of the UN General Assembly.

At its inaugural meeting of July 25, 1950, the Advisory Council designed and adopted its rules of procedure. It also elected Mohammad Abu al-As'ad al-Alim, the mufti of Tripolitania, as its chairman, while Khalil al-Qallal of Cyrenaica and Mohammad Bin Uthman al-Sayd of Fezzan were elected as secretaries. Another issue dealt with at this meeting was the size of the National Assembly. While some, for example representatives from Tripolitania, preferred proportional representation, others advocated for equal representation. At the end of its deliberations on August 7, 1950, 17 members voted for equal representation, while three representatives abstained from voting, and one was absent. Consequent upon this, Libya's National Assembly composed of 60 representatives, 20 representatives from each province.

On whether to elect members of the National Assembly or select them, Ali Rajab, representing Fezzan, spoke eloquently in support of election, while representatives from Tripolitania and Cyrenaica preferred selection. At the end of deliberation, opinions coalesced around selection. At the behest of the Council, Muhammad Idris al-Sanussi, the emir of Cyrenaica, selected representatives for Cyrenaica, while Ahmed Saif al-Nasr, the chief of Fezzan, selected the representatives for Fezzan and Mohammad Abo al-As'ad Al-Alim, the mufti of Tripolitania, selected Tripolitania's representatives. However, the Advisory Council declined the request to allow non-nationals, especially the remaining Italian colonialists, to have a representation in the National Assembly. While the Advisory Council also chose November 25, 1950 for the Opening Session of the National Assembly, Tripoli was chosen as the headquarters of the National Assembly.

The United Nations approved Pelt's report early in September of 1950, and a UN draft resolution, which empowered the commissioner, aided by the Council of Libya, to take all necessary steps toward the attainment of unity and independence of Libya, as mandated in UN General Assembly Resolution of 1949, was tabled and approved on October 19, 1950. The draft resolution passed by 53 votes.

From Pelt's letter to the Advisory Council on January 23, 1951, it can be argued that Pelt conceived a federal system of government for Libya. In the letter, Pelt advised the Libyan National Assembly as follows:

(i) The constitution to be drafted by the National Assembly should be enacted in a provisional form;

(ii) Provisions should be made in the constitution for a Parliament, which should consist of two chambers, a Senate that should be composed of elected representatives of the three territories on a basis of equality and a Popular Chamber to be elected by the People of Libya in a General Election.

(iii) The Parliament, to be elected by Libyan people in a General Election, shall have the power to finally approve or amend the Constitution, if necessary

(iv) Amongst its competencies, the Popular Chamber should have sole control over the budget.

(v) The Libyan government, that is the Libyan Cabinet, should be responsible to the Popular Chamber.

Before the Libyan independence in June 1949, an Arab self-governing administration was established in Cyrenaica. While many Libyans recognized this as important for the proposed federal government, especially as a way to integrate the three provinces, no effort was made to establish similar governments for Tripolitania and Fezzan. Emir Idris, for instance, discussed this with Bashir al-Sa'dawi, leader of the National Congress Party (NCP), at a meeting in Benghazi on February 2, 1950. Although Libyans recognized the advantages of self-rule in the provinces before national independence, when the UN passed its resolution of November 21, 1949, granting political independence to Libya, no provision was made to prepare Tripolitania and Fezzan for self-rule. The establishment of self-rule in Cyrenaica before independence therefore prepared Cyrenaica for eventual self-rule. It was in light of its importance to prepare the provinces for eventual independence that at both of its meetings of November 1950 and February 21, 1951, the Libyan National Assembly called for the establishment of regional governments in Tripolitania and Fezzan, as a preliminary step toward the establishment of the Libyan federal government.

At its meeting of February 21, 1951, the National Assembly invited King Idris, who had been proclaimed king of the Kingdom of Libya on December 2, 1950, to select members of local provisional governments for Tripolitania and Fezzan. In March 1951, a local provisional government was established for Tripolitania and Fezzan. After the Assembly's meeting of March 1951, a similar provisional government was established for Benghazi. In addition, the National Assembly also appointed Mahmoud al-Muntasir as the prime minister, minister of justice, and minister of education. Omar Shinneeb was appointed minister of defense, while Mansour Qadara was appointed minister of finance. Ibrahim Bin Sha'ban and Mohammad Bin Uthman were appointed minister of communications and minister of state, respectively.

The most troubling development in the evolution of an independent Libyan state was the composition of the Constitution Drafting Assembly. Crises erupted when the Bashir al-Sa'dawi-led National Congress Party rejected the list of representatives that Abou al-As'ad al-Alim, the mufti of Tripolitania, submitted to the Advisory Council. As the NCP argued, the Libyan National Assembly was incompetent to draw up a constitution for Libya; hence, the party appealed to both the UN and the Arab League to reconsider the whole question of Libyan independence. Bashir al-Sa'dawi and members of the NCP took to the streets of Tripoli. Lending its voice to the protest, Abdulrahman Azzam, the secretary-general of the Arab League, told the *Tempo*, an Italian newspaper that the proposed constitution of Libya must be proclaimed by a freely elected National Assembly that represented the Libyan people based on population. Anything other than that, Azzam maintained, would be a false foundation, which the Arab League would not recognize.

To resolve this impasse, the National Assembly enacted two laws. On the one hand, it established Libya as a federalism and, on the other hand, proclaimed Libya as a monarchy. By this law, the throne was offered to Emir Idris al-Sanussi of Cyrenaica. In addition to these, the National Assembly on January 22, 1951, sent a delegation to the Arab League to protest Azzam's position on Libya.

While federalism was wholly supported by representatives from Cyrenaica and Fezzan, members representing Tripolitania were reluctant to support it. The National Congress Party never hid its opposition to a federal system. The party and the Cyrenaican Omar al-Mukhtar Group considered federalism as an imperialist scheme of the European imperialists aimed at dividing Libya into three separate states.

Notwithstanding this development, the Libyan National Assembly adopted federalism and proclaimed the Emir Idris al-Sanussi of

Cyrenaica as the king of the Kingdom of Libya on December 2, 1950. The decision taken by the Assembly was communicated to the king, and, on December 17, 1950, a delegation of all members of the National Assembly presented the Assembly's resolution to the emir in Benghazi. al-Saqizli, the prime minister of Cyrenaica, Bashir al-Sa'dawi, leader of the NCP, and other dignitaries were also in attendance at this event.

It was only after all these that a Constitution Drafting Assembly, called the Committee of the Constitution, composed of 18 members, was assembled on December 4, 1950. The committee held its inaugural meeting on December 6, 1950. At this meeting, a Working Group, which met 96 times, was constituted. While the Working Group drafted the constitution, the committee, acting as a clearinghouse, read, amended (where necessary), and approved the various chapters of the constitution. The Committee of the Constitution submitted the draft constitution to the National Assembly, and discussions on the draft constitution began on September 10, 1951. All articles, provisions, and clauses were rigorously examined, and on October 7, 1951, the National Assembly completed deliberations on the constitution and unanimously passed a resolution adopting the entire constitution at its 43 meeting on November 6, 1951. The National Assembly remained in session until the proclamation of Libya's independence on December 24, 1951.

Upon independence, Mohamed Abulas'as El-Alem was the president of the Libyan National Assembly. He had two vice-presidents—Omar Faiek Shennib and Abubaker Ahmed Abubaker. According to the constitution, Libya was a hereditary and constitutional monarchy, with a representative system of government.

In light of all this, it is clear that Libya was the first African nation to become independent and the only nation established by the United Nations General Assembly. As shown, Libya obtained its independence because international disagreement between East and West in the immediate postwar period was greater than Libya's national disunity. The role of Great Britain, France, the Soviet Union, and the United States in granting Libya independence cannot be dissociated from the power politics of the Cold War. As Adrian Pelt brilliantly puts it, the United Nations assisted the people of Libya in the formulation of their constitution and in the establishment of an independent government. What was the nature of this constitution? What were its basic provisions, and how did the constitution contribute to and inform nation-building? What was the nature of the independent Libyan government? These questions are answered in the remaining parts of this chapter.

LIBYA'S INDEPENDENT CONSTITUTION

Led by King Idris, the independent Libyan government was a constitutional and hereditary monarchy. Its constitution, which came into force on October 7, 1951, was the first document that focused exclusively on the fundamental rights of Libyans. Besides a preamble, Libya's Independence Constitution contained 12 chapters, which, among other things, provided for the protection of the fundamental rights of Libyans, the establishment of the Libyan State, and the establishment of the main institutional apparatus of the state and their functions. It also detailed the nature, ways, and manners through which these institutions could be regulated. Altogether, the 12-chapter constitution had 213 articles.

Chapter 1 of Libya's constitution defined the "Form of State and System of Government of the Country," while Chapter 2 described the "Rights of People." Chapter 3, which had two sections, provided for a federal system of government. Section one of Chapter 3 of the constitution defined the "Powers of the Federal Government" and defined the "Joint Powers" of the government in the second section. Chapter 4, which focused on the "General Powers" of the Libyan State, was further developed and expanded upon in Chapters 5–8. These four chapters covered the powers of the "King," "Ministers," "Parliament," and the "Senate." Other items in these chapters included the powers of the "House of Representatives," "Provisions Common to the Two Chambers," and the "Judiciary." Chapters 9–12 focused on Libya's "Fiscal System," "Local Administration," "General Provisions," and "Transitory and Provisional Provisions."

Article 4 of Chapter 1 of the constitution defined the physical and geographical boundaries of Libya as covering from the Mediterranean Sea in the North and the United Arab Republic and the Republic of Sudan in the East. While the Republic of Sudan, Chad, Niger, and Algeria were in the South, Libya was bounded by the Republics of Tunisia and Algeria in the West. Libya, as noted in Article 5, was an Islamic state.

The Libyan constitution delicately balanced power between a hereditary monarchy and a federal state. In both Articles 44 and 45, the constitution set the governing parameters of the hereditary monarchy. In term of the procedure for succession, the articles mandated transmission of the Throne of the Kingdom of Libya only through the male line. By this, the constitution recognized and incorporated Libya's traditional political system into the newly established state. Under the constitution, the king was exempted from all responsibility. Notwithstanding these, the constitution also established a healthy democratic machinery and provided for the fundamental human rights of Libyans.

Libya's Independence Constitution provided for a three-arm government. The Executive arm of government was composed of a Presidential Council and a Cabinet. The second arm of government was a bicameral legislature, which was composed of a House of Representatives and a House of Senate. The Judiciary was the third arm of government, composed of a Supreme Court, Courts of Appeal, and Courts of First Instance. The constitution also provided for an elaborate administrative system.

In addition to the federal government, the constitution also provided for governance at the provincial level. Each of the provinces had its respective Provincial Legislative Councils and Executive Councils. In addition, each of the provinces had its own provincial head and a wider range of administrative office holders. While the federal government was small, provincial administration in the provinces involved a huge number of native workers, numbering in the thousands.

In addition, the constitution also established rock solid mechanisms for guaranteeing the human rights of Libyans. Among others, the constitution provided for equality before the law, rights to personal liberty, rights to no forced labor, right to recourse to the courts, the presumption of innocence until proven guilty in accordance with the law and in a trial, which guarantees citizens' defense, and the rights not to be arrested, detained, imprisoned, or searched except in the cases prescribed by law. Other rights guaranteed by the constitution included not to be deported from Libya under any circumstances, not to be compelled to reside in any locality or any specific place or prohibited from moving in Libya; freedom of conscience, freedom of thought, freedom of the press and of printing, freedom to use any language in private, religious, or cultural matters, rights of peaceful assembly and association, rights to address public authorities, rights to education, and rights to own property and the prohibition of general confiscation of property. Not only did the constitution make public elementary education compulsory for males and females in Libya, it also charged the state with the responsibility of providing an appropriate standard of living for every Libyan. In general, the constitution guaranteed to Libyans the same rights guaranteed by the constitution of any Western nation.

While it established the representative nature of Libyan government, it also granted members of the Parliament autonomy in their legislative function. Although the king had broad powers, the constitution established a bicameral legislature—the Senate and Chamber of Deputies. While members of the first house were selected based on proportional representation, members of the second house were elected representatives. The constitution also established an independent Judiciary, and, in Article 136, it prevented an autocratic monarch by spelling out clearly the procedures for overturning a king's veto and ensuring that government was by law and not by the whims and caprices of an absolute monarch.

Undoubtedly, Libya's 1951 constitution aimed primarily at ensuring ethnocultural cohesion and safeguarding the fundamental rights of Libyans while ensuring good governance, transparency, and the prevention of autocracy. The constitution was, however, silent on periodic and democratic elections. How did the first postcolonial government implement the provisions of the constitution? Put in another way, what was the nature of government and administration under King Idris, who ruled the first postcolonial Libyan state? How did the various organs of government fare under the constitution and hereditary monarchy of King Idris? How did the new government meet the expectations of its people and the expectations of the international community, especially in the light of Libya's being the first country granted independence by the United Nations? These and other questions are answered in the next section.

KING IDRIS AND THE UNITED KINGDOM OF LIBYA, 1951–1969

Born on March 12, 1889, El Sayyid Muhammad Idris bin Muhammad al-Mahdi al-Sanussi assumed power as the king of the independent state of Libya on December 24, 1951. Before this, he was the emir of Cyrenaica and a well-respected political and religious leader across Libya. Following the Italian invasion of Cyrenaica in 1913 and the abdication of his cousin and leader of the Order, Ahmed Sharif al-Sanussi, Idris became the head of the Sanussi Order, a position he held until 1922. Although the Ottoman rulers wanted the Order to attack the British in Egypt, Idris instead allied with the British. Through this alliance, he was able to secure two agreements with the Italians: at Al-Zuwaytina in April 1916 and Akrama in April 1917. These two agreements preserved the Sanussi's rights over Cyrenaica.

Following Benito Mussolini's ascension in Italy in 1922, Idris, fearing that the new leader of Italy would retaliate against the Order's anticolonial resistance, went into exile in Egypt. As Idris had feared, Mussolini's rule marked a turning point in the Italian occupation of Libya. Not only did the colonial conquest resume in earnest, but also it did so with such monstrosity that only Cyrenaica was left unconquered by December. Thousands of Libyans were killed in concentration camps, the deserts, and gas chambers. When World War II broke out, Idris supported Great Britain, a decision that paid off.

When in December 24, 1951, King Idris became the leader of the United Kingdom of Libya, it was the culmination of a long journey—a journey that could effectively be dated back to the periods of trade relations between different Libyan ethnic groups and the Phoenicians, Greeks, Romans, Vandals, and Ottomans. It was a historical moment not only for the indigenous people of Libya such as the Berbers, Garamantes, Tebous, among others in Cyrenaica, Benghazi, Tripolitania, and Fezzan but also for settlers like the Arab, Jewish, Greek, Turkish, and Italian minorities—all of whom saw Libya as home.

Like in all postcolonial state, the newly established United Kingdom of Libya was not a successor to any known precolonial Libyan groups. Neither Cyrenaica nor the leader of the new and independent government, King Idris, had any history of monarchy and royalty. King Idris, as noted in previous chapters, was appointed as emir of Cyrenaica, a title that showed its religious origin and purpose. Although increasing

Idris I, king of Libya (right), prepares to broadcast a speech in honor of Libya's independence, declared on December 24, 1951. (PNA_Rota/Getty Images)

military engagements with Italian colonial forces led to a metamorphosis of this religious position into a purely political one, King Idris's control and administration of Cyrenaica were not on account of any form of precolonial history of a monarchical system.

The practice of investing ordinary people with titles and positions was common throughout the colonial period. In its administration of Nigeria, British colonial administration invested ordinary people in both Central Nigeria and among the Igbos with traditional titles, appointing them as heads of communities where no such heads existed before the colonial period. Given that the indirect rule administrative system worked with existing traditional political institutions, this system, called the warrant chief system, allowed Britain to establish an indirect rule political administrative system on Nigeria's noncentralized societies, where traditional political institutions were different from what obtained in centralized societies.

Similar to the situation in Nigeria, the imposition of King Idris on Libyan people, especially Fezzan, Tripolitania, Benghazi, and other parts of Libya where no such institution had previously existed, directly affected ethnic relation and nation-building. Mutual suspicion, ethnic animosity, and ethnic hatred were rife, with serious implications for national development. For instance, on the issue of whether to adopt a federal or unitary system, Cyrenaica and Fezzan opted for a federal system, claiming that a unitary system will be dominated by Tripolitania, given its huge population. Tripolitania, on the other hand, preferred a unitary system, arguing that a federal system would render the central government impotent, especially on matters of national interest. This problem resurfaced immediately after independence. The constitution was inadequate to safeguard and prevent frictions between the Central government and the Provincial governments.

As noted in the previous section, Libya's Independence Constitution vested the king with extensive powers. The Cabinet, composed of a prime minister and Council of Ministers, was responsible to the king. Notwithstanding this, the king also had a group of unofficial royal advisers (*diwan*). Although the king selected both the prime minister and other members of the Council of Ministers, the government was responsible to the lower legislative house, the Chamber of Deputies. As leader of the executive arm, the king was undoubtedly the head of the federal government.

The Senate, which was the upper legislative house, was composed of eight selected representatives from each of the three provinces. The king nominated half of these senators, while the political parties nominated the other half.

The constitution also delineated the powers and responsibilities of the federal government and those of the provinces. In areas such as defense and foreign relations, the constitution invested the federal government with exclusive legislative and executive powers. In internal matters within the province, the provincial governments had exclusive legislative and executive powers. However, on matters relating to banking and income tax, imports and exports, mining and subsoil wealth, electoral laws and national economic policies, both the federal and provincial governments had joint powers. In these types of issues, the powers of the federal government were limited only to legislation, while powers of execution and implementation were vested in the provincial governments. Although this constitutional arrangement affected the federal government's ability to implement national policies, the processes involved in amending the constitution were tedious. For instance, Article 199 of the Libyan Independence Constitution required that to change the federal government or a portion of the constitution, not only a two-thirds majority in each of Libya's two chambers must approve but also all of the Legislative Councils of the provinces.

Given this power structure, it could be said that while appearing on paper as a constitutional monarchy, in practice, Libya's Independence Constitution fostered a monarchical dictatorship. As a person, King Idris was a scholarly individual whose life was punctuated by a studious reluctance to engage in politics. He was also a well-meaning, pious, deeply religious, and self-effacing man. Notwithstanding his personal attributes, the constitution transformed him from a spiritual leader into an autocrat disguising as a parliamentary democrat.

It must be noted that the constitution, not minding its flaws, provided a check on the powers of the king. For instance, the Senate reserved the power to veto any legislation. It could also dissolve the lower house, the Chamber of Deputies. By granting the provinces autonomy under the federal system, the provincial governments and their respective legislatures had powers and responsibilities that were similar to those of the king and the two houses of the National Assembly. In this way, the constitution limited the powers of the king to only the federal level of government.

In practice, the constitution proved difficult to implement, and no sooner did Libya became independent than the flaws of the constitution became manifest. One of the most palpable problems with the constitution was the power of the king. Besides his control of members of the Cabinet, the king also had great control over the Senate. For instance, he appointed the entire 24 members of the Senate. While members of the House of Representatives were elected on proportional representation, this House depended on the Senate. In addition, because the Cabinet was in charge of elections, the Legislative arm could not control the Cabinet. Given this, the king had control not only of the Cabinet but also of the Legislative arm of government.

In theory, the provinces—with their respective Legislative Assemblies and Executive Councils, were autonomous. Notwithstanding this, the constitution vested the king with the power to appoint all the provincial governors (*wali*). To bring governance to the grassroots, the constitution divided the provinces into departments, and districts and, in the day-to-day administration of these departments, the king appointed heads of these departments—*nazirs*, at the advice of the governors. Without the approval of the king, the governors could not dismiss any of these departmental heads. Between independence and 1963, the king's unofficial advisers, which were composed essentially of the kings' Cyrenaican elders and friends, controlled the Libyan state.

Although King Idris had extensive powers, he was unable to use this power to achieve national objectives, inasmuch as ethnic hatred, suspicion, and animosity ensured that policy objectives that would have life-changing impact on the nation got entangled in provincial politics and infighting. This development owed its origin to the very nature of the colonial state. Except in few places, colonial administration in Africa was wary of incorporating Africans, especially educated ones, into government. As was the case in Nigeria and Ghana, educated elites were seen as bastions of anticolonial agitation; hence, many of them were denied inclusion in state administration. In the case of Libya, it was a double jeopardy.

On the one hand, Italian colonizers denied Libyans access to education beyond elementary school. From the beginning, Italian colonial administration had no intention of providing any structured educational program for Libyans. When it finally decided on creating some form of institutionalized educational system, the Italians left no one in doubt that Libyans should be *Italianized*; hence, Italian schools in Libya not only used Italian but were also anchored on the teaching of Italian culture and education. No effort was made to incorporate any alternative perspective that privileged local languages, cultures, and customs. For instance, when the Ministry for the Colonies introduced a primary-level education in 1913, it aimed at training and preparing Libyan children for manual jobs in the colonial service. The system did not aim at providing them any intellectual education that could bring about an informed society.

Even at that, the segregation of Italian and local children in schools began by 1914. While children of Italian parents were to be taught in schools with standards that resembled their counterparts in Italy, the focus of education in the few Libyan communities with Italian schools aimed at assimilating these Libyan children. To ensure that the processes of assimilation were complete, not only did the Italians take over Libyans' Quranic schools, but also new Italian-Arabic schools, which provided a three-year program of Italian language and history, Koran, and Arabic classes, were established. In these newly established Quranic schools, Italian authorities supervised the Quranic education of Libyans and also selected those Libyan children whom they considered good enough for the newly established *Scuola di Cultura Islamica* (Higher Islamic School). This school, which was set up in 1935, aimed at providing personnel for Islamic religious, legal, and educational institutions.

Except for areas where Italians lived, secondary schools, *Scuole Medie*, were not established anywhere in any areas that Libyans lived until after World War II. During this time, not only were secondary schools established, but the Italian colonial government also took over all Quranic schools and established technical and agricultural schools, and for the first time in Libyan colonial history, girls were admitted into elementary schools. It was also the first time that that the Italian colonial administration paid any attention to the preservation of indigenous culture, language, and religion. Owing to this development, many local "elites" were incorporated into colonial administration. Anticolonial rebellion and the limited spread of these schools ensured that their impacts were noticeable only in theory, not in practice. For example, in Tripolitania, only 1,525 Libyans enrolled in Italian-Arabic schools in 1921. The number rose to 4,931 in 1931.

Given this, it could be argued that even during the post–World War I era, schools appeared only in a few special villages built for Libyan supporters of Italian colonialism. These fewer schools offered only elementary, Quranic, and secondary education. Unlike in Italian occupied areas, the Italian educational system was geared toward the teaching of Italian language and culture, while paying lip service to promoting African or Libyans' indigenous cultures and customs, Islamic religion, and education.

Although not for a lack of interest or efforts, Libyans who attended the Italian schools in Libya's special villages were deliberately prevented from continuing their education in the special villages built for Italian colonizers and farmers. Products of this limited educational system were employed in the lower rung of the administrative ladder, a situation that occluded them from such administrative position that could afford them any knowledge of administration and political participation.

On the other hand, agitation for Libyan independence differed remarkably from other independence agitations in Africa, Asia, or Latin America. Unlike others that were products of long-drawn-out political negotiations involving different independence movements and, oftentimes, differing political ideologies, afforded the colonized opportunities and platforms to learn politics and political administration, Libya's independence was orchestrated by the Great Powers involved in World War II and the United Nations.

The implications of these two unusual developments include a lack of highly educated elites who were administratively inclined enough to run a nation. Writing about this in early 2015, Hisham Matar—the American-born British-Libyan writer and winner of the 2017 Pulitzer Prize for Biography or Autobiography and the 2017 PEN America Jean Stein Book Award, noted, "The departing Italians left a traumatized and uneducated colony"[2] in Libya. To borrow from Gino Cerbella, the Italian educational system in colonial Libya aimed at the establishment of the requisite spiritual climate that was capable of fostering the mutual harmony of national and indigenous interests and of establishing, to Italian benefit, an emotional rapprochement of the native soul, stifling the naturally hostile feelings harbored by subject populations toward the ruling nation.

As already demonstrated in previous chapters, Libyans were politically conscious. However, their political consciousness was not to a nation but to the ethnic group. Italian colonial administration not only took specific advantage of this lack of loyalty to a nation but also fostered the colonial enterprise through it. The impact of this on the newly independent Libya was not just a lack of loyalty to a nation but also a wholesale lack of a politically conscious citizenry whose sense of loyalty was strong enough to support a truly federal system. In other words, independent Libya was filled with citizens whose loyalty was not to a Libyan state but to their ethnic groups.

This situation was not helped by the independent constitution, especially with a concentration of power on the provinces. The Provinces had different political orientations. This, coupled with the ambiguities of the king, ensured that both the federal government and the provincial governments were constantly working at cross-purposes. Provincial considerations and politics overshadowed national development. Constant squabbles with provincial administrators over jurisdiction ensured that no meaningful decisions could be taken, and the federal government was rendered ineffectual.

The terrible impact of ethnic issues on government and administration was not lost on the provinces. For instance, the Bashir al Sa'dawi–led National Congress Party campaigned for the abolition of the federal system of government in the general election of February 19, 1952. The party argued for the adoption of a unitary system of government. Sadly, other political leaders feared that a unitary system would reduce their powers and clout in government and administration, as well as negatively affect their respective provinces. Besides losing in the election, the NCP was not only proscribed, but also Bashir al Sa'dawi, the party leader, was deported from Libya. Given the politicians' inability to put parochial provincial concerns behind them and work for Libya's national development, the king proscribed all political parties and outlawed party politics immediately after the general election.

The outcomes of this development cannot be overemphasized: Violent protests erupted in major cities, which were put down by a strong police reaction, involving dozens of deaths; the press was curbed, and virtually no opposition party or group was allowed. While this enabled the federal government some room to operate, it obliterated everything called democracy in Libya.

Independent Libya was a poor country. It depended on the international community for its economic wealth. For instance, in 1953, under King Idris, the Kingdom of Libya joined the League of Arab States, a conservative regional traditionalist bloc that aimed at cultural, economic, and political codevelopment of the Arab-speaking peoples. Libya also had a close affinity with both the United Kingdom and the United States. In exchange for financial and military assistance, Libya concluded a 20-year treaty of friendship and alliance with the United Kingdom in 1953. Under this alliance, the United Kingdom established military bases in Libya. In 1954, Libya also signed an agreement with the United States, which allowed the United States to establish military bases in Libya, the most important of which was the Wheelus Air Base, near Tripoli. In return, the United States provided Libya with financial assistance running into millions of dollars.

It must be noted that both the United States and the Union of Soviet Socialist Republics (USSR) supported the United Nations' resolution demanding independence for Libya in 1951, as the two world powers were interested in securing Libya as an ally in their Cold War ideological battle. Inadvertently, Libya forged economic and strategic alliances not only with both world powers but also with France, Greece, Italy, and Turkey. Although USSR did not establish any military presence in Libya, both the United Kingdom and United States did. The military bases were parts of the United Kingdom and United States' strategic measures to counter the growing influence of the USSR in Africa. Besides stationing military aircraft in these military bases, the United Kingdom and United States also used the Libyan deserts as practice firing ranges.

The United Nations, through its Technical Assistance Board (TAB), also invested heavily in Libya. For instance, TAB provided technical assistance in the agricultural and educational development of Libya. It was instrumental in the establishment of the University of Libya, which was established by royal decree in 1955. Although economic development was slow, it, however, coalesced to lift Libya from a bleak economic future due to these multiple foreign efforts.

Two significant developments under King Idris were the discovery and exploration of high-quality crude oil in commercial quantity and the abolition of the federal system of government. These two developments, although different, were nevertheless related. As noted earlier, Libyans were conscious of the negative impact of ethnicity and provincial politics on national development. Party leaders were, however, wary of losing power to the king under a unitary system; hence, as the campaign of the Bashir al Sa'dawi–led NCP demonstrated, they were not prepared to effect the necessary change. The discovery and exploration of high-quality crude oil made political change possible, as the preceding discussion has shown.

In June 1959, the story of Libya changed radically when Exxon, then known as Esso, discovered high-grade crude oil in commercial quantity in Cyrenaica and other parts of Libya. Libya, unexpectedly, grew from a beggar state that depended on the generosity of foreign donor nations and the United Nations to a major crude oil exporter.

OIL EXPLORATION IN LIBYA

While many have described King Idris as a clueless and reluctant leader who presided over an autocratic and pseudo-democratic independent government, the king's remarkable and professional handling of Libya's oil industry presented a totally different picture. The impetus to prospect for crude oil in Libya was derived from a general observation along Libya's coastal cities. Prior to World War II, the Italian colonial administration, having noticed traces of crude oil in well water, employed the *Aziendi Generale Italiana Petroliche* to prospect for oil in the Sirtica Basin and along other coastal cities. Not long after the engineers moved to site, World War II began, forcing the engineers to abandon their assignment.

Not long after the war, a number of British, American, and Dutch oil companies—British Petroleum (BP), Royal Dutch Shell, and Standard Oil (Esso Standard of New Jersey, US) began prospecting for oil in Libya. As noted in Libya's *Official Gazette* of September 18, 1953, Libya's Parliament passed the Mineral Law of 1953, which stipulated a number of stringent conditions guiding the activities of these foreign companies. While the Mineral Law allowed oil companies to survey and prospect for oil, it prohibited seismic operations and drilling. In addition, the law opened the door for a possible future oil licensing but offered no guarantees. Rather than guarantees, it delineated between prospecting for oil and oil production. In other words, the law granted these foreign companies the license to prospect, not to produce.

In this way, King Idris and his advisers presided over Libya's oil industry. In drafting the Libya's Petroleum Law of 1955, the king hired expatriates who combined with Libyans to craft the country's first petroleum law. This law granted license to survey and prospect for oil only to nine companies. The duration of their licenses was one year. In addition, Libya's Petroleum Law divided Libya into four zones of exploration. Zones one and two, lying along 28° Latitude, were parallel to the north of the country, while zones three and four were parallel to the south.

Western interests, especially those of Great Britain and the United States, in Libyan oil could be explained in two key ways. On the one hand is Cold War politics. This involved curtailing the growing spread and influences of the USSR and Communism on the African continent. This was important to Western powers not just because of the importance of crude oil to the postwar world but also given the strategic closeness of Libya and Africa to Europe, especially Western Europe. On the other hand was the increasing impact of crude oil on the economic recovery of Western Europe after World War II. At the time, the Middle Eastern oil fields that fueled Western Europe's postwar economic recovery were experiencing a lull; hence, the discovery of new oil fields in Algeria and Libya in 1955 offered Western Europe the much needed alternatives to the Middle East oil fields. Another important point to be noted included the fact that, although not much was known about the extent of the oil reserves in Libya, the prospect and subsequent announcements of oil finds in Libya afforded Western Europe the prospect of a diversification from the oil fields in the Middle East. As a pro–Western Europe kingdom, Libya offered a better alternative, and, more fundamentally, Libya involved a short trans-Mediterranean voyage. As it turned out, Libya's crude was of a higher quality, light, and low in Sulphur and, hence, easily refined.

Given these multiple advantages, British, American, Dutch, and smaller oil companies trooped to Libya and were granted concessions to prospect for oil in Libya. By agreements, these companies paid 50 percent of their profits in taxes to the Libyan government. In a bid to increase its share of oil revenues, Libya's government introduced a number of changes to the country's petroleum law between 1955 and 1965. Given the numerous advantages that Libya's oil offered and, as later events showed, its huge oil deposits, none of these oil industries considered Libya's increasing demands and amendments to its oil laws as cumbersome. Libya's oil quality and proximity to Europe therefore played dramatic roles in the country's economic growth, as a direct linkage to Europe by sea guaranteed marketing benefits.

With crude exploration rising from a modest 6 million barrels in 1961 to 1,120 million barrels in 1969, Libya grew from a nation whose sources of revenue were derived mainly from foreign aid, especially from Great Britain and the United States, corsairing along the Mediterranean, raiding for slaves, trading across the Sahara, and/or working on Italian farms to becoming a major player in global oil trade. Table 5.1 shows Libya's revenues from crude oil exportation between 1961 and 1969.

The unexpected discovery and exploitation of crude oil changed the course of Libyan history. Shortly after the discovery of crude oil, Libya launched its first Five-Year Economic Development Plan, which lasted between 1963 and 1968. Under this plan, the country massively injected

Table 5.1   Oil Export and Revenues 1961–1969

Year	Million Barrels	$ Million
1961	6	3
1962	67	40
1963	167	108
1964	314	211
1965	443	351
1966	547	523
1967	621	625
1968	945	1,002
1969	1,120	1,175
Total	**4,230**	**4,038**

Source: Petroleum Economist, OPEC Oil Report, 1979.

funds into infrastructural developments in coastal highways and road construction, the building of 100,000 cheap houses, health care, education, farming and stock raising, and the like. Among other things, these and other developmental projects transformed the social, political, and economic lives of all Libyans. For instance, thousands of youths migrated from the rural areas to either the oil fields or the urban centers, which were the major recipients of government developmental projects. Not only did rural–urban migration stimulate overpopulation without corresponding urban planning, it also led to the emergence of shanty towns in Libya's coastal cities.

Between 1954 and 1964, the population of Tripoli rose to 200,000, a two-thirds growth over a 10-year period. Population in Benghazi doubled from 70,000 to 140,000. Although wages were higher in these towns and cities, housing and diet were poor. Suburban houses that were devoid of basic infrastructure, serving as a breeding ground for crime and criminality, developed everywhere. Resentment against politicians and government grew, as many argued that the new national wealth was not equitably shared.

The impact of the plan also included the emergence of a new class of educated elite who were desirous of power. This was composed of teachers, businesspersons, and bureaucrats—a group that ought to understand the precarious nature of the nation's economy. This new class of educated elite was not just a bastion of resentment against the government, it was also the main consumer of Arab Nationalism that Radio Cairo dished out daily.

Although King Idris's economic development plan was well intended, as later events showed, its source—crude oil wealth—was also its major problem. While oil wealth powered this development plan, it also raised popular expectation among Libyans. Overnight, Libya grew from penury to enormous affluence. This sudden wealth affected the people in unanticipated ways. At independence, not only was the nation poor, every standard of living was low. About 90 percent of the population was engaged in agricultural production and animal husbandry. Owing to irregular rainfall and the light, sandy soil, agriculture contributed a paltry one-third to the nation's gross domestic product (GDP). Overnight, oil wealth began to flood a nation that lacked the requisite manpower, resources, knowledge, and skills to make meaningful use of this new and unexpected wealth. Food production declined almost immediately, as Libyans began to see agricultural activities as demeaning. Traditional skills, such as gardening along the desert oases and productive herding along the predesert ranges, disappeared. What was the most fundamental impact of this development? While in 1955,

Libya's food import stood at $2 million, by 1968, Libya was spending over $80 million dollars on the importation of food.

Libya's economy became dependent on oil and thereby remained distorted, unbalanced, and underdeveloped. All state and personal consumptions were readily imported. National and personal incomes rose owing to oil. Productivity and achievement became disrupted. A culture of easy life, characterized by lavish state subsidies without any meaningful returns, followed. Libya transformed from an impoverished and sparsely populated country into a wealthy and independent country with enormous potential for rapid economic growth and development.

This unexpected discovery and exploitation of crude oil crippled agricultural production and turned Libya into a monocultural economy. In addition, the government—from the federal level to provincial level, became exceedingly corrupt. Favoritism and ethnic chauvinism became rampant, and social, political, and economic gaps between the rich and the poor widened dramatically.

Development projects were limited only to the cities, a development that accelerated rural–urban migration at a level that was never seen before. It also led to a high turnover in the central government. For example, besides the formation of 11 new cabinets between independence and 1968, 32 cabinet reshuffles—involving over 100 ministers— occurred. In addition, both the central and provincial governments became exceedingly corrupt.

While massive injection of funds into the economy ensured economic development and therefore ensured a stable polity, Libyan politicians were not unaware of the damage being done to democracy, nationalism, and national development by the federal system of government. Not only had the discovery and exploration of crude oil proven how inefficient and cumbersome the system was, it also showed that unless there was a radical change, competition between the federal government and the provinces would grind the new nation to a halt. So, in April 1963, Prime Minister Mohieddin Fikini presented a bill to the parliament calling for the abolition of the federal system and the institution of a unitary system, under the king and with a dominant central government. The bill, which was endorsed by the king, abolished the old provincial governments of Cyrenaica, Fezzan, and Tripolitania and, in their stead, divided the country into 10 new provinces, each headed by an appointed governor. The bill saw the end of federalism and the introduction of a unitary state.

Table 5.2 shows the number of prime ministers and the lengths of their time in office.

Mahmud al-Muntasir, the pioneer, who served between March 29, 1951, and February 19, 1954, was reappointed for a second spell in office between January 20, 1964 and March 20, 1965. While the kingdom lasted, he remained the longest serving prime minister. Wanis al-Qaddafi, the last prime minister under King Idris, was not a relation of Muammar Gaddafi who took over in 1969, after a military coup.

Under these prime ministers, the federal government was corrupt. Abdul Majid Kabar, who served as prime minister between May 26, 1957 and October 17, 1960, was dismissed from office on alleged corruption charges. Whether serving in the cabinet or as advisers to the king, many elites saw politics and office holding as a means to wealth, prestige, and power. The situation in the provinces was not different from the one at the federal level. Libya, by 1968, was both a rentier and a welfare state.

Coupled with a leadership dogged by endemic corruption, ineffectual leadership, especially at the federal level, and popular disenchantment with Libya's relationship with the duo of the United Kingdom and United States, King Idris's government also found itself faced with a growing pan-Arab nationalism.

Although rural–urban migration began in earnest in the 1930s when the Italian labor demands stimulated the movement of youth to the coastal cities, two other developments that fostered mass migration into the cities were the 1955–1959 drought and oil exploration. Faced with the drought, many farmers dumped agriculture and animal husbandry for positions in the newly established European coastal trade, industrial

Table 5.2 Prime Ministers of Libya, 1951–1969

	Prime Minister	From	To
1	Mahmud al-Muntasir	March 29, 1951	February 19, 1954
2	Muhammad Sakizli	February 19, 1954	April 12, 1954
3	Mustafa Ben Halim	April 12, 1954	May 25, 1957
4	Abdul Majid Kabar	May 26, 1957	October 17, 1960
5	Muhammad Osman Said	October 17, 1960	March 19, 1963
6	Mohieddin Fikini	March 19, 1963	January 22, 1964
7	Mahmud al-Muntasir	January 20, 1964	March 20, 1965
8	Hussein Maziq	March 18, 1965	July 2, 1967
9	Abdul Qadir al-Badri	July 2, 1967	October 25, 1967
10	Abdul Hamid al-Bakkoush	October 25, 1967	September 4, 1968
11	Wanis al-Qaddafi	September 4, 1968	August 31, 1969

plants, and oil rigs. Job prospects from the newly established oil industries and their satellite service industries lured many young men and
women from the interior to the coastal cities. Tripoli, like Benghazi, saw
a massive rise in population. In most coastal towns and cities, urban
development failed to catch up with population increases.

Poor housing and feeding conditions in the face of higher wages were
some of the distinguishing characteristics of Libyan urban lives. Shan-
ties emerged almost everywhere, as did crime and criminality. As
more and more Libyans were educated, a small class of educated elites
emerged who believed that the nation's wealth was not judiciously
spent. This class of businessmen and -women, teachers, and professionals found the growing Arab nationalism, which was growing almost
everywhere in North Africa, appealing. To them, Libya's new oil wealth
was enough to ensure that there were no poor people in Libya.

Although all of the preceding served the course of Arab nationalism,
Israel's war against the Arab states in 1967 almost led to a civil war in
Libya. The establishment of military bases in Libya by Great Britain and
the United States and crude oil exploration in Libya ensured a better
relationship between Libya and its Western allies. Many Libyans
considered this relationship with the West as neocolonialism and
would stop at nothing to stop their country from Western influences
of all kinds. They were not only demanding that the government
should sever relationships with the West but also that Libya should
join forces with other North African states against Israel.

On June 5, 1967, Libyan youth took to the streets in support of other
Arab states' war with Israel. This development, which cannot be dissociated from the influences of Radio Cairo, led to the murder of many
Jews. Properties belonging to British and Americans in Benghazi and
Tripoli were also destroyed in the attacks. By June 7, many government
ministers had fled Libya for their lives. Oil exploration declined, as oil
workers refused to load waiting tankers—as a way of supporting the oil
embargo agreed to by Arab oil producers. By July, the oil embargo was
directed solely at the United States, Britain, and West Germany. Within
weeks, no semblance of any government remained, and Libya was at the
verge of a total collapse.

To restore order, the king joined Saudi Arabia and Kuwait in Khartum
in August and injected huge financial outlays into Egypt's recovery
effort after its devastation in the war with Israel. At home, a number
of other steps was taken. First, the king dissolved the government
and appointed Abdul Hamid al-Bakkoush, a 35-year-old lawyer, as prime
minister. In turn, al-Bakkoush appointed many young and highly educated technocrats into government. To counter growing antigovernment

sentiment, al-Bakkoush announced a five-year security plan, which would help transition Libyan security and rid Libya of British and American military bases. In addition to these, Libya began to deploy its oil wealth as a "weapon of war" in support of other Arab states.

The peace and stability that followed were, however, short-lived, as al-Bakkoush abruptly resigned after a year. He was believed to be too radical in his approach, and Wanis al-Qaddafi, an older conservative was appointed as prime minister.

At independence, no one expected Libya to succeed: The country depended on the United Nations, rents, and foreign aid to exist. Its people were poor, uneducated, and divided. There were neither common traditions nor common ideologies to unite townspeople of Tripolitania with either the nomads of Fezzan or the tribesmen and -women of Cyrenaica. There were few trained technicians and experienced administrators, as Italian rule limited such careers to only Italian settlers. With barely 10 percent educated Libyans in 1951, Libya, under King Idris in 1968, had 85 percent of Libyan children enrolled in schools. This giant leap was occasioned by Libya's huge crude oil wealth, which was not only sudden but also unexpected. While in truth, King Idris might appear as a disinterested monarch, and the government he presided over might be corrupt, crude oil wealth fueled social and economic growth and positioned Libya in global trade in ways never anticipated or thought possible in 1951. Unfortunately for Libya, it also brought about a phenomenon whereby productive traditional skills such as animal herding and cultivation of crops were regarded as unsuitable for educated Libyans. This has led to a situation whereby sustained economic growth was not fueled by disruptive social and organizational changes.

As at the end of 1968, many Libyans considered King Idris's reign in Libya as unsuccessful. Given that King Idris had no heir, different rival groups emerged, plotting to seize power. Realizing this, King Idris took leave of the kingdom in June 1969, delegating his offices to a surrogate. On September 1, 1969, Muammar Gadaffi, a 27-year-old army captain, led a group of army officers—the Free Unionist Officers Movement—in a successful coup d'état that put an end to the monarchy.

NOTES

1. Geoff Simons, *Libya and the West: From Independence to Lockerbie* (Oxford: Centre for Libyan Studies, 2003), 27.

2. Hisham Matar, "What's Left in Libya," *The New Yorker*, January 14, 2015. Accessed on September 14, 2018, at https://www.newyorker.com /news/news-desk/whats-left-libya

LIBYA

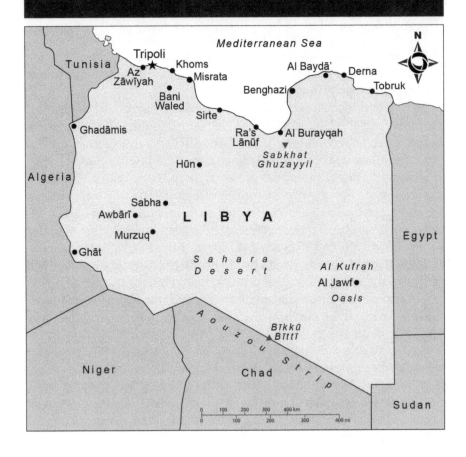

Mediterranean Sea

Tunisia

Tripoli
Az Zāwīyah
Khoms
Misrata

Al Baydā'
Derna
Tobruk

Benghazi

Bani Waled

Ghadāmis

Sirte

Ra's Lānūf
Al Burayqah

Sabkhat Ghuzayyil

Hūn

Algeria

LIBYA

Sabha
Awbārī
Murzuq

Egypt

Ghāt

Sahara Desert

Al Kufrah
Al Jawf
Oasis

Bīkkū
Bīttī

Niger

Chad

Aouzou Strip

Sudan

0   100   200   300   400 km
0   100   200   300   400 mi

6

The Gaddafi Years, 1969–1977

INTRODUCTION

On September 1, 1969, a small band of army officers who called them-selves the Free Unionist Officers Movement carried out a coup d'état, which ended the monarchy. The Free Unionist Officers Movement was composed of about 70 army officers and a few enlisted men from the signal corps. The coup, which was launched in Benghazi, lasted for only two hours. At the head of this group was a 12-man Revolutionary Com-mand Council (RCC), which initiated a major shift in Libya's domestic and foreign policy. Initially, members of the Free Unionist Officers Movement were anonymous; the group later announced the promotion of Captain Muammar al-Gaddafi to the rank of colonel and Gaddafi's appointment as the leader and commander-in-chief of the Armed Forces of Libya.

Other members of the group included Major Abd as-Salam Jallud, Major Bashir Hawadi, Captain Mukhtar Abdallah Gerwy, Captain al-Khuwaylidi al-Hamidi, Captain Muhammad Nejm, Captain Ali Awad Hamza, Captain Abd al-Munim Tahir al-Huni, Captain Mustafa al-Kharubi, Captain Abu Bakr Yunis Jabr, and Captain Omar Abdallah al-Muhayshi. Like Captain Muammar al-Gaddafi, all of these men attended the Royal Military Academy.

At the time of the coup, King Idris was seeking medical treatment in Greece. The RCC imprisoned Crown Prince Sayyid Hasan ar-Rida al-Mahdi al-Sanussi, who was ruling Libya at King Idris's absence. Fearing that the new leadership in Libya might imprison him if he returned to Libya, King Idris left Greece for Turkey and later for Egypt, where he lived and died on May 25, 1983. The crown prince, along with other senior civil and military officials of the royal government, spent between two and five years in jail. When he was eventually released, he was placed on house arrest for another seven years.

Gaddafi, the leader of the RCC and the de facto head of state, was born in the central Libyan Desert, 50 miles southward of Sirte in 1943. His parents were Bedouin whose education was limited to elementary school. Although his parents had other children, he was the only surviving son. Gaddafi's early education consisted mainly of traditional religious subjects and principles taught mostly by the local leader. He later began elementary school in Sirte, where he completed six grades in four years. He transferred to Sebha, a small market town in south-central Libya, where he enrolled for his secondary school education. It was while in Sebha that he developed an interest in politics, as he was exposed to Arab newspapers and radio broadcasts, most importantly the *Voice of the Arabs,* a news program that was broadcast from Cairo.

The Arab newspaper and radio broadcast were not the sole factors in Gaddafi's political development; his teachers, most of whom were Egyptians, stimulated his interests in the Egyptian revolution. Under the influences of these different sources, Gaddafi developed into a radically and politically active young man, whose most engaging interest was to distribute subversive literature and to organize violent political gatherings. He was so ardent at these that he was expelled from high school. Rather than bowing his spirit, his expulsion further convinced him that the path to any meaningful socioeconomic and political change in Libya cannot but be violent. Arab's defeat in the hands of the Israelis in 1948, the Egyptian revolution of 1952, the Suez crisis of 1956, and the alliance between Syria and Egypt in 1958 reinforced his pan-Arab nationalist fervor. It was from all of these that Gaddafi became convinced that nonviolent political change was impossible.

Having been expelled, Gaddafi sought and gained admission to Misurata High School, where he completed his higher education. Although Gaddafi did not join any factional group, his ideologies crystalized under the influences of groups like the Arab Socialist Resurrection (Ba'athist) Party, the Muslim Brotherhood, and the Arab Nationalist Movement. With his outlook to world politics colored by these developments in the Arab world, he became a fervent admirer of Egyptian

President Gamal Abdel Nasser and looked forward to implementing a revolution similar to the Egyptian revolution in Libya. He was not only anti-imperialistic but also aspired to the implementation of Arab nationalist foreign policies and the establishment of egalitarian, socialist domestic reforms in Libya. Like many of his generation, he was desirous of ending Western influences not just in Libya but across the entire North Africa.

After completing his education in Misurata High School, Gaddafi was admitted to read history at the University of Libya, where he met like-minded youths, with whom he established the Free Unionist Officers Movement. From inception, the movement was limited to the university, and most of its activities were clandestine, as there was a ban on political parties, and politics of any kind was severely regulated under King Idris.

The actual number of initial members of the movement remains unknown. However, it was generally known that one of the major concerns of the movement was how to reform Libya. Within the first two years of its existence, Gaddafi appointed 12 of his most trusted allies as members of the central committee, whose responsibilities included the day-to-day administration of the movement. In many of their deliberations, members of the movement discussed the obstacles to reforming Libya and unanimously agreed that politics, especially while the monarchy lasted, cannot bring about any meaningful change. Unlike a career in politics, a career in the army held possibilities of better and well funded education, especially for poor but talented Libyans like Gaddafi and his friends, better opportunities in the economy, and better assurances of upward sociopolitical mobility.

Two years into their programs, in 1963, Gaddafi and his friends left the University of Libya and enrolled in the Royal Military Academy, Benghazi, where they graduated in 1965. Upon graduation, Gaddafi was commissioned as a communication officer in the Signal Corps—a position that later served him in the planning and execution of the coup. He proceeded in 1966 to the United Kingdom, where he studied English language and later an advanced military training in signal science.

At the end of his training, he returned to Libya and was posted to a military facility near Benghazi, where he coordinated the coup of September 1, 1969. Unlike Gaddafi, not much was known of the 12-man RCC members. Nevertheless, the new government reflected Gaddafi's thinking and disposition, as the committee announced the following goals as the underlying reasons for the military takeover: freedom for all, establishment of a socialist state, and unity of all ethnic groups in Libya and the Arab world. These were the very same policies of the

Egyptian revolution led by Gamal in 1952. Reinforcing the view of the Gaddafi-led administration as a replica of the Egyptian experience were the policy statements that followed the coup. In a speech in 1970, Gaddafi declared loudly: "Tell President Nasser we made this revolution for him. He can take everything of ours and add it to the rest of the Arab world's resources to be used for the battle against Israel, and for Arab unity."[1] He then went on to declare Libya's neutrality in the ideological disputes between the United States and the Union of Soviet Socialist Republics (USSR), noting that Libya would take active roles in espousing and spreading Arab nationalism and especially that Libya would support the Palestinian course against Israel.

Gaddafi and his coup plotters left no one in doubt about their intentions. Shortly after taking office, the new military government invited diplomats and ambassadors of France, Great Britain, the United States, and the USSR to series of meetings where major issues, ranging from the need to dissolve U.S. and British military bases and the gradual reduction of Western influences on Libya, were discussed. Britain was unequivocal in its lack of comfort with the new government.

Although the United States was equally uncomfortable, it supported the new government in the hope that it could secure a favorable deal, especially in maintaining a commercial and military presence in Libya. As declassified Central Intelligence Agency (CIA) records have shown, steps were taken to truncate the new government, but neither the United States embassy in Libya nor the officials in Washington knew who was in charge of the new government until much later. In addition, the CIA, carried away by the need to curry the favor of the new government, revealed a series of intelligence on countercoups to members of the new government. Not only was the United States actively supporting the new government, it also refused to support any effort at removing the coup plotters by a U.S. military operation, as canvassed by the promonarchy elements in Libya.

Realizing its precarious position, the new government also pivoted to the United States' duplicitous behavior. Diplomatic correspondences between Britain and the United States during the 1970s showed that both countries were sharing intelligence on how best to deal with the new government, including the possible assassination of its leaders. As noted in its assessment report of September 30, 1971, David L. Mack[2] noted, for the first time, that Gaddafi was not just a member of the central committee of the new government but also the "Alpha Male." He then went on to maintain Gaddafi's indispensability, thereby putting to rest any thought of either assassinating him or engaging the new government militarily. David L. Mack was then a junior diplomat at the

U.S. Embassy in Libya and, because of his fluency in Arabic, served as translator between the ambassador and the new government.

It was not only the United States that was doing all in its powers to curry the favor of the new government; the British were also doing the same. In fact, many expected Britain to intervene in the coup and restore Libya to King Idris, a view that the British government denied. Notwithstanding the denials, evidence abounds to support the fact that British entities made efforts to remove Gaddafi and his men.

In a 1960 U.S. National Security Council Report, intelligence officials had noted that younger urban elements in Libya had little or no respect or loyalty to King Idris, describing the king as a British puppet. As the report noted further: "Although there are no political parties in Libya there are a number of loose political factions and interest groups and pan-Arab nationalism has considerable appeal, particularly to the younger urban elements."[3] The report concluded, "Although the British would be reluctant to intervene with force in Libya to maintain a regime favorable to their interests, they would probably do so if it seemed the only way to preserve their position."[4]

Five years before Gaddafi led the coup that toppled King Idris, the British government already had a fully loaded file concerning Gaddafi, his views, and his ambitions. In 1965, a British intelligence officer, Colonel Ted Lough, noted in his reports that Gaddafi was "a murderer, a possible assassin, a revolutionary, and a major suspect"[5] in a planned coup plot. Rather than sharing the intelligence on Gaddafi either with the army or with King Idris, the British accepted Gaddafi into their military academies, where he was trained further on behalf of the Libyan Army. Whether in the Royal Military Academy in Libya or in training academies in Britain, the kind of treatment that British trainers and advisers gave to Gaddafi, as David Blundy and Andrew Lycett noted in their biography of Gaddafi, amounted to cultivating the young officer. Not only were the British military advisers well aware that Gaddafi was planning some form of subversion, they also kept the knowledge away from the King Idris–led government of Libya.

The British's concern was that these younger urban elements, who did not have significant political power during King Idris's rule, would soon have such power. So, rather than sharing intelligence on Gaddafi, he was admitted to British military academies where he spent four and nine months, respectively.

It was not only Gaddafi and his men who were interested in upstaging King Idris. As British intelligence showed, British Minister of Defense Dennis Healey noted to intelligence officers that when in Libya, it was obvious to him that the King Idris–led government had fallen apart and that at any moment, Colonel Omar al-Shelhi might take over in a coup d'état. In the same report, the British Labor politician also noted that the British ambassador in Tripoli informed him that when Colonel al-Shelhi's batman informed him of Gaddafi's coup on the morning of September 1, 1969, the colonel said: "Don't be silly, it is tomorrow."[6] In other words, had Gaddafi and his men not struck on September 1, the colonel and his men would have overthrown the monarch on September 2, 1969.

Even after Gaddafi's coup, several attempts were made by Libyans, aided actively by British elements, to overthrow Gaddafi. For instance, following the arrest and detention of promonarchy politicians and elements in the military, including Colonel al-Shelhi, David Stirling, a British war hero and founder of the British Special Air Service (SAS), hatched a plan with his Watch Guard, a company of British mercenary soldiers. The plan was that Stirling and his mercenary soldiers would raid Tripoli and release a number of political prisoners, including al-Shelhi, from jail. The Watch Guard would then withdraw, having set the stage for an al-Shelhi takeover. Stirling had to call off the plan due to fear of a possible leak. The details of the plan were contained in the book, *The Hilton Assignment*. Stirling, with the active support of French mercenaries, later made two more attempts at reviving the plan but was compelled to abandon it, as it became clear that the Gaddafi-led government was involved in multimillion military-related business with the French government.

Given all this, it is clear that both Britain and the United States knew ahead of time of Gaddafi's coup before it took place and directly or indirectly played roles to either facilitate the coup or to overthrow the government once in power. So, when in 1969, Gaddafi led a successful coup that removed King Idris, many were of the belief that it was with the active but clandestine support and blessings of both the United States and Britain. Attempts by both to remove Gaddafi were made because he always failed to cooperate with his CIA and MI6 backers.

Other evidence has come to light supporting the fact that even America's CIA was also aware of the coup plot but did nothing to prevent it. For instance, al-Bakoush, a former Libyan ambassador to France, who later became a prime minister, was briefed about the coup plot two months prior to the coup. He claimed to have reported the coup plot to CIA officials and station chief at the U.S. Embassy in Paris. He also went to Turkey to report the plot to King Idris.

As Gaddafi demanded in his public broadcast of October 16, 1969, Libyans would not continue to live with "foreign bases side by side," and the Libyan army would not continue to watch its people living side by side "with the bases of imperialism . . . in Libyan territory."[7] Among other personal experiences that mirror the state of things in Libya under the monarchy, Air Force General Daniel "Chappie" James, who assumed control of Wheelus Air Base following the 1969 coup, recounted a day Gaddafi came to Wheelus Base:

> One day, Khadafy ran a column of half-tracks through my base, right through the housing area at full speed. I shut the barrier down at the gate and met Khadafy a few yards outside it. He had a fancy gun and a holster and kept his hand on it. I had my .45 in my belt. I told him to move his hand away. If he had pulled that gun, he never would have cleared his holster. They never sent any more half-tracks.[8]

If the head of government and commander-in-chief of the Libyan military is treated in this way, how much indignity would an ordinary Libyan suffer at the hands of these Americans? It is clear from the preceding report of the American base commander that he had little or no respect for Gaddafi.

Following this experience, Gaddafi asked:

> How can a soldier remain passive and salute a king who has filled the country with foreign forces? How can you accept being stopped on the street by an American? That happened to me personally. When I wanted to enter Wheelus base, I was turned away. [9]

He maintained that, just like the bases, the lives of their occupiers had become limited in Libya, as Libyans would accept "no bases, no foreigner, no imperialist and no intruders."[10] Consequent upon this, Britain evacuated its Al-Adem Base in March 1970. After its initial tardiness, the United States evacuated in June 1970.

In a cable that the U.S. Embassy in Tripoli sent to Washington on June 11, 1970, it was clear that the United States left reluctantly. It originally refused to leave, arguing that the initial agreement reached with the King Idris–led independent government was to occupy Wheelus Base until December 24, 1970. While this was not enough to alter Gaddafi and his men's position, the United States also suggested a joint use of the base, a proposal that was also rejected. On October 7, 1970, the Gaddafi-led government also nationalized all Italian-owned assets in Libya. Also, Barclays Dominion, Colonial, and Overseas Bank were nationalized, and a series of arms contracts granted to the British by the previous regime were withdrawn.

In 1972, the Libyan government also ordered a reduction of staff at the British, U.S., French, and USSR embassies to a paltry 15 officials each. The U.S. Embassy had to send 70 staff back to the United States in accordance with government directives. In addition to these, a number of other foreign institutions were nationalized. For example, the Seventh Day Adventist Hospital, Benghazi, was nationalized. British, French, and American stakes in Libyan oil and gas were nationalized. The United States' claim to the entire Gulf of Sirte was rescinded, and the entire gulf reverted back to Libya.

While Britain and the United States continued to have torrid times with the Gaddafi-led government of Libya, France had a totally different experience. At the outset, Libya approached the United States for the procurement of C-130 cargo planes, a request that the United States accepted but denied an export license to Libya after accepting Libya's money. The embargoed cargo planes rotted away for more than 30 years in Marietta, Georgia. Given this experience, Libya approached France and bought 110 Mirage warplanes. In addition to this US$300-million-dollar business deal over a three-year period, France also trained the Libyan army on the use of these supersonic warplanes. Underlying this benign relationship with the French was France's policy in the Middle East, which favored the Arab states.

Just as the French were enjoying a lofty and beneficial relationship with Libya, the USSR also officially recognized the Gaddafi-led government of Libya and entered into trade relationships with Libya. By July of 1970, Libya received a consignment of USSR military equipment, and, over the next five years, the Gaddafi-led government's investment in Soviet military equipment rose to US$1 billion.

Libya's relationships with both the French and the USSR were to the displeasure of the United States and Britain. While both could tolerate Libya's relationship with France, they found the relationship with the Soviets an abhorrent one and therefore distanced themselves from Gaddafi-led Libya.

These and other policies of the Gaddafi-led government increased Libyan support for the government, as more jobs were created, and Libyans felt a sense of nationalism toward the nation rather than toward their ethnic or regional alliances. Libyans also rejoiced at the evacuation of military bases and the nationalization of Italian and other European assets in Libya. To many Libyans, the declaration of the dates when the various military bases of the United States and Britain were dismantled as national holidays was not only a commemoration of the evacuation of foreign military bases but also a celebration of Libya's true emergence as an independent nation. It was also considered the end of

Western influence and control of Libyan politics, power, and economy. Libyans received these policy decisions very well. For the first time, an average Libyan could boast of a government that cared for the common man and not only for the rich politicians and their foreign collaborators. The new government was a dramatic change from the conservative King Idris–led government. During its early days, the new government removed bureaucrats and businessmen put in place by the previous administration. The army was also not spared of these purges. While members of the National Guard were absorbed into the regular army, many above the rank of major were compulsorily retired.

The various reforms were well received by Libyans. Although there is no denying the fact that these reforms irked promonarchy politicians and elements in the government, not a single antigovernment protest occurred either in the wake of the coup or in response to any of the socioeconomic and political reforms of the new government. Gaddafi's statement of September 1969 adequately captured the mood of Libyans:

> The armed forces are an integral and inseparable part of this people, and when they proclaimed the principle of liberty, socialism, and unity, they proclaimed nothing new. It is the people who believe in liberty, socialism, and unity and inspired the armed forces, their vanguard, which imposed them on the enemies of the people with the force of arms.[11]

Given all this, it could be argued that while pockets of promonarchy Libyans existed in politics and government, they accepted the new government. To the extent that the British, Americans, and other Europeans desired a reversal to monarchical system, the new regime treated them as enemies.

Positive perception (and invariably acceptance) of the Gaddafi-led government was not limited to Libya. Gaddafi's pan-Arab nationalism made him a voice for many Arab leaders. On behalf of the Arab world, Gaddafi spoke truth to power, he attacked friends and foes alike and with a dignified righteousness. As later events showed, he was as much for the unification of the Arab countries as he was for the unification of Africa—two ideas that failed to catch up in both the Arab world and Africa.

THE 1969 CONSTITUTION

While announcing the coup d'état, the Free Unionist Officer Movement announced the suspension of the old monarchical constitution, and, on December 11, 1969, it announced the promulgation of a new constitution, which remained in force until the adoption of an interim constitution on August 3, 2011. The constitution restored Libyans' freedom, guaranteed the enjoyment of the wealth of Libya, and ensured a society in which every loyal citizen has the right to prosperity and well-being, where there were no restraints impeding their growth and development. The new constitution also provided safeguards for Libyans' association with other Arabs from all parts of the Arab Nation in the struggle for the restoration of every inch of Arab land desecrated by imperialism and for the elimination of all obstacles that prevent Arab unity from the gulf to the ocean.

The constitution asserted that peace could not be achieved without justice; hence, it supported all the people of the world who were struggling against imperialism and corruption and who were desirous of establishing a national, democratic, progressive, and unitary government. Above all, the constitution renamed the country from the Kingdom of Libya to the Libyan Arab Republic and declared the objectives of the revolution as freedom, socialism, and unity.

Article 1 of the constitution made Libya an Arab, democratic, and free republic, where sovereignty is vested in the people. It also declared that Libyan people were parts of the Arab nation and at the same time a part of Africa. It changed the country's name to the Libyan Arab Republic. In Article 2, the constitution declared Islam as the religion of the state and Arabic as Libya's official language. Notwithstanding this non-secular nature of the state, the constitution guaranteed religious freedom for all Libyans—Muslims and non-Muslims alike.

Chapter II, Article 18 of the constitution made the Revolutionary Command Council (RCC) the supreme authority in Libya. The powers and responsibilities of the RCC were set out from Articles 19–31. In Article 19, the constitution provided for a Council of Ministers, whose members were to be appointed by the RCC.

Articles 27–29 of the constitution provided for an independent judiciary whose primary objective was the protection of the principles of the community and the rights, dignity, and freedom of individuals. Although the constitution provided for an independent judiciary, it denied this arm of government the power to undertake constitutional or institutional review. Notwithstanding this, the constitution provided for equality before the law for all Libyans, making the provision of health care, education, property-ownership and so on basic rights for all citizens.

The last part of the constitution, Chapter III, "Miscellaneous and Transitory Provisions," differentiated between the old laws of the King

Idris era and the new ones of the new dispensation. In addition to declaring the old laws null and void, it also made the RCC the sole law-making body in Libya. Article 37 of the constitution noted that the 1969 constitutional proclamation would remain in effect until a permanent constitution was made. In order words, the 1969 constitutional recognized and enshrined the work-in-progress nature of the constitution and provided for a new constitution in the future.

A closer look at the 1969 constitution shows that the new regime had three cardinal objectives: to ensure freedom from foreign intervention in Libya's internal economic, social, and political affairs; to build nationalism among Libyans; and to attain national unity among the different ethnic groups. How did the new government pursue these three broad objectives? How successful or effective were government efforts, and how did Libyans and the international community react to these? Before examining these, it is important to examine the various institutions and offices provided for by the 1969 constitution.

THE REVOLUTIONARY COMMAND COUNCIL (RCC)

The new constitution designated the RCC as the highest political authority in Libya. It vested the RCC with the power to exercise all powers attached to national sovereignty, promulgation of laws and decrees, taking decisions in the name of the people, the general policy of the state, and the making of all decisions that it might deem necessary for the protection of the revolution and the regime. It was also vested with the powers to direct the country's national policy and to make all decisions on national security. The RCC was also tasked with declaring war and ratifying treaties. Only the RCC had the power to make decisions concerning martial law, states of emergency, and matters involving the Armed Forces.

In addition to the RCC, the constitution also provided for two other key institutions: the president and the Council of Ministers. According to Article 19 of the constitution, the RCC appoints both the president and members of the Council of Ministers. Besides the president, the constitution provided for the office of prime minister, minister without portfolio, and premier. The RCC was also charged with appointing deputies for the prime minister and ministers without portfolio. The council also may discharge the premier and ministers and accept their resignation. In a situation whereby a premier resigned, the constitution mandated that all ministers must also resign.

While the president and the RCC were charged with the responsibilities for formulating policies and programs for the country, the

Council of Ministers were to execute national policies and programs in accordance with the decisions of the Revolutionary Command Council. The Council of Ministers must also prepare and study all laws and make recommendations to the RCC where appropriate. While the Council of Ministers was collectively responsible to the Revolutionary Command Council, each of the ministers was responsible to the prime minister.

THE COUNCIL OF MINISTERS

Following the promulgation of the 1969 constitution, Mahmud Sulayman al-Maghribi, an educated, young radical opponent of the monarchical government, Adam Said Hawwaz, Musa Ahmed, and five others were appointed into the Council of Ministers. Mahmud Sulayman al-Maghribi was the prime minister and head of the eight-member council. Major Adam Said Hawwaz was the minister of defense, while Major Musa Ahmed was the minister of interior. Unlike others, Adam Said Hawwaz and Musa Ahmed were military officers. Although both represented the military in the council, none of them was a member of the RCC.

As noted in the constitution, the Council of Ministers was mandated to implement any policy—specific or general—as the RCC might have decided. It could therefore be seen as an executive arm of government. The legislative functions of government were performed exclusively by the RCC. This division of government powers followed closely with Gaddafi's declaration after the coup that the government would not run a government akin to King Idris's regime that was characterized by individual leadership. The new government was rather a collegial system of government where decision making involved all Libyans and their representatives.

Things, however, took a new turn for the Council of Ministers in December 1969, when Majors Adam Said Hawwaz and Musa Ahmed were indicted in a countercoup. Following this development, the RCC announced a shake-up in the Council of Ministers. This shake-up not only widened membership from eight to 13 but also saw the emergence of Gaddafi as the prime minister and Major Abdel Salam Jallud, Gaddafi's second-in-command, as deputy prime minister. In addition to these changes, five members of the RCC were among the new 13-member Council of Ministers.

In July 1970, the council once again witnessed a major shake-up following another countercoup involving Abdullah Abid Sanussi and

Ahmed al-Sanussi—two distant cousins of King Idris and members of the Sayf an Nasr clan of Fezzan. Prince Abdullah funded a force of mercenaries recruited in Chad. Things, however, took a different turn for the coup plotters when the French got wind of it and reported it to the RCC. The foiled coup led to a significant change in the composition of the Council of Ministers, as many of the civilian members were sacked, and new members, this time members of the RCC, were appointed to the Council of Ministers.

THE JUDICIARY

Chapter II of the 1969 constitution made a number of provisions on the judiciary. Article 27 noted that the aim of judicial decision was the protection of the basic principles of the community and the dignity of Libyans. Article 28, which focused on judges, did not discuss types of courts and their powers but limited itself to the constitutional expectations of judges—being independent, free from governmental intervention, and maintaining adherence to their consciences. The constitution in Article 29 maintained that the verdicts from the courts would be pronounced and executed in the name of Libyans. In Article 30, the constitution provided for the rights of every Libyan to the courts and in accordance with the law.

Although the constitution provided for an elaborate court system in its different parts, it, however, provided little direction on the composition of the judiciary. As Gaddafi noted later in his *Green Book*, Libya's legal system was based on the *Sharia*—Islamic law as enumerated in the Quran. The legal system made the Supreme Court of Libya, whose members are appointed by the General People's Congress, the highest appeal court.

Unlike the 1969 constitution that made no clear distinctions between the courts and their respective powers, *The Green Book* divided the Supreme Court into three chambers. While the first dealt with civil and commercial matters, the second dealt with purely criminal, administrative, and constitutional matters. The third chamber of the Supreme Court dealt only with religious matters.

In addition the general court system, Libya also had a number of revolutionary and military courts. A distinctive characteristic of these courts was that none of them abided by the procedural rules and judicial precedent established in the constitution. Rather, these courts heard all kinds of matters against the state, state officials, and politicians. They were primarily used in trying political, military, and government opponents. Hence, their activities could be classed as extrajudicial and unconstitutional. Until 2004, these kind of extrajudicial and unconstitutional tribunals and courts were in existence in Libya.

POLITICAL CHANGE IN POST-1969 LIBYA

The 1969 constitution provided for the preceding few institutions and offices. As the constitution itself showed, there is no gainsaying the fact that while the new government possessed abundant charismatic and revolutionary appeal, it grossly lacked experience in government and expertise in administration. In the first four years of the new government, efforts were concentrated on consolidation. Except in crude oil exploration and marketing, there was no clear-cut economic policy. The political direction of the government was sketchy and ad hoc. It was essentially whatever caught the fancy of members of the RCC, especially Gaddafi. With these few institutions and offices, how, then, did the new government attain its socioeconomic and political objectives? How successful or effective were these institutions and offices in attaining the goal of postcoup nation-building, and how did Libyans and the international community react to these efforts?

As early as January of 1971, Gaddafi identified a number of things that he considered wrong in Libya. He located problems of nation-building globally within the ambit of "problem of authority." He condemned representative democracy, parliament, political parties, class-based society, plebiscites, and popular conferences. In his argument, all of these fostered, in one way or the other, the oppression of the masses by political parties, parliament, class, race, and other means. He maintained: "The party allegedly governs on behalf of the people, but in reality, the true principle of democracy is based upon the notion that there can be no representation in lieu of the people."[12] He described the role of parliament, race, class, plebiscites, and the like in the same way as he described political parties and concluded that "the party represents a segment of the people, but the sovereignty of the people is indivisible."[13]

Parliaments, political parties, race, class, and the like, he argued, was a minority with its narrow, common sectarian interests and beliefs, from which a common and deceitful outlook of democracy was formed. Considered in this way, he likened political campaigns, parliamentary squabbles, and so on to tribal and sectarian struggle for power that paid little or no attention to what the populace wanted but rather to what benefits party members. If a party, a class, tribe, sect, or other group dominated a society, the dominant system becomes a dictatorship that catered only for its members and not for the masses outside such membership. Owing to this, he made it clear that the military government would foster a system of government that facilitates a popular rule that was composed of all Libyans.

On January 14, 1971 at Zawiya, Gaddafi announced the creation of Popular Congresses, which were later established in different districts and provinces in Libya. In addition, a Higher Council on National Orientation, a committee saddled with the responsibility for facilitating the exchange of ideas among top members of the government, was also established. Other committees that were established included the Popular Revolution, Popular Committee, Libyans' Peoples Court, and the like. As the government noted, the Popular Congresses, Popular Revolution, and Popular Committee were different means toward engendering popular rule. Members of these different committees were ordinary Libyans. Conceptually, the idea behind the establishment of these and other committees was to foster mass participation in government and administration.

Popular Revolution, for instance, was meant to remove all administrative and legal obstacles to revolutionary change. At its beginning, it focused primarily on local and regional officials—mayors, managers, heads of government institutions, and others who opposed the revolution. This committee sacked managers and heads of government agencies such as the Libyan Broadcasting Service, Libyan Television, Libyan Arab Airlines, Libyan Petroleum Institute, and so on. At the height of its power, the committee removed the governors of Benghazi, Darna, and Gharyan, as well as the president of the University of Libya from office.

In all government offices and businesses, Popular Committees were established to oversee the activities of these offices and businesses. No less than 3,000 such committees were established by the end of 1973. Across Libya, the over 800 Popular Congresses established were tasked with the main responsibility of appointing representatives to Libya's parliament, members of whom directly elected the president.

On June 12, 1971, the Free Unionist Officer Movement (FUOM), the vanguard of the revolution, was rechristened the Arab Socialist Union (ASU), and its membership was thrown open to all Libyans. Although modeled after Egypt's Arab Socialist Union, Libya's ASU was made the only political party in Libya. Underlying this development was the internal war and violence that political parties wreaked in Libya during the Italian occupation and, later, during the monarchy. So it could be rightly argued that the underlying assumption behind the establishment of ASU was to ensure that an ethnic-dominated party or regional party did not develop again in Libya. The ASU was a vanguard for the mobilization of the masses for political participation and consolidation of the revolution.

In general, the ASU served as a "vehicle of national expression," which aimed to raise Libyans' political consciousness and to "aid the RCC in formulating public policy through debate in open forums."[14] Trade unions were incorporated into the ASU and strikes, protests, and sit-ins were outlawed. The press, already subject to censorship, was officially conscripted in 1972 as an agent of the revolution.

Other institutions created by the government included the General People's Congress (GPC), a 1,000-member congress of Libyans, drawn from different districts and sections of Libya, whose responsibilities included voting for the president and for general control of government. There was also a General People's Committee, also voted in from among the 1,000-member GPC, who controlled the GPC. The Basic People's Congress (BPC), which was the largest congress of Libyans, was a grassroots-based parliament of the people. In total, there were 84 Basic People's Congresses in Gaddafi-led Libya. Below the Basic People's Congress was the Municipal People's Congress (MPC), which, like the BPC, was grassroots based and spread across Libya. In total, there were 47 such congresses. The responsibility of the Municipal People's Congress included the control and administration of the different municipalities and districts. At the head of affairs in government institutions, agencies, and parastatals was the People's Committee, a body of people's representatives whose charge included the control and administration of these institutions, agencies, and parastatals.

As noted in Gaddafi's *Green Book*, the aim behind the establishment of these committees and congresses was to restore state power and control of government and administration to the people. In principle, the divisions of Libyan society into units, municipals, and districts allowed ordinary, everyday people to have a say in government; however, a theme that features prominently in the literature on Libya was that it was extremely difficult to rally the people around these different committees and congresses. The difficulties associated with rallying nationalist fervor around these committees and congresses cannot be dissociated from the very nature of Italian colonization. Not only were Libyans excluded from government and administration, they were also prohibited from seeking education beyond the elementary school stage. There were also the outlawing of political parties, even during King Idris's time, and the long distances between city centers and the hinterland. It was therefore the combination of these factors that ensured that many Libyans were apathetic to politics and unenthusiastic about Gaddafi's numerous committees and congresses.

In spite of the RCC and Gaddafi's best efforts to bring Libyans into the political arena and to kick-start a true people's revolution, the new government was not ready to open some key areas to the people. Petroleum, armed forces, national security, and foreign policy were treated differently from other areas. Unlike petroleum, security, in principle, involved the people, as a number of committees and congresses were established that incorporated the people. For instance, the highest-security committee was the Jamahiriya Security Organization (JSO). There were also the Intelligence Bureau of the Leaders and the Brigade of the Armed People. At the grassroots level, there was also the Security Battalion, a band of well trained and well equipped security personnel and spies who existed at different levels of society. In general, these organizations, composed of mainly military men and a handful of government sympathizers, formed the cornerstone of Libya's Armed People. Rather than the People's Committees, the control and administration of these organizations revolved around either members of the RCC or Gaddafi's henchmen. For example, the 32nd Brigade of the Armed People was led by Gaddafi's son, Kamis Gaddafi; hence, the brigade was known locally as Kamis's Brigade.

In spite of Gaddafi's best efforts, Libyans did not manifest the revolutionary zeal he enunciated in his *Green Book*. ASU, the main vanguard organization established to achieve this, failed to facilitate political participation and galvanize Libyans along revolutionary lines. Like the Popular Congresses, ASU aimed at ensuring that Libya was not turned into a state where ethnically based political parties would subvert the nation, as was the case during the Italian occupation and agitation for independence. ASU might not have achieved its main goal; it, however, succeeded in recruiting many middle-class and politically neutral citizens into positions of power.

Owing to ASU's failure, the government established the Executive Revolutionary Committees (ERCs), whose duties included the mobilization of the people and safeguarding of the people's rule as exercised via the People's Congresses and People's Committees. Divided into eight different commands, each of the ERCs reported directly to Gaddafi. The ERCs' boundless powers also allowed Gaddafi unlimited powers that enabled him to control state affairs in Libya for so many years.

THE THIRD UNIVERSAL THEORY

In *Libya: The History of Gaddafi's Pariah State*, John Oakes noted that Gaddafi's childhood as a Bedouin animal herder tremendously influenced his adult life, especially his choices and worldview after assuming the highest political office in Libya.[15] Dirk Vandewalle, Ronald Bruce St. John, and John Wright expressed similar views about Gaddafi's outlook on politics, social life, and family relations.[16] As these and many other authors argued, the influence of Gaddafi's early childhood on his politics, whether within the Libyan state or globally, was predicated on his harsh upbringing in the Libyan desert. While not discounting the influence of early socialization in attitudinal change, especially in adulthood, these writers and others who believed that Gaddafi's choices, as head of the Libyan state, were predicated on the harsh reality of his upbringing, especially in his first six years of life, neglected the important roles of education and learning, as well as experiences and reflections on life choices, in their estimations and conclusions.

Undoubtedly, Gaddafi was a product of his environment. As a young man, he experienced Italian colonization and the monarchy, with its markedly important and sometimes overbearing influences of Europeans in Libya's emergence as an independent nation. While his early education in his local village in Sirte was important, it could not have explained his understanding of politics and the world around him. His activities as a student in Misurata and later as an undergraduate were enough pointers to the fact that his life choices as an adult and politics were shaped by what was happening around him, his education, and global politics.

In his *Green Book*, Gaddafi left no one in doubt as to his understanding of politics, political representations, and the dividends of democratic governance. All of these could not have been shaped by his experiences in his first six years of life. A six-year-old, contrary to the claims in the literature, is too young to understand the ways of his people. Consequently, it is wrong to suggest that his writing on politics, political representation, and the Third Universal Theory were products of his experiences in the Libyan desert community of Sirte. The Third Universal Theory, also known as Third International Theory, is a style of government proposed by Gaddafi in the early 1970s based on the principles of direct democracy.

Gaddafi, in his *Green Book*, insisted that democratic politics and representative democracy are, in practice, undemocratic, as elected representatives are usually isolated from voters after elections. He also condemned voting as an undemocratic procedure that could not give birth to a truly democratic government. His critiques of representative democracy and voting cannot be divorced from his experiences under King Idris. It was the dangerous influences of party politics and political maneuvering that compelled King Idris to ban party politics. In addition to the above is also his desert experience. Rather than a

Muammar al-Gaddafi delivers a speech to a large crowd of Libyan demonstrators in 1973. Those who gathered were hoping to show support for al-Gaddafi's return in response to his resignation as leader of the Revolutionary Command Council. The council refused to accept his resignation, and he eventually returned to the RCC. (Genevieve Chauvel/Sygma/Sygma via Getty Images)

blanket ban on politics, Gaddafi introduced a multitiered, indirect legislative system.

As practiced after the publication of *The Green Book* and the promulgation of the Third Universal Theory, the lowest level of representation was the Basic People's Congress. The BPCs were divided by region, and every Libyan had to be a member of a Congress in his or her region. Each of the three Congresses in the three regions had a People's Committee whose members were chosen by the Congresses. These were the men and women who were tasked with the responsibility of administering basic services. Professional Committees also existed within each of the Congresses. These bodies of professionals and technocrats protected the interests and rights of their specific professions. In a national conference, the two committees—People's Committees and Professional Committees—met to form the General People's Congress, the main legislative body in Libya.

Leaders of the Arab Socialist Union chose members of the General Congress. These people's representatives were, in themselves, chosen indirectly from the local Congresses and among government officials.

It was at this level that all decisions relating to the declaration of wars, ratification of treaties, and consideration of general government policy were taken. The chair of the General Congress, selected by members at their first meeting, had the power to either accept or reject the credentials of foreign ambassadors.

Further reviews of governmental processes were done in 1979. The two most fundamental changes were the replacement of Revolutionary Command Council with the General Secretariat of the General People's Congress, as the highest executive authority and the replacement of the Council of Ministers with the General People's Committee. Although the General Secretariat, composed essentially of members of the former Revolutionary Command Council, and the functions of the Council remained to oversee the functioning of government and execute state policies, the General People's Congress now had the power to appoint members to this body in case any member died or resigned. As of old, Gaddafi, now serving as the Secretary General, was the head of the General Secretariat. Gaddafi later resigned his position as the Secretary General and titular Head of State to concentrate on foreign policy.

In addition, the Council of Ministers was changed to the General People's Committee. The General People's Committee, like the defunct Council of Ministers, also provided support services to the General Secretariat.

In general, the Third International Theory was inspired by the combination of Islamic socialism, Arab nationalism, and African nationalism and partly by the principles of direct democracy—a common system of government in traditional African society. It was similar to the system of Yugoslav municipal self-management between 1960 and 1980 under Edvard Kardelj. Gaddafi proposed the Third International Theory as an alternative to capitalism and communism, both of which he considered as failed options.

At the heart of the Third International Theory was the Higher Council for National Guidance, a body that was charged with the task of disseminating and implementing the theory. In addition to restoring powers to the people, the theory also believed that political power belongs to the people. Hence, it sought to create a special hierarchical structure of people's congresses and committees that would foster socioeconomic and political management through the people themselves.

Despite the fact that Gaddafi was a devout Muslim and, as shall be shown in subsequent chapters, a great advocate of Islam, he opposed the position of Imams and Islamic clerics in government and religious activities in Libya.

THE JAMAHIRIYA: A GOVERNMENT OF THE MASSES

When in March 1977, Gaddafi proclaimed Libya as a Jamahiriya—a "government of the popular masses by themselves and for themselves"[17]— it was in conformity with his espoused criticism of representative democracy. As conceived, the Jamahiriya was a higher form of direct democracy whereby the people themselves were the president. Under this system, Libya was divided into series of "mini autonomous states" that controlled their districts and made decisions on day-to-day administration and economy, including the allocation of oil revenue and budgets.

There were three main bodies within these mini autonomous states: local committees, People's Congresses, and Executive Revolutionary Councils. In total, there were 800 local committees in the country. Representatives from these committees met many times yearly at People's Congresses, where they passed laws based on the people's expressed views in their various local meetings. The People's Congresses possessed legislative power, and the various laws made at these congresses remained binding, even on Gaddafi. Although Gaddafi was presented in the literature as a dictator, in actual fact, there is evidence to show that the People's Congresses had enormous powers over Gaddafi. In 2009, for example, Gaddafi proposed the abolition of the central government. Also, in the same year, he proposed a direct payment of oil proceeds into Libyans' bank accounts. In these two cases, the People's Congresses overruled Gaddafi. Gaddafi also proposed the abolition of capital punishment, a proposal that was rejected at the People's Congresses. Similarly, when he proposed home schooling as opposed to the traditional school system, the People's Congresses pitched their tents in support of the traditional school system.

These various committees and congresses replaced precolonial traditional institutions of government, and, through them, power was restored directly to the people. Jamahiriya was therefore intended to involve all Libyans in decision making, as opposed to representative democracy. Thousands of Libyans, male and female, took part in deliberations in local committees and congresses. Through these committees and congresses, a broad-based national consensus was built.

Although members of the People's Congresses elected members of the Executive Revolutionary Councils, the councils were accountable to ordinary citizens who had the power to change, recall, or dismiss them at any time. The Executive Revolutionary Councils were responsible for the implementation of national policies, as formulated by the people. From this arrangement, it can be argued that in the Jamahiriya, the actions of the Executive Revolutionary Councils were, indeed, the will of the masses, not of a political party or an ethnic or religious group.

The Jamahiriya political structure functioned as a direct democracy that afforded all Libyans the opportunity to participate directly in decision making and therefore in administration. In this way, Libyans contributed to governance directly and not through elected representatives in a parliament filled with elite politicians but through hundreds of committees and congresses.

Like any human institution, the Jamahiriya had its drawbacks. As already noted, committees and congresses were poorly attended, and not many Libyans had the initiative or the resources to travel long distances to city centers in order to participate in deliberations. There was also insufficient supervision. Perhaps the most significant drawback of the Jamahiriya was that Gaddafi appointed a sizable number of his cronies as members of these committees and congresses. This subversion of the system lends credence to the popular conclusion that the Gaddafi-led government was a dictatorship. Notwithstanding these drawbacks, it must be noted that under the Jamahiriya, all exploitative private ownership, except private family businesses in the service sector, were abolished. The Jamahiriya blended Arab nationalism and African socialism with Islamic religion. As a consequence, it was far more representative than any other form of democracy.

Another important thing to note about the Jamahiriya was that Islam was the official state religion. Although Islam was adopted as the state's religion, the influence of the *imams*—Muslim clergy—was limited. While the Quran provided the basis for justice, the legal system was not wholesale Islamic. For example, there were four distinct courts of justice where judicial proceedings were held in secular forms. These were the Magistrates' Courts, which was the lowest court, the Courts of the First Stage, the Appellate Courts, and the Supreme Court.

ECONOMIC AND SOCIAL CHANGE IN POST-1969 LIBYA

The discovery of crude oil in commercial quantity in Libya turned a country whose initial main sources of economic existence revolved around foreign aid from the United Nations and donor nations into an oil giant. In the real sense of the word, crude oil exploration changed Libya from a beggar nation to one of the richest nations on earth. Under

King Idris, crude oil exploration and marketing were seen as a means of financing Libya's socioeconomic development; under Gaddafi, Libya's oil became a weapon of politics and war, especially in the Arab–Israeli relations. Although Libya's oil reserves were small compared to those of other major Arab crude oil-producing nations, the Gaddafi-led government deployed it not only locally in its relations with foreign oil companies in Libya but also internationally in its relations with the wider world, most especially the nations of the West.

A number of factors made the deployment of oil as a weapon of politics and war possible under Gaddafi. For instance, Libya's nearness to Europe and the quality of its oil attracted many European and American oil companies. Another and perhaps most important factor was the 1973 global oil crisis.

At inception, the Gaddafi-led government was cautious with the economy, concentrating its efforts on consolidating the revolution instead. Although a great majority of Libyans were employed in the non–oil sector, oil export constituted 99 percent of Libya's total revenue in 1970. However, the sector employed just 1 percent of the total population. Given the government's methodic approach to the sector, it could be argued that the new government realized the precarious nature of the economy and was willing to correct it. For example, by 1970, Libya had one of the most sophisticated oil industries in the world. It, however, lacked the requisite manpower to man the sector. Since oil was discovered in commercial quantity, the workforce in the sector was composed almost entirely of European and American technocrats. So, rather than nationalizing the Libyan oil industry, the government allowed these expatriates to continue running the sector. By the end of 1970, the government's intervention in the sector was limited to oil pricing.

Under King Idris, oil prospecting permits and exploration licenses were issued to many independent producers and a handful of major producers. Advisers to King Idris were familiar with the activities of the Seven Sisters—an oligopoly of major oil producers that dominated global oil trade between 1940 and 1970—and therefore prevented them from gaining a foothold in Libya's oil economy. The Seven Sisters were Anglo-Iranian Oil Company, Gulf Oil, Royal Dutch Shell, Standard Oil Company of California, Standard Oil Company of New Jersey, Standard Oil Company of New York, and Texaco.

Prior to the 1973 global oil crisis, the Seven Sisters controlled over 85 percent of the world's petroleum reserves. By setting up a single consortium, Aramco, the Seven Sisters were able to monopolize Iran and Saudi Arabia oil concessions in ways that, if they wished, they could "shut the country down." Given this, Gaddafi appointed Abdullah

Tariki as his adviser on petroleum matters. Tariki had served as an oil minister in Saudi Arabia. He was sacked from his position after opposing the nefarious activities of the Seven Sisters. He was therefore familiar with their activities. Owing to this, Libya remained the only nation in the Middle East where the Seven Sisters had no presence. The two big oil-producing companies in Libya were Bunker Hunt and Occidental, with the latter having the largest and richest oil fields.

By granting permits and licenses to a large number of small-scale companies, Libya successfully prevented the rise of an oligopoly like those of the Seven Sisters. In order to encourage these small-scale companies, the Petroleum Amendments of 1961 gave them lower taxes and levies per barrel, while major producers paid more taxes and levies. This system proved very useful under the Gaddafi-led government.

When in 1970, Gaddafi revoked the oil concession of Chappaqua, a part of Occidental, on the ground that the concession was obtained fraudulently, it dawned on other companies that the new government would stop at nothing in its effort to gain control of Libya's oil trade. No sooner did the government revoke Chappaqua's oil concession than it opened up an investigation into the processes that led to successful procurement of Occidental concessions. A number of people, including Omar al-Shelhi, were indicted and, as in the case of Omar, charged in absentia. George Williamson, head of Occidental in Libya, claimed that by June 1970, the government had subpoenaed all documents related to the company's concessions. When the government announced that Occidental's concessions had been cut by 40 percent, Armand Hammer, the president of Occidental, flew to Libya, seeking to avoid a complete shutdown of the company. Hammer, on September 1, 1970, after meeting with Major Jalloud, Gaddafi's second-in-command, ceded 55 percent of Occidental's oil export to the Libyan government as a way to prevent a total shutdown.

These events had implications on two main fronts. On the one hand, the Gaddafi-led government, having demonstrated that it could revoke concessions, successfully impressed on small-scale independent producers that they either played by the new government's rules or shut down. So, when the government suddenly increased the price per barrel and imposed other taxes on small-scale independent producers, rather than losing their licenses and trading opportunities, the producers simply acquiesced.

Given that this category of producers had always enjoyed lesser taxes and levies, major producers saw nothing wrong in the new tax regime and saw no reason to ally with the small-scale independent producers against the new prices and taxes. For the next five years, the government continued to take advantage of the weak bargaining position of small-scale operators to introduce cutbacks in production, expropriation, and so on. Because these small-scale independent producers depended on Libyan oil for a substantial portion of their revenue, they were in no position to argue with the government. With small-scale independent producers paying new taxes and agreeing to new quotas, the government turned its attention to the major producers.

Having achieved this with small-scale independent producers, the government turned its attention to major producers. Acute oil shortages in Europe at the time and Gaddafi's drastic cutback of production quotas meant that not only the small-scale independent producers were affected by the new government's oil politics but also major producers who were also forced to acquiesce. By playing small-scale independent producers against major producers, the government got all foreign petroleum companies to agree to a price hike from US$0.90 to US$3.45 per barrel in 1971. This was a significant increase, as it was more than three times the going rate.

As if this were not enough, by the middle of 1971, individual company's production quotas were reduced, as Libya cooperated with Algeria. Toward the end of the year, all producers in Libya met with the government, hoping to secure a better bargaining position in what was to be known as the Libyan Producers' Agreements of 1971. The Gaddafi-led government, using its divide-and-rule tactics, successfully frustrated this Agreement. Prior to the 1971 Agreement, efforts by producers to force Libya to implement the Organization of Petroleum Exporting Countries' (OPEC) Tehran Agreement of 1970 met with stiff opposition, as the government argued that OPEC's prices and premiums were inadequate.

In the Tripoli Agreement of 1971 that followed, Libya once again raised the posted price to $3.32 per barrel, a figure that incorporated a Suez Canal Allowance, freight, and low sulfur premium. The agreement also allowed for an annual price increase. By 1974, Libyan oil, compared to its counterparts from the Middle East, had a price deferential of $4.12. Using price increases, higher income tax rates, elimination of marketing allowances, and adoption of a new system that forced the oil companies to agree to a retroactive and supplemental payment on every barrel of oil exported for the duration of their concession during the monarchy, Libya realized an estimated $1 billion in additional revenues in 1971.

Libya, under Gaddafi, therefore began a nationalization process that was aimed primarily at restoring full control of the oil sector to the Libyans. By December 1971, Libya nationalized British Petroleum (BP) and the Sarir field, which belonged to Bunker Hunt. In addition, Libya also withdrew its sterling balances, amounting to approximately US$550 million invested in various British banks. BP rejected Libya's offer of compensation for nationalizing BP's export concession, arguing that the compensation was inadequate. Coming to the aid of BP, the British government announced that it had banned Libya from participation in the sterling area.

By 1973, Libya's efforts at ensuring a complete control of its oil trade reached a new height when it announced a takeover of controlling interests in all petroleum companies operating in Libya. With this step, Libya gained about 60 percent of its domestic oil production. Further nationalization in 1974 gave Libya control of about 70 percent of its oil wealth. Libya's inability to produce a workforce that could effectively man its oil industries ensured that the country could not achieve total control of its oil wealth. In other words, 30 percent of Libya's oil wealth was under the control of expatriate workers who were providing technical services in the sector.

At the outset of the 1973 global oil crisis, Libya had emerged as a major oil power whose policy decisions helped in shaping global trade and its associated politics. The way and manner in which the Gaddafi-led government went about the politics of oil during the period belied the general conclusion in the literature that the new government was filled with inexperienced and unprofessional men and women. In fact, the politics of oil played by Libya from 1969 till the end of 1973 contributed immensely to Libyans' acceptance of Gaddafi's government. Not only did the government embark upon large-scale infrastructural and economic development programs, it also raised Libyans' standard of living.

ECONOMIC DEVELOPMENT IN THE NON–OIL SECTOR

Libya was not new to a multiyear socioeconomic and political development plan. Under the monarchy and following the discovery of oil, King Idris embarked on a three-year socioeconomic development plan. Under Gaddafi, Libya witnessed a number of multiyear development plans, which gave expressions to Gaddafi's social and economic aspirations and dreams for Libya.

In April 1973, the Gaddafi-led government launched its *Three Year Economic and Social Development Plan, 1973–1975*. It was an ambitious socioeconomic plan that projected an 11 percent economic growth, despite the crushing effect of the global oil crisis. The plan focused primarily on adjusting the structure of the economy. Rather than depending solely on crude oil for national revenue, the plan focused on developing Libya's non–oil sector and expected a 6.5 percent annual growth in that sector.

As planned, by 1975, Libya's non–oil sector, most especially agriculture and industrialization, was expected to contribute about 50 percent of the national revenue. To realize these goals, the government pumped considerable amount of its oil gains into the non–oil sector. Gaddafi also made it clear that his government would adopt a state-led economic system, as the government had no trust in private sector's capacity to drive a national economic development that would benefit the generality of Libyans. Serving as impetus for this was the endemic nature of graft and corruption that bedeviled King Idris's government. The government also noted that a private sector–led economy, with its obtuse fascination with private gains, would not help Libya in the development of its non–oil sector. So, while the government retained private sector operators in the service industry, all other sectors of the economy came under direct government control.

Although the oil sector remained the most fundamental revenue earner, Libya witnessed significant economic development in its non–oil sector under Gaddafi. While the oil sector grew exponentially, economic realities in the non–oil sector were quite different. During the last decade of King Idris's rule, the oil sector's contribution to the economy grew from 7.8 percent to 76.5 percent. Between 1969 and 1973, crude oil's contribution to the Libyan economy rose from 77.4 percent to 85.3 percent. Table 6.1 presents 10-year data on oil production and its contribution to total national revenue and shows that oil sector contributions to the economy began to nosedive by 1973. The reduction in the contributions of the oil sector to Libyan economy was on account of contributions from other sectors of the economy.

At the inception of Gaddafi's military dictatorship, agriculture contributed just 2.4 percent to the nation's gross domestic product while manufacturing contributed just 2.0 percent. Gaddafi was concerned about the lopsided nature of the economy and sought an immediate solution to the problem. Table 6.2 presents the total state expenditure in the non–oil sector between 1973 and 1974.

Just as in the case of the 1973–1975 development plan, the *Five Year Plan 1976–1980* also gave considerable attention to housing, agriculture, electricity and water, transport and communications, and industry. This showed how important it was for the government to develop the non-oil sectors, especially these five key areas.

As stated in Gaddafi's *Green Book*, "The house is a basic need of both the individual and the family, therefore it should not be owned by others."[18] To the Gaddafi-led government therefore, provision of

Table 6.1 Oil Production and the Contribution of Oil Revenues to
Total Revenues

Year	Oil Production (in millions of metric tons)	Total Revenues (in millions of Libyan dinar*)	Oil Revenues (millions of Libyan dinar)	Oil Revenues (percentage of total revenue)
1962	8.7	25,803	2,000	07.8
1963	21.8	36,027	7,200	20.0
1964	40.7	63,369	23,800	37.6
1965	57.5	86,020	54,500	63.6
1966	71.9	126,000	83,416	66.6
1967	82.1	321,700	268,298	83.4
1968	122.8	249,500	191,014	76.5
1969	146.3	358,900	277,789	77.4
1970	156.2	444,000	363,484	82.0
1971	136.8	551,541	468,741	84.9
1972	109.2	738,118	652,318	88.4
1973	107.9	732,075	624,575	85.3

Source: For Production: (1) Libyan Oil, Ministry of Petroleum, Tripoli, Libya, 1972,
p. 22. (2)
International Petroleum Encyclopedia, New York, 1974, p. 306.
For Revenues: (1) Fourteenth Annual Report: Bank of Libya, Tripoli, Libya, 1970,
p. 116. (2)
Seventeenth Annual Report: Bank of Libya, Tripoli, Libya, 1973, p. 110.
*One Libyan dinar (LD) equals US$3.38 (IMF. Statistics, April 1975).

housing for all Libyans was considered a fundamental human right. In
order to attain this, the government directed funds not only toward
the provision of education and health care but also toward housing.

In the development plans, the revolutionary government hoped to
provide adequate housing for all Libyans by the 1980s. It must be noted
that King Idris's government undertook a similar project, building
100,000 housing units, in order to meet the need for housing. King Idris's
housing project ended badly, as the government lacked the much
needed labor and financial power. The project was eventually abandoned in early 1969.

When Gaddafi came to power, housing shortages were acute, with
about 180,000 families lacking decent homes. In response to this problem, Gaddafi earmarked 361.3 million Libyan dinars for the provision
of housing in the 1973–1974 fiscal year. Also, in the 1975–1980 development plan, the sum of 794.236 million Libyan dinars was earmarked

Table 6.2 Allocations among Sectors in the 1973–1974 Plan

Sector	Allocation (in million Libyan dinar)	Percentage of Total
Housing	361.3	18.4
Agriculture	327.8	16.6
Electricity and water	257.4	13.1
Transport and communications	253.8	12.9
Industry	231.6	11.8
Education	192.1	9.8
Public services	186.7	9.5
Health	71.0	3.6
Petroleum	48.9	2.5
Construction	6.2	0.3
Other minerals	2.9	0.2
Banking and insurance	0.4	N/A
Reserves	23.9	1.2
Total	**1,965.0**	**100.0**

Source: The Three Years Plan (1972–1975), Ministry of Planning, Libya, p. 90.

for housing. In order to attain its goal, Resolution 4 of the General Secretariat of the General People's Congress of 1978 established a number of resolutions aimed at combating the housing problem. First, the resolution called for housing appropriation and compensations to individuals whose houses were taken away by the government. Second, the resolution established guidelines for the redistribution of homes among Libyans. For instance, the resolution established that no Libyan, except widows with a son who is over 18 years and whose source of income depended on rents, can own two houses.

In order to implement the housing policy, Gaddafi, in spite of his abhorrence for the role of private sector operators and capitalism in ensuring general welfare, used private investment, and many private contractors constructed the new property. In addition to enlisting the resources and services of private sector operators, Gaddafi also enlisted the services of foreign firms, most especially from France, the Federal Republic of Germany (West Germany), Spain, Italy, Turkey, the Republic of Korea (South Korea), and Cuba.

Moreover, committees were set up in every province to implement the resolution. These committees were in charge of expropriating houses and apartments and redistributing them to Libyans. Between 1970 and 1986, the government experienced a declining budgetary allocation, which shrank its housing budgetary allocation. Notwithstanding, the government constructed and distributed a total of 277,500 new housing units. This was in addition to private houses and apartments appropriated and redistributed by the government.

In addition, in 1978, new ownership laws, which limited each family to only one house, went into effect. Among others, the provision of houses to Libyans remained one of the most fundamental achievements of Gaddafi in Libya. As from 1971, shanty towns began to disappear in Libya, and, by the 1980s, modern apartment blocks with electricity and running water developed almost everywhere in Benghazi, Tripoli, and other urban areas.

There is no denying the fact that if not for the shortfall in housing allocation, which necessitated suspensions and cancellations of housing contracts with many foreign firms, the Gaddafi-led government would have achieved more in the housing sector. Even with the constraints, the provision of housing remained one of the landmark achievements of Libya under Gaddafi.

The confiscation of private homes and apartments was not without its criticisms. Many whose houses and apartments were taken away and distributed among less privileged Libyans found the policy obnoxious. Compensation for confiscating houses and apartment was another source of dissatisfaction. More often than not, the government undervalued houses and apartments and, to make matter worse, paid 40 percent of the houses and apartments' true value to their original owners. Unlike the original owners, beneficiaries found the policy popular, especially because the government not only subsidized mortgage payments on the homes but also gave the houses out at about 40 percent of their actual costs.

Two other most notable sectors that were the immediate foci of the government's economic policies in the 1970s were agriculture and industries, and it is to these two sectors that this discussion will now turn.

During the colonial period, Libyans were chased off their land, and the Italian colonial administrators gave the most arable land to the Italian settlers. While many Libyans were railroaded into internment camps, others were forced to flee into the deserts. Owing to this, the agricultural sector was effectively in the hands of the colonialist. Following independence, King Idris's government irrigated a total of 260,000 acres of land, of which over 220,000 acres were owned by the Sanussi family. As at the time of Gaddafi, most arable lands were under the control of either the Italian settlers or members of King Idris's ethnic group or his associates.

While the Italians developed a mechanized farming system, ordinary Libyans continued the practice of slash-and-burn, rain-fed agriculture. With many Italians departing following Libyan independence, most of their mechanized farms either laid in ruins or were taken over by powerful political office holders. The masses were left with the most unproductive dry land that was poorly suited for farming. Consequently, Libya was barely able to feed its population and had to depend on importation of food items. Unfortunately for the nation, only about 34 percent of its active citizens worked in the agricultural sector as of 1969.

This reality was not lost on the new government, and, within the first few months, the Gaddafi-led government embarked upon a land redistribution project that took away land from the Sanussi and Italians for redistribution to poor Libyans. Jefara Plain, among other places, witnessed substantial land confiscation and redistribution. Between 1969 and 1973, about 40 percent of arable land had been restored to ordinary Libyans, many of whom were unskilled in mechanized farming practices.

To facilitate rapid agricultural development, the government provided soft-term loans to Libyan farmers. The loans were intended not only to establish them on their lots but also to boost production, as farmers were expected to pay back about 40 percent of the loans. In addition, crops and equipment were also made available, while the government also established fertilizer companies whose products were sold to farmers at a highly subsidized rate.

In addition, the Gaddafi-led government invested heavily in irrigation, building one of the largest water pipelines in the world. Built as an aid to agriculture, the trans-Sahara water pipeline, which pumped water from the Nubian Sandstone Aquifer System to major cities such as Tripoli, Sirte, and Benghazi as well as providing water for irrigation projects around the country, is part of the Great Man-Made River project that commenced in 1984. This trans-Sahara water pipeline connected all major aquifers to a network of reservoirs that took water from one part of the country to others.

Although there was significant growth in agricultural production following the implementation of the land redistribution policy, it is disheartening to note that many Libyans preferred employment in the oil sector or in the government than in the agricultural sector. Farming, for the most part, was looked down upon, derided as beneath any reasonable

Libyan. This perception of farming or any backbreaking job, for that matter, was fueled by the easy money coming out of the oil sector. Libya's sudden and stupendous wealth impacted the citizens negatively in that it built a culture of unmerited wealth, an easy life, and the tendency to regard any task or job that does not bring instant riches, like the oil sector, as a bad job.

Because Libyans had no manpower and technical resources, skills, and knowledge to channel the nation's oil wealth into productive uses, it was difficult to put the increasing flow of petroleum dollars to a use capable of facilitating long-term sustainable benefits. Many of the youths migrated from the hinterland to the cities in search of jobs in the oil sector. National and personal incomes, which were usually products of economic growth in a well managed economy, witnessed substantial growth. Organizational and disruptive changes, the very engine of sustainable growth, were, however, lacking in Libya—fostering an attitude of "something for nothing" and a sense of easy superiority over the less fortunate.

One of the major outcomes of the land reform and redistribution policy was the exodus of the remaining Italian settlers and usurpers. This development, coupled with a dismally low level of available skill in Libya, had a serious impact on agricultural production. Hence, in spite of government efforts, Libya managed to produce only one-third of its annual food requirements. As it had always done since the monarchy, it continued to make up for the shortfall in its food requirements through importation.

Despite its tough position on the private sector, the government was, however, not oblivious to the role of private sector operators in economic development. A number of private sector operators cooperated with the government in the establishment of a number of industrial projects. Key among these industries were a petrochemical company in Marsa al-Buraya, two steel plants in Fezzan, three new refineries, a number of construction firms, and many other industries specializing in consumer goods.

By-products of these industrial complexes were not only job opportunities but also the extension of basic services into towns and cities where these industrial complexes were based. For example, water, electricity, and road construction followed all these industrial projects, and host communities, many of whom had been neglected during King Idris's regime, witnessed significant socioeconomic and infrastructural developments. It was during this time that electricity and power were extended to all Libya's coastal cities and towns. In addition, many of the existing roads were extended and new ones were built, connecting different economic centers. The harbors at Misurata and Tripoli were also extended.

As shown in Table 6.1, electricity and water, transport and communications, as well as public services, received considerable attention in the 1973/1974 development plan. In Table 6.3, it is clear that the Gaddafi-led government realized the importance of these sectors to rapid economic and social development. Hence, budgetary allocations for electricity and water resources jumped from 257.4 million Libyan dinars in the 1973/1974-year plan to 543.645 million Libyan dinars in the 1975/1980-year plan. The same huge jump could be seen in transportation, which jumped from 253.8 million Libyan dinars in the 1973/1974-year plan to 632.134 million Libyan dinars in the 1975/1980-year plan. It is significant to note that, compared to its predecessor, the 1975/1980-year plan was more nuanced, with, for example, a separation between sea transportation and other forms of transportation. Marine transportation was prioritized and allocated 373.500 million Libyan dinars.

Given this, it can be argued that Libya's economic and social development policies since the early seventies gave greater attention to the industrial sector and decreased dependency on the oil sector. The policies also decreased dependency on imports. In order to achieve these goals, the Gaddafi-led government increased expenditures on the industrial sector and established other enterprises allied to the industrial and agricultural sectors. The government's reasoning, as captured in Gaddafi's numerous speeches and policy papers, was to channel oil revenue into diversifying the nation's economy, creating new job opportunities, and the replacing imported goods with local manufacture.

To these ends, the Three-Year Economic and Social Development Plan (1973–1975) focused essentially on the food industries. The government deployed state resources into revamping the agricultural sector in order to boost production. In the subsequent Five-Year Economic and Social Development Plan (1975–1980), allocations to the industrial sector jumped significantly, a development that showed where the Gaddafi-led government's attention lay. Besides, considerable emphases were also placed on mineral and chemical industries, as well as the iron and steel industry. In the Five-Year Economic and Social Development Plan (1980–1985), attention was shifted to the export industries, and the government pumped huge amounts of money into a number of intermediary industries.

During these years, available organic and mineral materials in Libya were brought into the production sector, which made significant changes in the industrial production structure. In addition, the government successfully cultivated a new work culture based on what

Table 6.3   Five-Year Development Plan Allocations by Sector (in millions of Libyan dinars)

Development Sector	Total Expenditure (1976–1980)
Agriculture and agrarian reform	445.296
Integral agricultural development	781.300
Nutrition and marine wealth	41.351
Industry and mineral wealth	1,089.753
Oil and gas exploitation	648.196
Electricity	543.645
Education	470.430
Information and culture	91.340
Manpower	41.799
Public health	171.405
Social affairs and social security	43.157
Housing	794.236
Security services	35.000
Municipalities	552.650
Transport and communications	632.134
Marine transport	373.500
Planning and scientific research	56.745
Trade and marketing	32.730
Reserve	325.333
Total	**7,170.000**

Source: *Middle East Economic Digest*, January 30, 1976, 20 (5), 22.

Gaddafi called "partners not wage-workers," a work culture that aimed at increasing production, securing the continuity and stability of the workforce, and lessening work rotation by treating workers as partners and not wage-workers. In addition, industrial credits were introduced and broadened, leading many private sector operators into establishing cooperative societies, many of which invested huge resources in research and development. These cooperative societies formed industrial partnerships, many of which enjoyed series of material incentives, including customs duty waivers and tax exemptions.

The culmination of these economic and social development plans was the higher rates of growth in industrial and agricultural production. Despite achieving good results in the industrial and agricultural sectors, it must be noted that neither the industrial nor agricultural sector could supplant the oil industry as the mainstay of Libyan economy. It could be argued that the bane of these economic and social development plans was the focus on production for domestic consumption rather than on production for export. Inasmuch as Libya's industrial and agricultural production targeted the local economy, their capacities were, by default, limited, as they were not competitive.

The global oil crises between 1982 and 1986 led to a major shortfall in oil revenue, which, inadvertently affected the government's investment in other sectors. Consequently, Libya's economic and social development efforts were stymied. Between 1986 and 2000, the multiyear development plans were abandoned for annual budgets. This, coupled with the global politics associated with Libya's role in global terrorism, brought the economy to the brink of collapse.

Notwithstanding all of this, under Gaddafi, Libya had the highest GDP per capita and the highest life expectancy in Africa. Libyans enjoyed not only free health care and free education at all levels but also free electricity and interest-free loans. Although Gaddafi inherited one of the poorest nations in Africa, he built a state where legal protections existed for its citizens and where respect for human rights was a major priority of the government. The United Nations specifically scored Libya higher on improving women's rights, including granting equal educational opportunities to all sexes. As the United Nations Human Rights Council noted, Gaddafi successfully built a nation unlike others in the Muslim world in terms of women's rights. Libyan women had the right to education and to hold jobs and earn equal pay for equal qualifications, jobs, and experience as their male counterparts. Libyan women also had the rights to divorce and to own property.

Prior to Gaddafi's regime, only a few Libyan women had university education. Since 1970 when the Gaddafi-led government passed a decree on education, more and more Libyan girls enrolled and completed schools, including university education. More women were also absorbed into government services and businesses, including teaching in the universities. In addition, working mothers enjoyed cash bonuses for raising children and free day care services, and the retirement age for women was set at 55. For these reasons, the United Nations ranked Libya as the 53rd best country in human development.

On the continent of Africa, Libya became a force to be reckoned with. From North and West Africa to Central and East Africa as well as to Southern Africa, Libya provided financial and training assistance to all African countries struggling against European colonialism. While apartheid lasted, Gaddafi contributed huge sums of money to the

African National Congress (ANC) and other anti-apartheid movements in South Africa. In addition, Libya also set up the World Revolutionary Center (WRC), a military training center near Benghazi where ANC combatants and other freedom fighters were given military training. From 1969 when he assumed power to 1994 when apartheid ended in South Africa, Gaddafi was a staunch opponent of white minority rule, the color bar, and all forms of colonization on the African continent.

Writing in 2011, Stephen Ellis described the WRC as the "Harvard and Yale of a whole generation of African revolutionaries."[19] Besides training, Gaddafi hosted recruits from different countries in camps in the desert, sometimes for a few weeks or, at times, more than a year. During this time, recruits were given training in weapons, intelligence, and techniques. Many of these recruits later led independence agitations against colonialism and white minority rule or led rebel groups in their agitation for participation in the post-independence government. Notable African leaders that were trained at the WRC included Blaise Compaore, Idriss Déby, Charles Taylor, Foday Sankoh, among others.

Gaddafi supported President Idi Amin of Uganda and sent troops to Tanzania in support of Amin's war against Tanzania. Gaddafi also aided Jean-Bedel Bokassa and, later, Ange-Félix Patasse in the Central African Republic. Haile Mariam Mengistu, a Soviet protégé, got enormous support from Gaddafi. In these and other cases, Libya was either directly engaging in overt warfare with other countries or was fighting in support of its allies. The only exemption to these two broad patterns was Libya's war with Chad.

The events that led to the Chadian-Libyan conflict of 1978 to 1987 started long before Gaddafi's coup in 1969. In 1968, a rebellious Muslim group, the Muslim National Liberation Front of Chad (FROLINAT) was involved in guerrilla warfare against President François Tombalbaye, the Christian leader of Chad. King Idris supported FROLINAT because of an existing relationship between the group and the Sanussi Group. Given the aid and other support that King Idris and Libya were receiving from the United Nations and others in the West, the king could not openly support FROLINAT but provided training, financial support, and safe haven for its guerrilla fighters on Libyan territory.

Following the coup, Gaddafi, depending on an unratified treaty between Italy and France in 1935, claimed Aouzou Strip in northern Chad as a part of Libya. It must be noted that in 1954, King Idris also considered making efforts to bring Aouzou Strip under Libyan control. French Colonial Forces, however, repelled and prevented the king's forces from occupying the area.

While Gaddafi made it clear that he did not support the FROLINAT, he continued to provide training, weapons, and funding to the insurgents. The politics associated with this Libyan–Chad relationship cannot be dissociated from the larger US–USSR ideological standoff of the Cold War. By the 1970s, Gaddafi began to consider FROLINAT as a veritable tool in Libya–USSR relations, as it allowed Libya to show its Soviet backers that Libya was not an ally of the United States.

Things took a new turn when, after an unsuccessful coup to oust Chadian President Mr. François Tombalbaye, Chad, on August 27, 1971, accused Libya and Egypt of supporting and aiding the coup plotters in the two countries' efforts to Arabize Chad. Consequently, President Tombalbaye severed all diplomatic relations between Chad and Libya and Egypt. In retaliation for Libya's support for FROLINAT, the president invited all Libyan opposition groups to Chad. In addition to providing funding, training, and weapons to these groups, Chad also laid claims to Fezzan, citing "historical rights."

Gaddafi's response was swift. On September 17, he officially recognized FROLINAT as the legitimate government of Chad. Chad, in turn, took the matter to the United Nations, with its foreign minister, Baba Hassan, condemning Libya and informing the UN of Libya's "expansionist ideas" with regard to Chad.

Gaddafi's impact on Africa was not limited to providing money and training to revolutionaries alone; he also fought against some African nations. Notable examples include the Libyan-Egyptian War in July 1977 and the Uganda-Tanzania War of 1978, where Gaddafi deployed about 3,000 troops to aid Idi Amin's government. Libya was also involved in the Second Congo War of 1998 and 2003. In this war, Libya provided the government of the Democratic Republic of the Congo with planes and transported soldiers from Chad. Of all these wars and other involvements across the continent, the war with Egypt was the most shocking.

Gaddafi undoubtedly admired Gamal Nasser. In addition to deriving inspiration from Gamal's ideology and politics, he also modeled his government after Gamal's. Like Gamal, Gaddafi desired a unification of all Arab countries. It was therefore shocking that seven years after Gamal, Gaddafi deployed Libyan forces against Egypt. What could explain this sudden deterioration in the Libya–Egypt relationship?

When Gamal Abdel Nasser suffered and died of a heart attack shortly after the conclusion of the Arab League summit on September 28, 1970, Anwar Sadat, his close confidant and vice-president, took over. Gaddafi fell out with Sadat very early in Sadat's presidency. Underlying this problem was Sadat's peace policy with Israel. Almost immediately upon being sworn in as president, Sadat departed from many of Gamal's political and economic policies. Under Gamal, Israel humiliated Egypt and the Arab world during the First Arab-Israeli War—also known as the Suez War or the Six-Day War. Under Sadat, Egypt led the Arab world in the Yom Kippur War—also known as the Ramadan War or October War, a war to "recover all Arab territory occupied by Israel following the 1967 war and to achieve a just, peaceful solution to the Arab-Israeli conflict."[20] Although the war ended in a stalemate, Sadat, however, gained considerable popularity across the Arab world. The outcomes of the Yom Kippur War included Israel's recognition of the fact that it could not militarily dominate the Arab world and the subsequent setting up of the Camp David Accords of 1978, which returned the Sinai to Egypt and normalized diplomatic relations between Israel and the Arab world.

These strings of events culminated in Egypt's gradual withdrawal from the Soviet sphere of influence. Much to the consternation of other Arab countries, Sadat unilaterally negotiated peace with Israel, a development that gave rise to a general perception that Sadat had capitulated to the United States and its allies. This was a deviation from Gamal's nonalignment and pan-Arab stance. The perception of Sadat's capitulation was reinforced not only by the Egypt–Israel Peace Treaty but also by the conferment of the Nobel Peace Prize on Sadat and Menachem Begin, the prime minister of Israel.

Although the treaty resulted in the return of Sinai to Egypt, Sadat's policies angered most leaders of the Arab world. Yasser Arafat and the Palestine Liberation Organization (PLO) strongly denounced Sadat. Like others, Arafat argued that Sadat ought to have discussed the treaty with Israel and with other Arab leaders; after all, Egypt led these Arab countries in fighting the Yom Kippur War. Within Egypt, members of the Muslim Brotherhood, many in the military, and others also felt betrayed by Sadat. These and others across Africa believed that Sadat had abandoned efforts to ensure a Palestinian state. Consequently, the Arab League suspended Egypt from 1979 to 1989. On October 6, 1981, members of a militant group led by Khalid Islambouli assassinated Sadat at a parade in Cairo. The Cuban ambassador to Egypt was also killed, while Hosni Mubarak—Sadat's deputy and successor—sustained multiple injuries. Given this, it could be argued that, despite the fact that Sadat successfully restored the Sinai to Egypt, he betrayed the entire Arab world—not Gaddafi alone. His assassination was, for many, a just desert for his betrayal of Gamal and the Arab world.

There were early signs that the relationship between Libya and Egypt was deteriorating. By the end of Yom Kippur War in October 1973,

President Anwar Sadat discontinued any talk of unification with Libya due to the former's opposition to Egypt's peace policy with Israel.

President Sadat, in a discussion with Henry Kissinger—the United States' 56th secretary of state—on February 28, 1974, requested that the United States prevail upon Israel not to attack Egypt in the event of any war between Egypt and Libya. Evidence also abounds to support Gaddafi's claim that Sadat assisted Majors Abd al-Munim al-Huni and Omar Muhayshi—both former members of the RCC—in an unsuccessful coup to topple Gaddafi in 1975. Although Sadat denied this claim, he harbored the majors and refused to extradite them after their indictments in the coup plot. Sadat, in turn, accused Gaddafi of sponsoring a coup plot to remove him. As Sadat's deputy, Hosni Mubarak, told Mr. Hermann Eilts, the U.S. ambassador to Egypt, on January 26, 1976, the Egyptian government was exploiting internal crisis within Libya to topple Gaddafi. In response to a series of Egypt's subversive actions, on July 22, 1976, Gaddafi declared that Libya would break all diplomatic relations with Egypt and, subsequently, ordered the closure of the Egyptian Consulate in Benghazi.

When, on August 8, 1976, an explosion rocked a government office in Tahrir Square, Cairo, the Egyptian government and media blamed the attack on Gaddafi and his Libyan agents. A few days later, Egypt paraded two Egyptians who were allegedly trained by Libyan intelligence to carry out the attack on Tahrir Square and other incidences of sabotage in different parts of Egypt. On August 23, an Egyptian passenger plane was hijacked. The incident, which involved no casualties, was believed to have been carried out by persons commissioned by Libyan intelligence. Libya denied any knowledge or involvement in the incident.

The relationship between the two erstwhile allies therefore deteriorated. On July 21, 1977, armed forces of both countries exchanged fire. It took the timely intervention of both Houari Boumédiène, the president of Algeria, and Yasser Arafat, the leader of the Palestine Liberation Organization (PLO) to bring the gun battles—both on land and air strikes—to a halt on July 24, 1977.

Not only did Gaddafi's stupendous oil wealth and strong military support afford him allies within Libya, he was also involved in philanthropy and warfare in different parts of Africa. His domestic policies shall be discussed in the next section; however, it is important to state that the two most important events that showcased Gaddafi's clout in the continent remained his fraternity with traditional rulers and his clamor for a United States of Africa. With more than 200 African traditional rulers and kings in attendance in 2008, Gaddafi invested himself with the title "King of Kings of Africa" and had himself crowned.

At the 53rd African Union Summit in Addis Ababa, Ethiopia, on February 1, 2009, he was elected head of the African Union. In his address to the assembled African leaders, Gaddafi declared, "I shall continue to insist that our sovereign countries work to achieve the United States of Africa."[21] This is discussed fully in the next chapter.

IMPLEMENTATION IN LIBYA

How were Gaddafi's lofty ideals, as documented in his *Green Book*, implemented in Libya? As this section shows, Gaddafi found it difficult to fully implement his own theory. While different reasons could be advanced for this, the following two were the most fundamental.

On the one hand was political apathy on the part of Libyans themselves, while on the other hand was Gaddafi's overt ambition to perpetuate himself in power. Rather than governing a democratic state, Gaddafi established a military regime that blended the ideas of Arab nationalism and Islam with African socialism. Given this, the state was in constant flux, characterized by constantly changing laws.

In part one of his *Green Book*, Gaddafi faulted representative democracy and identified the problem of democracy as the issue of peoples' authority. To solve this problem, he advocated for a General People's Congress (GPC) and other institutions and committees to wield state authority. The GPC, Libya's highest decision-making body, was designed as a committee of people's representatives. In practice, while some members of the GPC were elected at local and regional levels, a large majority were appointed by Gaddafi himself. This practice was not limited to the GPC, Gaddafi also appointed a sizable number of his henchmen and women as members of other institutions and committees. In this way, the GPC and other institutions and committees became mere contradictions, as none of them represented the will of the people.

As noted in Chapter 4, while Italian colonization lasted, Libyans were prevented from any form of political participation. European colonial rulers dreaded an enlightened citizenry, as this would derail the economic goals of colonization itself. So keeping Libyans uneducated aligned with Italian colonial goals. Following independence, King Idris also banned party politics and political parties. King Idris's abhorrence of party politics cannot be dissociated from the fact that the earliest political parties in Libya operated along ethnic lines. Consequently, the king viewed party politics and political parties as antithetical to nation-building and discouraged it. It was the combination of these two developments that created a general lack of political education and interest in politics among Libyans.

From the Arab Socialist Union and General Peoples' Congress to Basic Peoples' Congress and Municipal Peoples' Congress, Gaddafi's primary desire in establishing these and other institutions was to foster popular participation in politics and administration. Political apathy and the special political landscape that the government found itself in meant that Gaddafi had to revisit and tweak his policies and programs to suit emerging developments almost on yearly basis. For example, it was as a result of the failure of the Arab Socialist Union to generate popular political participation that led to the establishment of the General People's Congress. In his effort to ensure popular control of government departments and agencies, Peoples' Committees were established in all government agencies and institutions.

There is no denying the fact that no political institution can survive in a situation of political apathy. Rather than embarking upon a mass political literacy program and building political participation from the ground up, the Gaddafi-led government simply filled positions with friends and loyalists. In this way, the government successfully maintained a semblance of a people-led governance, while in actual fact it was a one-party state under a military dictatorship.

Given the pernicious environment in which the Gaddafi-led government found itself, its options were limited. The ideological standoff between the United States and the Union of Soviet Socialist Republics created an environment whereby Libya found itself under the unholy influences of the two superpowers. The United States, basking in the dismemberment of its Wheelus Air Base and its eventual expulsion from Libya, saw nothing good in the Gaddafi-led government of Libya. As already noted, the United States also reneged on an agreement to supply Libya with cargo planes after payments had been made. As the evidence has shown, the United States' Central Intelligence Agency (CIA) and British intelligence toyed with the idea of removing Gaddafi militarily at different times. In addition, the United States and its Western allies overtly and covertly supported anti-Gaddafi elements within Libya. All this contributed to Libya's abandonment of its initial non-alignment stance in the Cold War ideological standoff and the eventual fraternization with the Soviets. In fact, it could be argued that the United States and its anti-Libyan policies played decisive roles in pushing Gaddafi and Libya unto the waiting arms of the Soviets.

NOTES

1. Dirk J. Vandewalle, *A History of Modern Libya* (Cambridge: Cambridge University Press, 2012), 79.

2. Ethan Chorin, *Exit the Colonel: The Hidden History of the Libyan Revolution* (New York: Public Affairs, 2012), 63.

3. Rebecca Adler-Nissen and Vincent Pouliot, "Power in Practice: Negotiating the International Intervention in Libya" in *European Journal of International Relations*, 20, no. 4 (2014), 889–911.

4. Adler-Nissen and Pouliot, "Power in Practice," 901.

5. Islamic Revival, "Was Britain behind Gaddafi's Coup in 1969?" in *Khilafah Magazine*, February 21, 2011. Accessed on September 14, 2018, at http://islamicsystem.blogspot.com/2011/02/was-britain-behind-gadaffis-coup-in.html

6. Vandewalle, *A History of Modern Libya*, 176.

7. "The Libyan Revolution in the Words of Its Leaders" in *Middle East Journal*, 24, no. 2 (1970), 203–219.

8. Ronald Bruce St. John, *Libya: From Colony to Revolution* (Oxford: Oneworld Publications, 2011), 185.

9. Ibid., 184.

10. Ibid., 200.

11. David J. Whittaker, *The Terrorism Reader* (New York: Routledge, 2012), 94.

12. Muammar Gaddafi, *The Green Book* (n.p., 1976), 13.

13. Ibid., 15.

14. Ibid., 15–32.

15. John Oakes, *Libya: The History of Gaddafi's Pariah State* (Gloucestershire, UK: History Press, 2011), 109.

16. St. John, *Libya*, 133–135; Vandewalle, *A History of Modern Libya*, 76–80; and John Wright, *A History of Libya* (New York: Columbia University Press, 2012), 199.

17. Gaddafi, *Green Book*, 58.

18. Ibid., 43.

19. Stephen Ellis, *The Mask of Anarchy: The Destruction of Liberia and the Religious Dimension of an African Civil War* (New York: New York University Press, 2001), 72.

20. Eugene Rogan, *The Arabs: A History* (New York: Basic Books, 2012), 35.

21. Linda Heywood, Allison Blakely, and Charles Stith (eds.), *African Americans in U.S. Foreign Policy: From the Era of Frederick Douglass to the Age of Obama* (Champaign: University of Illinois Press, 2015), 206.

7

Libya and the Wider World, 1969–Early 2000s

INTRODUCTION

As shown in Chapter 1, Libya had different kinds of relationships with different peoples and at different time in its history. Starting with Egypt and other African neighbors to the east, west, and south of the African continent, these relationships continued with Phoenician traders and the Vandals from Europe. Libya also cultivated trade and diplomatic relations with the Graeco-Roman empire builders and, later, the Ottoman Arab Muslims and Italian colonialists from outside of Africa. While some of these multiple relations lasted a few years, other existed for hundreds of years. Although some were tumultuous and fraught with violence, others were peaceful and friendly. Irrespective of time and circumstance or status, these relationships shaped not only Libyan trade and commerce but also its culture and politics.

Except in peacetime, the history of Libya revealed that, from the Vandals' invasion and the Graeco-Roman period to the Ottoman and Italian colonization, Libyans had little or no control over their external relations. During these times, decisions on foreign relations were, for the most part, taken by Libya's conquerors and colonizers. It was not until 1951, when Libya became an independent nation, that it effectively controlled its foreign relations. Notwithstanding whether the decision on foreign relation was imposed or willingly taken, it must be noted that Libya's relations with the outside world at these times actively and directly inserted Libya into the vortex of global trade and international politics.

As the lead-up events to Libya's independence have shown, Libya was inserted into the vortex of global trade and politics when it was less than likely to succeed. The United Nations not only took the decision on independence for Libya but also imposed a constitutional monarchy on Libya. Owing to the fact that the first king depended on the United Nations and the international community for the much needed aid to sustain Libya's poor economy, most decisions on international relations were in line with the dictates of the United Nations and the international community.

Things, however, took a new turn in 1969 when the Free Officers Movement sacked the monarchy and Gaddafi became the new head of state and government. The new government not only asserted itself as a sovereign entity but also charted a course that was completely different from the one the monarchy originally pursued. Much to the chagrin of the United States, Great Britain, and their allies who canvassed for Libya's independence, Libya opted for neutrality in the ideological struggles of the Cold War. Although professing nonalignment, Libya supported and funded the course of pan-Arabism, a position that rejected the establishment of the State of Israel on land that the Palestinians originally controlled. Not only that, Libya expelled the United States and Great Britain from Libya, disbanding their military bases and pressing Malta, a neighboring island country, to expel North Atlantic Treaty Organization (NATO) soldiers from it. NATO was an intergovernmental military alliance among 29 North American and European countries that aimed to prevent USSR's external attacks on member nations. Moreover, Libya, exasperated about the United States' refusal to sell cargo planes to it, purchased thousands of Soviet weapons and also engaged in multimillion-dollar businesses with the Russians.

As far as the government of Libya was concerned, colonization anywhere in Africa was colonization in Libya. Hence, Libya pursued anticolonial and anti-imperial policies both on the continent of Africa and globally. Libya supported anti-apartheid struggles in southern Africa— providing money and training to members of the African National Congress (ANC) and other anti-apartheid movements in South Africa.

Besides Libya's support for Uganda against Tanzania that was discussed in Chapter 6, Libya also provided financial assistance and training to the Eritrean Liberation Front and the African National Union in Rhodesia (now Zimbabwe). Just as Libya engaged Egypt and Chad, it also aided Guinea with arms and money in the Guineans' fight against its neighbors.

As was its wont, Libya supported the course of peoples and groups fighting European colonization and national liberation in Africa and globally. Its support for the Palestinian cause was unflinching. As a matter of fact, one of the main goals of Libya's foreign policy in the Arab world was to free Palestine from Israeli's occupation. In this regard, Libya provided both military and financial support to President Yasser Arafat and his Palestine Liberation Organization (PLO). In 1971, Libya deployed thousands of Libyan soldiers to support the government of the State of Palestine against Israeli incursion. Similarly, in 1978, Libyan forces, equipped with missiles, discouraged aerial Israeli raids in Lebanon.

Justifying Libya's support for the Irish Republican Army (IRA) in 1971, Gaddafi explained that sending a huge amount of armaments to the IRA should not be interpreted as an act against Great Britain but rather as support for the Irish people, like any other people who were fighting for their rights to self-determination.

LIBYA AND THE COURSE OF PAN-ARABISM

In general, using its huge oil wealth, Libya supported the course of national liberation, the abolition of color bar, and all kinds of movements fighting against one form of oppression or the other across the world. In the process, the country successfully built a vast network of contacts, both across Africa and globally. On account of its provision of logistic, military, and economic aid to liberation movements and groups, many, especially the United States and Britain, considered Libya to be a state sponsor of terrorism. The General People's Congress's declaration of May 28, 1981, which acknowledged that Libya would support all peoples that are struggling for self-determination in whatever way the people might see fit, mainly served to reinforce this view.

Not only did all of the preceding mark Libya's place in the wider world; Gaddafi's pan-Arab sentiment and the oil politics he embarked on since the 1970s ensured Libya's place in global politics. Libya's 1969 constitution proclaimed the country's affinity with all peoples and nations of the Arab world. As an ideology, this pan-Arab sentiment seeks to unite all countries from the Atlantic Ocean to the Arabian Sea, essentially uniting countries of North Africa with those of West Asia. The overarching idea behind this sentiment was that Arabs should constitute a single nation; hence advocates canvassed for sociocultural, economic, and political unification of all Arab-speaking countries. In addition, advocates canvassed for socialist principles, worked for the empowerment of all Arab states against outside forces through military and economic alliances, and were stoutly against any Western sociocultural and political involvement in the Arab world.

The clamor for pan-Arabism in Libya predated Gaddafi. Under King Idris, Libyan youths took to the streets when the king decided not to join other Arab-speaking states during the Six-Day War. The war, which ended with a decisive Israel victory on June 10, 1967, was led by a coalition of Egypt, Jordan, and Syria and formed the basis of later pan-Arab coalition of these countries. When Gaddafi came to power, he made no secret of his intention of join the coalition. Together with Egypt and Syria, Gaddafi created a United Arab state called the Federation of Arab Republics. Each of the member countries approved the merger by September 1, 1971, but their inability to agree on the terms of the merger led to the dissolution of the coalition five years later.

While the coalition lasted, it had its capitals in Tripoli (Libya), Cairo (Egypt), and Damascus (Syria) and was established as a republic. A Federal National Assembly that had equal representation of the member states was also established. The language of the coalition was Arabic. Irrespective of the fact that the coalition lasted only five years, it must be noted that the idea was widely supported by citizens of the member states. For example, in the September 1, 1971 referendum, 99.6 percent of Egyptians, 98.6 percent in Libya, and 96.4 percent in Syria supported the referendum.

Gaddafi was unrelenting in his efforts to unite North Africa with other Arab-speaking Islamic republics. Between 1969 and 1977, five other attempts were made at coalition. These included a federation among Libya, Egypt and Sudan between 1969 and 1971, a federation between Egypt, Libya, and Syria between 1971 and 1977, the union between Egypt and Libya between 1972 and 1974, a union between Egypt and Syria between 1976 and 1977, and a federation involving Egypt, Sudan, and Syria in 1977. Others included the Arab Islamic Republic, a proposed union between Libya and Tunisia in 1972.

These efforts at rallying Arab-speaking and Muslim nations of North Africa with fellow Muslim nations in the Middle East were not without its critics, especially in the Muslim world. The most significant opponent was Iraq who, in 1958, established the Arab Federation, a coalition with Jordan. Iraq's formation of the Union of Arab Republics presented the most formidable opposition to Libya. It began in March 1972 when the Ba'athist Iraq proposed that Egypt and Syria should reestablish the United Arab Republic. Differences arose when Iraq proposed the inclusion of the Palestine Liberation Organization in the union. Iraq also wanted Libya to be excluded in the United Arab Republic for Libya's alleged role in sponsoring the Syria–Iraq conflicts. Libya, in turn, condemned Iraq over its alliance with the Soviet Union.

The most enduring and long-lasting union of Muslim countries in the world remained the unity of seven Arab emirates that now form the United Arab Emirates. This and, of course, the unification of North Yemen and South Yemen stand today as rare examples of actual unification.

The loss of the Six-Day War in 1967 put a dent in pan-Arabism, as the coalitions of different governments across the Arab world failed to generate sufficient economic and military strength to sustain the idea of an Arab unity. By the 1970s, the idea had become less visible in the socioeconomic and political lives of the Arab states. As far as Gaddafi was concerned, the government of Sadat after the death of Gamal in Egypt played critical roles in the weakening of Arab unity.

REGIONAL INTEGRATION AND CONTINENTAL UNITY

Libya had always been an important participant in African affairs. In 1963 under King Idris, it joined 31 other African nations to establish the Organization of African Unity (OAU). At the maiden meeting of the flagship organization on May 1, 1963 at Addis Ababa, Ethiopia, Alieu Ebrima Cham Joof noted that the OAU's main aim was to bring all African nations together in order to "speed up the freedom and total independence" of African countries and the "eradication of imperialism . . . colonialism . . . and neo-colonialism" from the continent.[1]

Libya was at the vanguard of these objectives from the founding of the OAU. There is no gainsaying the fact that Libya, under Gaddafi, was passionately committed to these objectives of OAU. Gaddafi committed not only Libya's oil wealth to achieving independence and freedom of other African countries from the clutches of European imperialism and apartheid but also played a dramatic role in the economic development of many African nations. Gaddafi fully committed himself and his nation's resources to the resurrection of African dignity.

From Morocco and Algeria in North Africa to South Africa and Zimbabwe in Southern Africa, Libya committed its moral and financial resources to training nationalist movements across Africa. Even under the monarchy, Libya, in November 1964, joined Algeria, Tunisia, and

Morocco to form a regional body that was committed to mutual economic growth and regional cooperation among North African states. Gaddafi continued in this work of African unity when, in 1974, he joined Tunisia to form the Islamic Arab Republic. Although poor planning was the albatross of the merger, he restored relations with Algeria and Morocco, after the debacle with the former over an alleged effort at overthrowing King Hassan of Morocco between 1971 and 1972.

Soon after he came into power, Gaddafi concluded a tripartite agreement with Egypt and Sudan for the formation of the Arab Revolutionary Front in December 1969. Although the union was short-lived, as infighting between Libya and Sudan over policies ruined the idea, Libya left no one in doubt that it was for the integration and unification of the African states.

Libya and Algeria entered into a defense pact in 1975 under the terms of the Hassi Messaoud Treaty, which saw Algeria defending Libya in July 1977 when Egypt launched air and ground attacks against the Libyan border. Libya also supported Algeria over Western Sahara, supplying arms and ammunitions to the Frente Popular para la Liberación de Saguia el Hamra y Rio de Oro (Polisaro Front).

All through the 1970s, Libya's stake in African affairs was higher than most countries in Africa, if not in the world. Libya was most visible in Islamic countries in Africa, where Gaddafi not only spent millions of dollars in facilitating Islamic religion and education but also in facilitating the elimination of all vestiges of colonialism, neocolonialism, and Western influences. Gaddafi worked to ensure that no Islamic country in Africa played host to America, British, or any European military bases. He was on the front line in opposition to apartheid in South Africa and in support for African liberation.

At the forefront of Gaddafi's foreign policy in Africa was opposition to the establishment of the state of Israel. He ensured that most Islamic countries in Africa severed diplomatic relations with Israel, providing, in return, economic assistance. By 1973, more than 30 nations in Africa, including Burundi, Chad, Congo, Mali, Niger, Uganda, and Sudan, severed diplomatic relations with Israel. Encouraged by this, Gaddafi made the severance of diplomatic relations with Israel a major issue on the floor of the Organization of African Unity.

To aid African nations, most especially nations with huge numbers of Muslims, Libya established the Jihad Fund in 1970. The fund aimed at strengthening Arab nations and Islamic countries in Africa against Israel. At the Fourth Conference of Foreign Ministers of Islamic Countries, which Gaddafi hosted in Benghazi, he noted that the purpose of the Jihad Fund was to provide welfare to Islamic states.

In 1973, he also established the Islamic Call Society, an organization for the propagation of the Islamic faith. Between 1973 and 1974, more than 132 Islamic Call societies had been formed in Africa. As part of its efforts at propagating the religion, Gaddafi provided loans to member states for the promotion of Islam and the Arabic language and culture.

Things, however, took a new turn in the 1980s for Libya when alleged sponsorship of terrorism took the center stage, and Libya lost some of its friends in Africa. By the end of the 1980s, the Central African Republic, Tanzania, Gabon, Gambia, Ghana, Senegal, and more than 10 other African states had expelled Libya's ambassadors from their countries. Globally, while the concern over Libya was global terrorism, in most of these African states, the concern was the intricate nexus between Libya and the spread of Islam through politics and foreign aid. These African states resented Gaddafi's use of Islam as an instrument of foreign policy and warned of the divisive nature of such a policy, especially in nations with huge numbers of non-Muslims. In other Africa states, Chad for instance, the concern over Libya was not about Islam but about Gaddafi's efforts to create an Islamic Republic of the Sahel and the Islamic Legion, both of which have implications for the territorial integrity of Chad.

LIBYA AND INTERNATIONAL TERRORISM

From the early days of Gaddafi's rule, Libya was alleged to be a state sponsor of terrorism. On January 4, 1974, *The Times*, a newspaper in Brussels, published a report on Gaddafi's presumed terrorist activities.[2] In the newspaper, the Revolutionary Command Council was accused of establishing the Arab Nationalist Youth for the Liberation of Palestine, an organization whose members were said to have committed severe crimes, including the terror attack at the Athens' International Airport on August 5, 1973, where four people died and 55 were injured. The group was also accused of the December 17, 1973, terror attack at Fiumicino Airport in Rome, where 32 people lost their lives. As the newspaper argued, during a speech in 1973, Gaddafi demonstrated his support for these two attacks and also for a Japanese terrorist group that massacred 26 people at the Lod Airport (now Ben Gurion International Airport, Israel) on May 30, 1972. In the same speech, Gaddafi was alleged to have exhorted all Palestinian dissidents to come to Libya, where full support in term of training, financing, and logistics for their cause awaited them.[3]

In the CIA's 1981 annual report on international terrorism, the organization reported that 760 terrorist attacks occurred in 1980 alone. Because the figure for 1980 was higher than those of the previous years, the spike in terrorist activities was blamed on the role of the government of Libya, especially Libya's support for dissident groups and terrorist organizations in the Middle East. As the report claimed, Libya deployed assassins and secret agents against diplomats in the Middle East and political opponents of the Gaddafi-led government, many of whom had fled to Europe.[4]

In addition, on January 8, 1985, the U.S. Department of State noted in a White Paper that Gaddafi had cultivated the culture of using terrorism as a tool of foreign policy and that he supported groups and organizations using terror tactics across Europe and the Middle East. Furthermore, the report claimed that Libya set up training camps where dissident groups and terror organizations were trained in acts of terrorism, guerrilla warfare, and similar activities. The report also claimed that Libyan embassies across the world were using their diplomatic privileges to purchase weapons and explosives.[5]

As the paper noted, Gaddafi intended to kill all moderate leaders of the Arab states for their support of the establishment of the State of Israel. Specific mention was made of Gaddafi's attempt to eliminate Hosni Mubarak, the Egyptian president. The report also claimed that Gaddafi harbored Abu Nidal, Leila Khaled, and Illich Ramirez Sánchez (aka Carlos the Jackal), three of the world's notorious terrorists.[6]

While Gaddafi denied these allegations, two terror incidences in 1986 and 1988 thrust Libya unto the world stage. On April 5, 1986, terrorists bombed a West Berlin discotheque frequented by American military personnel. Two U.S. soldiers and one Turkish civilian were killed in the attack. On December 21, 1988, Pan Am Flight 103 exploded over Lockerbie, Scotland, killing all 259 people on board and 11 on the ground. The two incidences were believed to have been sponsored by the Libyan government. Given the importance of these events to any understanding of Libya's place in the wider world, it is necessary to examine them closely.

1986 West Berlin Discotheque Bombing

On April 5, 1986 at 0145 CET, a bomb exploded under a table near the disc jockey's booth at the La Belle discotheque in West Berlin. Both Nermin Hannay, a Turkish woman, and Kenneth T. Ford, a U.S. Army sergeant, died instantly. James E. Goins, a second U.S. Army sergeant, died two months later. A number of victims sustained varying degrees of injuries.

Although there was no evidence to reveal the perpetrators, U.S. President Ronald Reagan accused Gaddafi. Reagan was acting on the fact that just two weeks before the terror attack, Gaddafi had called on Arabs around the world to attack American interests worldwide. Gaddafi's call was in reaction to a loss of 35 Libyan seamen during the U.S.-Libyan naval clash in the western Gulf of Sidra.

Shortly after the attack on the West Berlin discotheque, foreign intelligence intercepted a number of telex messages from Tripoli congratulating the Libyan embassy in East Berlin on the success of the attack. Notwithstanding the telex messages, Libya continued to deny any involvement or knowledge of the discotheque attack. Consequently, the U.S. president ordered retaliatory strikes on Tripoli and Benghazi on April 15, 1986. The retaliatory strikes were widely regarded as an attempt to kill Gaddafi himself.

Besides the telex messages, no other proof was found to link the attack to Libya until the end of the Cold War and the 1990 reunification of East and West Germany. The reunification of Germany led to the opening up of the Stasi archives. In different files at the Stasi archives, Detlev Mehlis, the German prosecutor, found evidence that linked the attack to Musbah Abdulghasem Eter, a Libyan who worked at the Libyan embassy in East Berlin. In the files, Eter was listed as an agent. In 1996, Eter and two Palestinians, Yasser Mohammed Chreidi Ali Chanaa, and one other person were arrested in Lebanon, Italy, Greece, and Berlin. Chreidi, who worked for the Libyan Peoples' Bureau in East Berlin at the time of the attack, had connections with Abu Nidal, a Palestinian terrorist who lived in Tripoli and was financed by Libya in the 1980s.

In a trial that lasted from 1997 till 2001, it was revealed that the Libyan secret service planned the bombing at the Libyan Embassy. As the prosecutor noted, although the three men assembled the bomb in Chanaa's flat, Chanaa's wife, Verena, and her sister, Andrea Hausler, brought it to West Berlin in a Libyan diplomatic bag. The two women subsequently took the bomb to the discotheque in a travel bag, five minutes before it exploded.

In 2001, Eter and the two Palestinians were convicted and sentenced to between 12 and 14 years in prison. Chanaa's wife, Verena, was also convicted of murder, while her sister was acquitted for want of evidence to prove that she knew about the bomb.

The 1988 Lockerbie Bombing

On December 21, 1988, Pan Am Flight 103 departed Heathrow International Airport, heading for New York. The last words sent from the aircraft were "Clipper 103 requesting oceanic clearance" as copilot Raymond Wagner requested clearance to begin the scheduled Flight 103 over the Atlantic Ocean. A little while after Wagner was issued clearance, Alan Topp, the air traffic controller (ATC) who watched Flight PA103 as it crossed Scottish airspace, noticed that the aircraft's transponder stopped replying somewhere over Lockerbie, Scotland. The ATC tried again and again to communicate with Clipper 103 but got no reply. Little did the ATC know that Pan Am Flight 103, a Boeing 747 with 259 people and crew members on board, had crashed, killing all on board and 11 more on the ground.

A bomb had detonated on the left side of the aircraft, leaving a hole in the aircraft skin. In less than 3 seconds, the pressure wave and the resistance of the contents of the cargo-hold reverberated, widening the opened holes of the container and the skin of the aircraft. The aircraft skin opened up like a zipper, as the plane broke apart. The aircraft, along with its passengers and crew, fell to the ground.

Spreading from Lockerbie east toward the coast, the debris from the aircraft covered a total area of 845 square miles. As the Scottish government instructed sector commanders in charge of the investigation,

A glimpse of the destruction caused by Pan Am Flight 103 after it crashed into the town of Lockerbie, Scotland, on December 21, 1988. The Boeing 747 'Clipper Maid of the Seas' was destroyed en route from Heathrow to JFK Airport in New York, when a bomb was detonated in its forward cargo hold. All 259 people on board were killed, as well as 11 people in the town of Lockerbie. In November 1991, arrest warrants were issued for two Libyan nationals in relation to the bombing. (Bryn Colton/Getty Images)

the aircraft and 211 tons of passenger and crew remains, cargo, mail, and other contents that were "not growing in the ground" had to be recovered.[7] Some 18,209 individual items, including 90 percent of the destroyed aircraft, were recovered. Investigators found Semtex, a kind of explosive, in the recovered aircraft debris, and the investigation was escalated to that of a major murder investigation.

Prior to Pan Am 103's crash, members of a cell group of the Popular Front for the Liberation of Palestine—General Command (PFLP-GC) had been arrested in Germany after a police raid—Operation Autumn Leaves—in October 1988. During the raid, four Toshiba Radio Cassette Players (model no. R0453D), laden with Semtex, were recovered. Members of the PFLP-GC told German investigators that the fifth one had been taken to Malta and would soon be deployed. The group was notorious for hijacking and bombing planes. German investigators had alerted all major airports to be on the lookout for an improvised electrical device (IED) hidden in a Toshiba radio cassette player, which had a basic timing mechanism in it. With Semtex found in the debris of the ill-fated plane at Lockerbie, the PFLP-GC became the focus of the criminal investigation.

Later, forensic experts found a fragment of another printed circuit board on a shirt in one of the explosive-blasted luggage containers, and the investigation took on a new but greater turn. The Royal Armament Research and Development Establishment (RARDE) of the United Kingdom, through extensive investigations, established that the fragment of printed circuit board came from a Toshiba radio cassette player. A fragment of the cassette player's owner instruction manual was also recovered, which allowed forensic experts to identify the cassette player model number as RTSF16, a different model from those that were recovered from the PFLP-GC.

Forensic experts concluded that the radio cassette recorder fragments were in close proximity to the IED that brought down Pan Am 103. Another fragment of printed circuit board found on a tailor-made gray shirt led the investigators to the following conclusion: "This fragment represents the only recovered piece of modification in the Toshiba radio which would have been necessary to convert it into a delayed action bomb."[8] When compared with the IEDs recovered by the German police, investigators found no correspondence between the fragment of the circuit board recovered from Pan Am 103's debris.

Other important recoveries made were an antique copper 26-inch Samsonite Silhouette 4,000 hard-shell suitcase and a fragment from a pair of trousers with a tag that bore Yorkie, which referred to Yorkie Clothing Company in Malta, and the number 1705. The number was an order number that referenced a retail outlet, Mary's House in Sliema, Malta. The outlet placed the order for the making of the said trouser. Following these discoveries, the investigation shifted to Sliema, Malta.

When confronted by investigators, Anthony Gauci, the proprietor of Mary's House—a family-owned business—told officers that he sold the trousers, shirt, an umbrella, and other items of clothing to a Libyan on Wednesday, December 7, 1988. Although Gauci made statements to investigators in December 1988, it was not until September 1989 that he described the mystery shopper as a Libyan of about 50 years of age, over 6 feet tall, and dark-skinned. He also added that the shopper had a large head, with a 36-inch waist and 18-inch collar. The shopper was heavily built, he noted, and could not fit into a 42-inch jacket. Gauci was able to recall these graphic details of the man because he spent time helping him fit into the new shirt.

Gauci also provided specific details about the merchandise bought by the shopper, which corresponded with the details of the blast-damaged clothing recovered at Lockerbie. The type of umbrella Gauci claimed to have sold to the mystery shopper also matched one recovered at Lockerbie. Forensic experts who examined the debris claimed that all of the items Gauci claimed to have sold to the mystery shopper were in close proximity to the explosion. Gauci's evidence led investigators to link the downing of Pan Am 103 to a Libyan citizen or citizens.

A number of questions could be asked about this development. For instance, why did it take almost one year before Gauci described the mystery shopper? Is it possible for human memory, especially of a shopkeeper who is dealing with different customers every day, to recall such graphic details about the mystery shopper, as given by Gauci? Is it possible that Gauci deliberately tailored his description of the items purportedly bought by the mystery shopper to match the descriptions of the recovered items from the ill-fated plane, after all the details of what was recovered had already been published in different newspapers?[9] How did Gauci know the mystery shopper was a Libyan? Is there any particularly reliable way to differentiate between Libyans and other Arabic speakers? Although Gauci said relatively little about the man's face and how he knew he was a Libyan, he nevertheless helped investigators to produce a photofit of the mystery shopper. His description fit a big man, roughly around or over 50 years.

It was ten months after attending to the mystery shopper in his shop that Gauci created two images for the police. However, the two images looked different; Gauci did not recall the man's face as well as he had remembered his body shape and build.

Given Gauci's evidence, the mystery shopper was believed to be the bomber and, given that Pan Am 103 took off from Frankfurt with some connecting passengers from Malta, investigators believed that the bomb must also have originated from Malta. To this end, the German BKA obtained a computer printout from the baggage handling system at Frankfurt Airport in order to trace the bags loaded onto flight Pan Am 103A, the feeder flight for Pan Am 103, on December 21, 1988. Although Air Malta claimed that no passengers transferred to Pan Am 103A from Air Malta, investigators believed that unaccompanied luggage, which contained the bomb or was the bomb itself, was transferred from Air Malta to Pan Am 103A and was eventually hauled to London.

Despite the investigators' claim, however, there was no record of any unaccompanied luggage transferring to the feeder flight Pan Am 103A from Air Malta on December 12, 1988. However, the printout and record sheet confirmed the presence of an unaccompanied piece of luggage accepted into the baggage conveyance system at 1307 hours, having been coded for that flight at Station 206. Who owned this luggage? Could this be the bomb or the luggage containing the bomb?

At Heathrow, two developments appeared to point at where the luggage could have emanated from. First, in the early hours of December 21, 1988, there was a break-in into that area of Heathrow airside where luggage was kept for transfer to outbound planes. The padlock on one of the doors was described as being "cut like butter."[10] Ray Manly, who discovered and reported the break-in on December 21, 1988, noted that it was the worst security breach in his many years on the job. As he noted on February 12, 2002, Manly was on a nightshift in Terminal 3 on the night of December 20/21, 1988. The police did not act on this information and also concealed it from the defense.

Second, at the baggage handling shed where all but one of the containers on PA103 originated, John Bedford, one of the security staff in charge of x-raying luggage as it arrived piecemeal into the shed, having sorted out luggage for the correct flights and loaded the containers, claimed to have placed a row of suitcases upright along the back of the container for PA103 by quarter past four, when he went for a tea break. When he returned, he found two additional cases in the container. Rather than placing them upright, these two new additional suitcases were lying flat, side by side at the front of the container for PA103. One of them was "a brown or maroon hard-shell, the kind Samsonite make."[11] As the loader responsible for the interline shed, John maintained that the two additional suitcases were not there when he went for his tea break. He noted that Sulkash Kamboj, another x-ray operator, claimed to have put them there after x-raying them. Bedford gave this statement to the investigators in early January 1989, but it was never used. Could Manly's and Bedford's accounts have provided a clue as to where the unaccompanied luggage containing the bomb that brought down Pan Am 103 emanated from? Why were these two pieces of important evidence never pursued?

In 1990, the investigators established that the fragment of circuit board found on the shirt was part of a printed circuit board from an MST-13 timer. MEBO, a Swiss company, owned by Erwin Meister and Edwin Bollier, mass-produced these MST-13 timers. MEBO shared an office building in Zurich with ASH, a company owned by Badri Hassan and Abdelbaset Ali Mohmed al-Megrahi, both Libyans.

In 1985, MEBO exclusively supplied Libya with 20 MST-13 timers. Libya was not the only customer of MEBO. In fact, earlier in February 1988, two members of the Libyan Intelligence Service and a Senegalese were arrested at Dakar Airport after a cache of weapons and explosives, including an MST-13 timer, was found on them. The FBI and CIA also recovered a number of MST-13 timers from Togo and Senegal.

Investigators found that, in addition to supplying Libya with the timers, MEBO also trained Libyan personnel at their training camp in the Sabha Desert on how to use the MST-13 timers. Besides the 20 MST-13 timers, MEBO later supplied Libya with 40 Olympus timers when it could not complete another order for the MST-13 timers.

Was the fragment of a timer found in the wreckage the same as those that MEBO supplied Libya? If so, does it mean that the Libyan government carried out the attack on Pan Am 103 flight? With MEBO confirming that it sold 20 units of the MST 13 timers to Libya, investigators believed that Libyan security forces had a hand in the Lockerbie bombing. In order to make this claim, the investigator embarked on a metallurgy testing of the fragment found in the wreckage. Allen Feraday, who delivered the metallurgy results on the timer fragment under oath, maintained that the PCB chip and the reference MST-13 timer were similar in all respects with those that MEBO produced and sold to Libya.

It must be noted that while there were considerable physical similarities between MEBO's timers and the one recovered from the wreckage, there were also considerable differences showing that the timers were different. In circuitry, it was a standard practice to coat or dye a PCB chip, a process called tinning. While the coating on the MEBO circuitry contained 70 percent of a tin/lead alloy, tin, and 30 percent lead, the tinning on the fragment was made of 100 percent tin. Confronted with this discrepancy, investigators argued that the lead vaporized in the explosion. However, both investigators and prosecution hid this important fact from the defense.[12] On appeal, it was, however, revealed that the explosion could not have vaporized the lead. In order words, the chip fragment found in the wreckage differs from the ones MEBO produced and sold to Libya, all of which were done to standard and had normal alloy tinning.

If the fragment was not made by MEBO, could it have been a copy? If so, could Libya or another terrorist group have made this fake chip? Could it even be a chip from the plane itself or from a photographer's camera? Could it be from a student's calculator? Many have argued that the CIA planted the evidence in order to blame Libya, especially since there was no love lost between the United States and Libya.[13] Whatever it was and wherever it came from, it did not appear to be MEBO's timer. Before the Lockerbie bombing, Majid Giaka, a garage mechanic with the Libyan intelligence service—the Jamahiriya Security Organization (JSO), who in August 1988 had volunteered as a CIA informer, named Megrahi and Lamin Fhimah as JSO operatives. Megrahi and Fhimah were, however, Giaka's bosses in the Libyan Arab Airlines. Given this information, which turned out to be false, the CIA was convinced that Megrahi was a JSO member, especially since he was seconded, as an airport security guard, to the JSO for a short period when training JSO staff. In addition, MEBO and ASH—Megrahi's company—were in the same office building in Zurich. Among other things, Giaka, who, for a time, worked for Libyan Arab Airlines at Malta, told the CIA that Megrahi and Fhimah also possessed explosives.

In addition, Megrahi and Fhimah were also in Malta the day Gauci sold some items of clothing to the mystery shopper. Unlike Fhimah, Megrahi traveled to Malta on a false passport issued to him by the state. For a fact, Megrahi flew back to Tripoli after an overnight stay in Malta. He checked in for his flight, LN147, at the at the adjacent check-in desk and at the same time as KM 180, which departed for Frankfurt. His use of his "coded" passport, which gave his name as Ahmed Khalifa Abdusamad, was to prevent his wife from knowing that he was on a trip to Malta.

The Libyan passport office issued the passport to him legally, as a flight dispatcher with the Libyan Arab Airlines. Different countries have rules associated with the use of coded passports. It is issued when there is a legitimate reason for an individual to conceal his real identity. In the case of Megrahi, the use of a coded passport was to facilitate the sourcing of aircraft parts for Libyan Arab Airlines during the time Libya was under UN sanctions. His official passport bore his real name and designated him as a staff of Libyan Arab Airlines.

Megrahi also had business dealings with MEBO, the manufacturer of the timers sold to Libya. When Gauci identified Megrahi as "resembling" the mystery shopper, every piece of evidence appeared to have pointed in his direction, as the terrorist who brought down Pan Am 103 over Lockerbie.

The allegations against Megrahi and Fhimah were based entirely on Giaka's words. However, the CIA said that Giaka's claims were "exaggerated," "fantastic," and "self-aggrandizing."[14] For instance, for close to three years, he disclosed no information on the Lockerbie bombing. But when the CIA threatened him with severance unless he produced information on Lockerbie, he testified that on December 20, 1988 he saw Megrahi and Fhimah with a brown Samsonite suitcase at Luqa Airport. For his effort at pinning Lockerbie bombing on Megrahi and Libya, Giaka and his wife were relocated to the United States and issued new identities.

On November 13, 1991, an arrest warrant was issued at Dumfries Sheriff Court for the arrest of Megrahi and Fhimah. The charges were murder, conspiracy to murder, and a contravention of the Aviation Security Act of 1982. Libya denied its citizens' involvement in the bombing and refused to hand over Megrahi and Fhimah for trial. As Gaddafi argued, according to Libyan laws, no Libyan could be extradited.[15] In addition, since neither the United States nor Britain had any extradition treaty with Libya, it was the right of Libya to conduct the trial internally and in accordance with the 1971 Convention for the Suppression of Unlawful Acts against the Safety of Civil Aviation.

Gaddafi's position aligned with Articles 6 and 7 of the convention, which stated that:

> any contracting state in the territory of which the offender or the alleged offender is present, shall take him into custody . . . and the contracting state, if it does not extradite, shall be obliged, without exception whatsoever and whether or not the offence was committed in its territory, to submit the case to its competent authorities for the purpose of prosecution. These authorities shall take their decision in the same manner as in the case of any ordinary offence of a serious nature under the law of that state.[16]

While adhering to these provisions of the 1971 Convention for the Suppression of Unlawful Acts against the Safety of Civil Aviation, Gaddafi maintained the innocence of Libyans indicted for both the Lockerbie bombing and the bombing of a French UTA DC-10 over the Sahara. In addition, he challenged the International Court of Justice over its support for United States and British extradition requests. For its refusal to extradite Megrahi and Fhimah, the United Nations and its member states imposed severe economic, diplomatic, and military sanctions on Libya.

GLOBAL RESPONSES AND OUTCOMES

Shortly before 7 p.m. EST on April 14, 1986, the United States launched air strikes against Libya in retaliation for the terror attack on the West Berlin discotheque. The air strikes, which targeted five military installations and terror centers in Tripoli and Benghazi, also affected Gaddafi's presidential palace. At least 30 soldiers and 15 civilians were killed in Tripoli and Benghazi. Gaddafi and some of his children were also injured in the attack. Gaddafi's foster daughter was believed to have been killed too.

The attacks, which involved more than 100 U.S. Air Force and Navy aircraft, was mounted by 14 A-6E Navy attack jets based in the Mediterranean and 18 FB-111 bombers from bases in England. Military facilities at Tripoli's main airport, the Benina Air Base southeast of Benghazi and three military barracks were hit in the raids. The operation, code-named El Dorado Canyon, was successful; although the United States lost one F-111, along with its two crew members, to Libya's surface-to-air missiles and conventional anti-aircraft artillery. Besides killing 15 Libyan civilians, many residential buildings, including the French embassy in Tripoli, were also bombed.

In addition to airstrikes, the United States also imposed economic, military, and diplomatic sanctions on Libya. In turn, Libya fired missiles at a U.S. Navy communications station on the Italian island of Lamedusa. Also, in 1981, Libya downed a U.S. aircraft in the Gulf of Sidra. In coordinated terrorist attacks at airports in Rome and Vienna in December 1985, five American citizens were killed. President Ronald Reagan of the United States blamed Libya for the attacks and expanded sanctions on Libya. Oil business contracts with Libya were cancelled. Libya's foreign reserve and assets in the United States were frozen, while Libya's businesses were taken over by the American government.

Following the retaliatory attacks, the United Nations and other member nations imposed severe sanctions on Libya. These sanctions—ranging from military and economic to diplomatic sanctions—crippled Libya's economy. In order to ease the economic stress, Libya accepted responsibility for the bombing, and on August 10, 2004, Libya paid a total of $35 million in compensation for it.[17]

Following Libya's refusal to hand over the two accused persons in the Lockerbie bombing trial case, the United Nations imposed its

Resolution 748 of March 31, 1992 on Libya. The Resolution imposed an arms and air embargo and a reduction of Libyan diplomatic personnel serving abroad. In addition, it also set up a Security Council sanctions committee.

Moreover, Resolution 883 of November 11, 1993, approved the freezing of Libyan funds and financial resources in other countries. It also prohibited provision of oil refining and transportation equipment to Libya. According to UN Security Council Resolution 748, all Member States should:

(a) deny permission of Libyan aircraft to take off from, land in or overfly their territory if it has taken off from Libyan territory, excluding humanitarian need;

(b) prohibit the supply of aircraft or aircraft components or the provision or servicing of aircraft or aircraft components;

(c) prohibit the provision of weapons, ammunition or other military equipment to Libya and technical advice or training;

(d) withdraw officials present in Libya that advise the Libyan authorities on military matters;

(e) significantly reduce diplomatic and consular personnel in Libya;

(f) prevent the operation of all Libyan Airlines offices;

(g) deny or expel Libyan nationals involved in terrorist activities in other states.

Resolution 1192 of August 27, 1998, reaffirmed sanctions set forth in Resolutions 748 of 1992 and 883 of 1993. In addition, Resolution 1192 paved the way for additional measures if Libya continued to refuse to extradite the two accused persons. In sum, the various resolutions of the United Nations called for suspension of aerial, arms, and diplomatic measures with the Libyan Arab Jamahiriya until it complied with the arrest warrant issued for the two accused persons.

In a September 1996 report, the Libyan mission to the UN submitted an impact assessment report on the effect of the UN sanctions against Libya to Boutros Boutros-Ghali, secretary general of the UN. As the report noted, the substantial damage caused in the humanitarian, economic, and social spheres by the coercive and unjust measures taken against the Libyan Arab people under Security Council Resolutions 748 (1992) and 883 (1993) continued to worsen day by day. In addition, all infrastructure development programs and plans had been adversely affected, thereby dashing the hopes and aspirations of the Libyan Arab people to achieve progress, well-being, development, stability, security, and peace.

Through the imposition of economic, diplomatic, and military sanctions and embargoes imposed on the Libyan Arab Jamahiriya by Security Council Resolutions 748 (1992) and 883 (1993), the total financial losses in the transportation and communication sector stood at $1,157,523,500 between April 15, 1992 and December 31, 1995. In the same period, Libya's industry and mining sector lost $4,150,677,942, while losses in finance and trade stood at $4,257,000,000. The mainstay of Libyan economy, petroleum and electricity, lost $3 billion within the same period.

Some particulars of the enormous physical, material, and financial damage sustained by the Libyan people following the implementation of the UN sanctions mentioned in the reports are reproduced verbatim here:[18]

(a) Some 15,750 persons living in the Jamahiriya are suffering from serious medical conditions (cardiovascular disease; fractures of the spinal column and thorax; fractured skulls; chronic eye diseases; detached retinas: serious burns; cancer and malignant tumors) which require emergency treatment (neurosurgery; spinal marrow transplants; kidney transplants; corneal transplants; fitting of prostheses). Owing to the continuation of the aerial embargo, these individuals, who could not be treated in local hospitals and health-care facilities, could not be evacuated by air for treatment in other countries or for necessary medical examinations and surgery in hospitals and specialized health-care facilities with modern equipment. Because they could not obtain treatment, most of these patients died in tragic circumstances.

(b) More than 780 seriously injured patients (most of whom were the victims of road accidents) died in ambulances en-route to airports in neighboring countries so that they could be transported by air for treatment abroad in spite of the difficulties of the overland journey.

(c) There have been 1,135 stillbirths and 514 women have died in childbirth in the various hospitals owing to the shortage of medicines, serums and vaccines. Prior to the aerial embargo, such supplies had been imported regularly by air, with the usual precautions being taken to preserve their efficacy and usability. The Libyan Arab Jamahiriya was able in that way to meet its needs in this area, particularly in emergency situations.

(d) Owing to the aerial embargo and the consequent increase in overland traffic, there has been a rise in the number of road accidents. As Libyans have had to take to the roads linking the major cities in the country, hundreds have been involved in accidents in which they have been killed or suffered permanent disability. There have been some 15,260 victims of road accidents, including 2,560 fatalities. The remaining 12,700 victims are suffering from serious injuries or permanent disabilities. More than 18,200 public and privately-owned vehicles have been damaged, for an estimated cost of $1,450,000.

(e) The number of diabetics who have died has increased, owing to the unavailability of serums and medicines.

(f) The shortage of poliomyelitis vaccine, which continues to worsen, has impeded the implementation of periodic or annual therapeutic, preventive and awareness-raising programs connected with national and international immunization campaigns with specific timetables. Many Libyan and other children have thus been prevented from receiving doses at the prescribed times in accordance with the guidelines of the World Health Organization (WHO) and national public health laws and regulations.

(g) Therapeutic and preventive services for school health programs have been suspended, as have the programs and activities of mother-and-child health-care centers and centers for the mentally retarded and physically handicapped.

(h) International pharmaceutical companies have been slow in supplying the health and social welfare sector and hospital establishments with essential pharmaceuticals and equipment needed to treat and prevent diseases.

(i) Companies specializing in the maintenance of air ambulances have refused to supply the spare parts needed to maintain the country's fleet and other on-board equipment. These aircraft, which service Libyan citizens and expatriates alike, are no longer able to perform fully their humanitarian mission, whether in Libya or abroad, given the country's extensive land area.

(j) Delays have consistently occurred in the delivery of some medical supplies (serums, vaccines, blood products, hormones, reagents used in AIDS testing, radioactive iodine, etc.) because they are now shipped overland or by sea. Such supplies are usually shipped by air (so that the normal measures can be taken to preserve their efficacy); special permission must now be sought for the purchase of such items. When they arrive in Libya, most of these supplies (in particular, poliomyelitis vaccine) have lost their efficacy (having been stored under improper conditions) which has resulted in an increase in the number of deaths among infants and women, particularly in childbirth, and disarray in the provision of health services generally.

(k) Losses estimated at around $180,800,000 have been experienced in the health and social welfare sector owing to the maintenance of the aerial embargo against the Libyan Arab Jamahiriya, which has caused delays in the shipment of medical supplies. The Libyan Arab Jamahiriya obtains supplies from specialized international companies to meet the needs of a variety of institutions (medical schools, technical institutes, rehabilitation centers and homes for the elderly).

(l) Maintenance of the aerial embargo has dealt a serious blow to preventive and curative health services provided under international technical cooperation agreements. The country is endeavoring to develop, strengthen and maintain such agreements with various countries in order to develop the health and social welfare sector and modernize its hospitals with the aim of providing improved medical, therapeutic and prophylactic services for all its citizens.

(m) The maintenance of the embargo has also impeded cooperation programs between the People's Committee for Health and Social Welfare and the bodies under it, on the one hand, and WHO, on the other. Most of the visits which international experts and WHO teams were to make to Libya have been cancelled or postponed, which has adversely affected all the major health care and preventive health programs and hampered efforts to promote and modernize the health and social welfare sector. The failure or stagnation of international cooperation in this area would prevent Libya from achieving the targets set by WHO and pursuing the WHO strategy of "Health for All by the Year 2000".

(n) More than 360 medical specialists and highly qualified instructors from universities and medical centers from around the world have been unable to come to the Libyan Arab Jamahiriya to treat patients with serious conditions, perform delicate surgical procedures in public hospitals, conduct examinations in the country's medical schools at different times of the year, and participate in conferences, symposia and courses organized in the country.

(o) The growing shortage of spare parts has resulted in a deterioration in the maintenance of modern medical equipment used in hospitals and medical centers. In addition, there is the lack of technical skills in most hospitals and health establishments in major cities and villages alike.

(p) More than 8,500 medical doctors of various nationalities have been unable to come to the country to work in the health and social welfare sector because of the difficulties and hardships presented by

the maintenance of the aerial embargo. Some 6,400 medical specialists in various fields have not renewed their contracts, which has
adversely affected the quality of health care in the majority of hospitals and other health facilities.

Tottering on the brink of social and economic collapse, Libya gave in
to UN sanctions, and, after extensive international negotiations, Megrahi
and Fhimah were arrested on April 5, 1999. The trial took place at a former American Air Force Base at Kamp Van Zeist near Soesterberg in
Holland. While Megrahi was sentenced to life imprisonment, Fhimah
was acquitted. Megrahi's sentencing was premised on the court's position that he was in Malta and bought clothes from Gauci on December 7—a conclusion not backed by any hard evidence; the court believed
that the bomb originated from Malta and that Megrahi was at the airport when the bomb was introduced. In addition, Megrahi's possession
of a false passport and dealings with MEBO, which, in the opinion of
the court, proved his alleged JSO connection. Other positions expressed
by the court in sentencing Megrahi included Frankfurt records, which
showed that an unaccompanied piece of luggage was carried on KM180
and that, since Megrahi was at the airport at the time, the said unaccompanied luggage was believed to have contained the bomb. Megrahi
maintained his innocence throughout both the main trial and his subsequent appeal.
    It is possible that Megrahi was not the Lockerbie bomber. For instance,
when the issue of the Heathrow break-in and the two newly introduced
suitcases at Heathrow are brought into the picture, it could be argued
that the bomb was actually introduced in Malta or Frankfurt. Perhaps
the most damning evidence against the verdict was the metallurgy
results on the timer fragment. Why did the prosecution hide this crucial evidence from the defense? It is difficult to link Megrahi to the
attack when it could not be proven that the chip found in the wreckage
was the same as those produced by MEBO. There was also the criminal complicity of the CIA over Giaka. The CIA believed that Giaka was
lying, and the same applied to Anthony Gauci, the shopkeeper. It was
clear from the beginning that Gauci never recollected the mystery shopper's face. In addition, it is possible that all his efforts were made in
order to aid the police in arriving at an easy conclusion. The CIA presented Gauci with Megrahi's photo, which possibly led him to state he
was definitely the bomber.[19] Far and above all these questions, it was
revealed that Paul, Gauci's brother, had already helped Gauci compile
photos and press cuttings of Megrahi prior to the police identification
parade of possible suspects. Both Gauci and Paul were motivated in

their course by the reward money, which they both shared. Despite that all this was known and presented at the appeal, Megrahi lost his appeal.

When these and other contradictions in the investigation and trial are put together, it is easy to see that, from 1991, investigators were interested in gathering evidence against Megrahi and Fhimah and that the guilty verdict on Megrahi was based on inferential evidence. Rather than the arcane practice of the prosecution discharging the burden of proof, it was Megrahi that had to proof his innocence. There was no presumption of innocence at all in the case.

Megrahi was at the threshold of another appeal when he was released on August 20, 2009, on account of a terminal prostate cancer. As detailed in his book, *You Are My Jury: The Lockerbie Evidence*, had his second appeal been allowed, the illogicality of the Scottish legal system would have been laid bare. His release, which was premised on discontinuing with the appeal, prevented the world from knowing the truth about whether or not Megrahi and/or Libya sponsored the Lockerbie bombing.

ENDING THE SANCTIONS

The United Nations Security Council suspended all sanctions immediately upon Gaddafi's handing over of the two accused Libyans in the Lockerbie bombing on April 5, 1999. Many member nations also did the same, except for the United States, which relaxed the sanctions. Gaddafi's immediate concern after the suspension of the sanctions was how to revamp Libya's economy. On the international scene, Gaddafi wanted to consolidate his stance in Africa and reestablished Libya's relationships with the outside world, most especially the United States and European Union.

Originally, efforts at revamping Libya's economy began in 1987 when, in May, Gaddafi called for a reform of the agricultural and industrial sectors. In what Gaddafi described as a "Revolution within a Revolution," the overarching plan was, on the one hand, to limit importation by growing and producing a majority of Libya's imports locally. On the other hand, the planned economic and industrial changes involved the adoption of contemporary management practices, which included the injection of the private sector into the economy.

As a measure to jump-start the economy, private sector operators were encouraged to form cooperative societies in order to pool labor and capital to start industries and commercial agricultural production. Within the first year of this effort, about 150 government enterprises were handed over to private sector operators to manage.

In order to ease and reduce the cost of business operations, the government also established the Ministry of Mass Mobilization and Revolutionary Leadership, a body that limited government involvement in public companies by curtailing the involvement of different agencies of government in businesses. As of September 1988, the government had divested itself from controlling trade. In a rather bold step, more and more private sector operators were given control of both import and export, ending many years of government control of this vital sector of the economy. Except for the petroleum, hydrocarbon, and heavy industries, all sectors were yielded to private sector operators.

Libyans' reaction to this new trend in governance in Libya was immediate. Privately owned industries of different sizes sprang up across Libya. Large and small-scale businesses, ranging from small shops to highly managed chain stores sprang up everywhere. Unlike the state-run enterprises of old, which were characterized by poor management and incessant shortages, endemic corruption, and disorganized distribution systems, the private sector–led businesses were effective and efficient, and Libyans were quick to praise the new system.

The most troubling aspect of this new development in Libya was the flight of expatriates following the sanctions. The impact of this on the economy was unprecedented, as the petroleum and hydrocarbon sector, the very sinew of Libyan economy, was the worst hit. Since 1985, a large number of Americans and Europeans who worked in the petroleum and hydrocarbon sector left Libya. Although the United States closed its embassy in Libya in 1980, it was not until 1982 that travel to Libya was banned, and American oil magnates, the single most players in oil exploration in Libya, left Libya's oil fields. The United States, Libya's major customer, also banned oil importation from Libya. In addition, the exportation of any good whatsoever to Libya was strictly controlled. The agricultural sector was not spared the sanctions that befell Libya. From 1985, a large number of foreign cultivators also left Libya, bringing agricultural production to a standstill and threatening food shortages across the country.

The flight of expatriates in the oil and agricultural sectors led to a precipitous decline in oil and food production. Libya's isolation by other member states of the United Nations made matter worse for Libya, as it could hardly turn to any other nation for any kind of relief. The decline in daily production of crude oil meant a decline in revenue and the government's ability to fund any of its socialist policies. The economic reform was therefore the Gaddafi-led government's internal response to the avalanche of sanctions and restrictions imposed on Libya by both the United Nations and its member states.

In the midst of these social and economic changes, the United States accused Libya of producing chemical weapons. As published on the front page of *The New York Times* on December 24, 1987, in a facility in Rabat, the Gaddafi-led government was said to be producing weapons of mass destruction in disguise at this facility. The article cited instances of poison gas use by Libya in Chad, a claim that remained unverified.[20] In addition to these claims, the United States also alleged that Libya's relation to Iran helped Gaddafi to facilitate the procurement of enriched uranium and other materials used in chemical weapon production.

While not denying the existence of a facility in Rabat, the Gaddafi-led government vehemently denied the allegation of producing chemical weapons and weapons of mass destruction. As Gaddafi argued, the severe pain associated with the sanctions made it incumbent on the government to establish its own pharmaceutical industry in Rabat. The United States, unconcerned about Libya's explanation, imposed further sanctions on Libya. As noted in Executive Order 12543 of January 7, 1986, all exports to Libya except donations for humanitarian relief, such as medical supplies and medicine, clothes, and food, should stop immediately.

This came to a head when, in 1987, the United States announced that Libya's facility in Rabat was the largest chemical weapon manufacturing facility in the world and that it was on the verge of full-scale production. In 1988, President Reagan announced that the United States was considering an all-out military action against Libya over the facility in Rabat. By early in January 1989, U.S. forces downed two unarmed Libyan warplanes. In numerous speeches and newspaper publications, Libya challenged the United States to prove its claim of Libya's facility as a chemical weapon production center. In addition, it demanded that the United States should destroy its own weapons of mass destruction, stop assisting Israel in acquiring chemical and nuclear weapons, and stop perpetuating false allegations against Libya.

Under George H. W. Bush in 1990, *The New York Times* also published a report whereby the U.S. government claimed that Imhausen-Chemie, a German company was aiding Libya's construction of the facility in Rabat and that Libya had begun to produce small quantities of mustard and sarin gases.[21] Bush called on the international community to pay special attention to Libya's alleged production of chemical weapons, warning that should any of the chemicals get into the hands of terrorists, the outcome would be catastrophic. Like Reagan, Bush also announced that the United States would not hesitate to unleash its military might on Libya.

Things, however, took a new turn in March when Libya's facility in Rabat was engulfed in fire. The Gaddafi-led government claimed sabotage and announced that the United States, Israel, and Germany sponsored the attack on its pharmaceutical facility in Rabat. The United States, in turn, denied any involvement and maintained that the fire was staged to divert attention and that an intelligence report available to the CIA was to the effect that Libya had started a subterranean chemical weapon facility, disguised as a water treatment plant, at Tarhuna. Libya claimed that the facility at Tarhuna was part of an irrigation system and challenged the United States to provide evidence to support its allegations.

It remained unclear whether Libya was producing or was attempting to produce chemical weapons or weapons of mass destruction at these two facilities. It could, however, be argued that while Libya was a signatory to the 1925 Protocol for the Prohibition of the Use in War of Asphyxiating, Poisonous or Other Gases and of Bacteriological Methods of Warfare, as well as the 1972 Convention on the Prohibition of the Development, Production, and Stockpiling of Bacteriological (Biological) and Toxin Weapons and on their Destruction, the Gaddafi-led government, however, declined to sign the 1993 Convention on the Prohibition of the Development, Production, Stockpiling and Use of Chemical Weapons and on Their Destruction. Had Libya signed this protocol, experts would have had access to the two facilities to ascertain their purposes.

It was, however, indisputable that Libya produced and stockpiled chemical weapons, as in 2004, the Gaddafi-led government voluntarily renounced the production of chemical weapons. As the Organization for the Prohibition of Chemical Weapons—an intergovernmental body, composed of 193 member states, that oversees global endeavor for the permanent and verifiable elimination of chemical weapons—supervised the destruction of Libya's stockpile of chemical weapons and announced that Libya had successfully produced a large quantity of mustard gas and was at the threshold of designing chemical weapon–carrying missiles or other delivery systems.

As early as 1997, many African nations expressed discontent over sanctions on Libya, especially given the near collapse of Libyans' socioeconomic lives. In October, Nelson Mandela, president of South Africa, visited Libya. Mandela noted the invaluable roles that Gaddafi and Libya played in South Africans' struggle against apartheid. He canvassed for the relaxation of sanctions on Libya and corroborated the Organisation of African Unity's position that the Lockerbie bombing trial be handled by an independent tribunal. Other African leaders that visited Libya immediately after Mandela were the presidents of Uganda, Gambia, Chad, Nigeria, Sudan, Liberia, and Tanzania. In order not to violate United Nations' sanctions on Libya, these African leaders flew to neighboring countries and completed their journeys into and out of Libya by road.

In October 1998, the United Nations General Assembly adopted the resolution, sponsored by Libya, calling for the repeal of laws that unilaterally sanctioned companies and citizens. By the adoption of this resolution, Americans and American companies can trade and work in Libya without violating any provision, a step that could reinvigorate Libya's ailing oil industry. The resolution passed by a majority of 80 in favor against a minority of 67 abstaining delegations.

With the removal or relaxation (as was the case with the United States) of sanctions, Libya began to cultivate goodwill and relations with African nations. In July 1999, Gaddafi was voted in as chairman of the Organisation of African Unity (OAU). In his maiden speech as chairman of OAU, Gaddafi called for the establishment of a pan-African Congress and a United States of Africa, as a system of states modeled along the line of the United States of America. He argued that, as a block of states, a pan-African Congress and a United States of Africa would provide a common front for Africa in global trade and politics. He went further to ask the gathering of heads of African states to establish the Economic Community of Africa.

Speaking specifically to the Arab-speaking countries of Africa, Gaddafi demanded these African states to consider the establishment of an Integration Bank that aimed at promoting Arab unity and economic cooperation. At this meeting, member states of what, in July 2002, became known as the African Union, called for ending all socioeconomic, diplomatic, and military sanctions on Libya.

The outcome of the meeting for Libya was the conclusion of socioeconomic and diplomatic cooperation treaties between Libya and a number of African countries, especially Niger in 1997, Eritrea in 1998, and Senegal and South Africa in 1999. These treaties covered areas from education to science and culture.

Despite the fact that Libya had barely recovered from its economic woes, it, in 2004, provided food aid and other humanitarian assistance to Sudan. The World Food Program coordinated Libya's food aid in the Darfur region and other refugee camps in Sudan. In order to bring more trade to Libya, in 2005, Libya joined a regional economic community—the Common Market for East and Southern Africa, an organization established in 2004 for regional economic cooperation and integration.

There is no doubt that Gaddafi, after many years of international sanctions and restrictions, felt the need not only to open and diversify its economy but also to improve its relations with other African nations.

Gaddafi's call for the establishment of a United States of Africa was borne out of his realization that it would be extremely difficult to treat the entire continent to a series of international sanctions and restrictions, as Libya experienced after its refusal to give up two of its citizens for trials. In addition, he reckoned that with a pan-African bank, African countries would escape any freezing of their foreign reserves in the circumstance of any intransigence on the international stage.

Other African leaders viewed Gaddafi's proposals with suspicion. For instance, concerns were raised on how a United States of Africa be governed, especially in the face of an uneven political development across the continent. In addition, given uneven economic developments in different African countries, a United States of Africa with a pan-African banking system would ensure that a developed region would be able to develop other areas.

Many also viewed Gaddafi's proposals as an attempt at continental domination. For instance, since his assumption of leadership in 1969, Gaddafi was critical of French-speaking African countries. Given his critiques of France's willingness to sell arms to all sides in the Middle East conflicts and also France's willingness to sell arms to Egypt during the Libya–Egypt border war, all Gaddafi's efforts at African integration and economic cooperation were viewed among French-speaking African countries as aggressive, exploitative, and sinister.

While Libya's relations with the United States and Great Britain had been frosty, Libya's relations with France teetered between friendship and enmity. As demonstrated in Chapter 7, France–Libya relations started on a good note when Gaddafi came to power. However, this friendly relation soured over Libya's relations with French-speaking African nations. When in April 1990, Libya aided in securing the release of three European hostages from the Abu-Nidal group—the Fatah Revolutionary Council—France released Libya's three Mirage fighter jets impounded since 1986. France also implicated Libya following Abu Nidal's group's hijacking of UTA Flight 772, which exploded over Niger. Since Abu Nidal was living in Libya during the time, Libya was accused of harboring and aiding the renowned terrorist.

It was not only the United States, Great Britain, and France that Libya had frosty relationships with. Its relationship with Germany was also not good. The La Belle discotheque terror attack in Berlin endangered the prospect of any good relationship with Germany, as the intercepted intelligence showed that the Gaddafi-led government had knowledge of or sponsored the attack where two Americans and one Turk were killed, while more than 200 other people, mostly Germans, sustained varying degrees of injuries. As previously noted, Libya, after 15 years, accepted responsibility for the discotheque terror attack and paid reparations to the families of the affected people.

There is no denying the fact that long years of sanctions and restrictions that almost ruined Libya's economy left in its wake a deep lesson for Gaddafi, especially on the Palestinian question. Speaking at the opening session of the OAU summit in 2001, Gaddafi completely avoided any mention of the Palestinian question. His views on the Palestinian question were later made known during an interview on Al-Jazeera in 2007, when he declared that he was convinced that the solution to Israel–Palestine problem was to establish a democratic state for the Jews and another one for the Palestinians. This support for a two-state solution differs remarkably from Gaddafi's earlier stance and advocacy.

Among other nations, Gaddafi also cultivated new relationships with the People's Republic of China and the Philippines.

Prior to the years of sanctions and restrictions, Libya's major customers in Europe were Germany, Italy, and Spain. In 2004, Gaddafi was at the European Union headquarters in Brussels. Following this visit, trade with the European Union markedly improved. Libya was admitted to the Euro-Mediterranean Partnership and the European Union, and those member states that still had sanctions and restrictions in place, withdrew all sanctions and admitted Libya, once again, into the comity of nations.

NOTES

1. Alhaji A. E. Cham Joof, "Message to the Founding Fathers of the OAU at Their First Conference at Addis Ababa," May 1, 1963. Accessed on September 14, 2018, at https://web.archive.org/web/20111123024430/

2. *The Times of Bruxelles* (January 4, 1974), cited in Enrica Oliveri, *Libya before and after Gaddafi: An International Law Analysis*. Dissertation submitted in 2012 to the Universita Ca'Foscari Venezia in partial fulfillment for the award of master's degree in comparative international relations, 20.

3. Dirk J. Vandewalle, *A History of Modern Libya* (Cambridge: Cambridge University Press, 2012), 128. See also Ronald Bruce St. John, *Libya: From Colony to Revolution* (Oxford: Oneworld Publications, 2011), 197–224.

4. Central Intelligence Agency, *The Supporters of International Terrorism*, accessed October 11, 2018, at https://www.cia.gov/library/readingroom/docs/CIA-RDP84B00274R000100040012-9.pdf

5. U.S. Department of State, *Patterns of Global Terrorism, 2003*. Accessed October 10, 2018, at https://www.state.gov/j/ct/rls/crt/2003/33771.htm. See also Patrick Seale, *Abu Nidal: A Gun for Hire* (London: Hutchinson, 1992), 99; "Acting against Libyan Support of International Terrorism,"

accessed October 31, 2018, at https://web.archive.org/web/20050203182653
/http://www2.gwu.edu/~nsarchiv/NSAEBB/NSAEBB55/nsdd205.pdf

6. U.S. Department of State, *Patterns of Global Terrorism, 2003.*

7. Sergey Ushynskyi, "Pan Am Flight 103 Investigation and Lessons
Learned" in *Aviation*, 13, no. 3 (2009), 79.

8. Ushynskyi, 80.

9. Severin Carrell, "US Paid Reward to Lockerbie Witness, Abdelbaset
al-Megrahi Papers Claim," *The Guardian*, October 2, 2009, accessed October 31, 2018, at https://www.theguardian.com/world/2009/oct/02/locker
bie-documents-witness-megrahi

10. BBC, "Lockerbie Appeal Hears Key Witness" in *BBC News*, February 13, 2002. Accessed October 10, 2018, at http://news.bbc.co.uk/2/hi/in
_depth/1817752.stm

11. Ushynskyi, 78.

12. John Biewen, "Shadow over Lockerbie," *American Radio Works*,
March 2000. Accessed October 31, 2018, at http://americanradioworks
.publicradio.org/features/lockerbie/story/printable_story.html

13. For different arguments on the handling of Manly's testimony on
the break-in at Heathrow Terminal 3, see the blog entitled "The Lockerbie
Case," accessed October 31, 2018, at http://lockerbiecase.blogspot.com
/2015/12/the-break-in-at-heathrow-terminal-3.html

14. BBC, "Lockerbie Witness Branded Liar" in *BBC News*, January 17,
2001, accessed October 10, 2018, at http://news.bbc.co.uk/2/hi/1121924
.stm. See also Gerard Seenan, "Lockerbie Witness 'Lied' to CIA to Secure
Life in US," *The Guardian*, September 27, 2000. Accessed October 10, 2018, at
https://www.theguardian.com/uk/2000/sep/28/lockerbie.gerardseenan

15. "The Lockerbie Cases before the International Court of Justice," *The
Hague Justice Portal*, accessed October 12, 2018, at http://www.haguejusti
ceportal.net/Docs/Miscellaneous/Lockerbie_info_EN.pdf

16. International Law Commission, *The Obligation to Extradite or Prosecute: Final Report of the International Law Commission* (New York: United
Nations, 2014), 8.

17. Peter Slevin, "Libya Accepts Blame in Lockerbie Bombing," in *The
Washington Post*, August 17, 2003. Accessed October 31, 2018, at https://www
.washingtonpost.com/archive/politics/2003/08/17/libya-accepts-blame
-in-lockerbie-bombing/9796f0de-7b4b-4197-bea4-bb1fc64265c5
/?noredirect=on&utm_term=.2d7fb39e7fca

18. Dapo Akande, "The Effect of Security Council Resolutions and
Domestic Proceedings on State Obligations to Cooperate with the ICC," in
Journal of International Criminal Justice, 10, no. 2 (2012), 299–324.

19. Robert D. McFadden, "Megrahi, Convicted in 1988 Lockerbie Bombing, Dies at 60" in *The New York Times*, May 20, 2012. Accessed October 31,
2018, at https://www.nytimes.com/2012/05/21/world/africa/abdel-basset
-ali-al-megrahi-lockerbie-bomber-dies-at-60.html

20. Seymour M. Hersh, "Target Qaddafi," in *The New York Times Magazine*, February 22, 1987. Accessed October 10, 2018, at https://www.nytimes
.com/1987/02/22/magazine/target-qaddafi.html

21. Stephen Engelberg, "U.S. Says Libya Moves Chemicals for Poison Gas away from Plant," in *The New York Times*, January 4, 1989. Accessed October 10, 2018, at https://www.nytimes.com/1989/01/04/world/us-says -libya-moves-chemicals-for-poison-gas-away-from-plant.html. See also U.S. Senate, Congressional Record—Senate (Legislative day of Tuesday, January 3, 1989), 1910; James Martin Center for Nonproliferation Studies, *Libya Chemical Chronology*, accessed October 10, 2018, at https://www.nti.org /media/pdfs/libya_chemical_2.pdf?_=1321482794

8

The Arab Spring and Death of Gaddafi, 2011–2012

INTRODUCTION

The Arab Spring or Arab Revolutions was a wave of violent and non-violent demonstrations, protests, riots, coups, foreign interventions, and civil wars that is widely believed to have been instigated by many years of dissatisfaction, particularly among a young generation rising up against oppressive and authoritarian regimes in North Africa and the Middle East. It began on December 18, 2010 in Sidi Bouzid, Tunisia, when Mohamed Bouazizi set himself ablaze to protest police brutality and government neglect. Following Bouazizi's self-immolation, a series of increasingly violent street demonstrations broke out, and, by January 14, 2011, it had led to the ousting of President Zine El Abidine Ben Ali, the Tunisian president.

The revolution spread from Tunisia to Egypt, Libya, Yemen, Syria, and Bahrain. In all of these countries, it led either to a regime change or to major uprisings and social violence, including riots, civil wars, and insurgencies. The overarching aim of the revolution was to secure a more democratic political system and a brighter economic future for

citizens. The Arab Spring was therefore a wave of sustained revolutionary campaigns that involved tens of thousands of ordinary citizens,
using different forms of civil resistance such as demonstrations and
marches, strikes and rallies. Common to and of primary importance to
these revolutions were protesters' use of social media, especially in
organizing and communicating, raising awareness and issuing danger
alerts in their attempts at ensuring successes and crowd control, evad-
ing arrest and other forms of state repression and censorship. Authorities, both in North Africa and in the Middle East, responded to these
antigovernment protests and demonstrations in violent ways.

What were the underlying reasons for this wave of revolutionary
demonstrations and riots? While similar demonstrations were later held
in other parts of the world, why did it start in North Africa and the
Middle East, and why did it record far more successes in North Africa
and the Middle East than elsewhere? These and other questions shall
be addressed in this chapter, using the case of Libya.

THE 2011 LIBYAN REVOLUTION

Following the Arab Spring's successes in Tunisia and Egypt, many
Libyans yearned for a similar development in Libya. Fathi Terbil, a Libyan lawyer and human rights activist who represented the relatives of
over 1,000 prisoners killed by Libyan security forces in Abu Salim
Prison in 1996, and others took advantage of the fifteen-year anniversary
of the Abu Salim Prison massacre in order to plan protests in Libya on
February 17, 2011. In the protesters' language, the February 17 was "the
day of rage." To forestall the planned protests, the Libyan government
arrested Terbil in Benghazi on February 15, asking him to stop the
planned protests.

Abu Salim, a major prison in Tripoli, which held about 1,700 inmates,
witnessed a prisoners' revolt over detention conditions in 1996. During negotiations, Abdullah al-Sanussi commanded the prisoners to
assemble in the prison's courtyards, whereupon security forces opened
fire on them, killing about 1,200 prisoners. The government made no
effort to contact the families of these prisoners, and the issue went unre-
ported. Over many years, many family members visited the prison,
leaving gifts and provisions for their imprisoned family members, not
knowing that those family members were long murdered. When the
news of the massacre broke, the government denied it, and Terbil represented the families of the massacred prisoners in the ensuing litiga-
tion. When Terbil was arrested on February 15, 2011, many families of
the victims of the Abu Salim massacre, believing that his arrest and

Supporters of Libyan leader Muammar al-Gaddafi hold pictures of him as they take part in a pro-government rally in Tripoli on February 17, 2011. The rally took place as the country faced a nationwide 'Day of Anger' incited by opposition cyber activists. (Mahmud Turkia/AFP/Getty Images)

detention were politically motivated, gathered in Benghazi to protest his arrest. Attempts to disperse the gathered protesters failed, and a spontaneous mass demonstration broke out in the city. Police's man-handling of the protesters led to a number of casualties, which sparked solidarity protests not only in Benghazi but across major cities and towns in Libya. The protests and demonstrations became countrywide by February 17, marking the beginning of Libya's Arab Spring.

In a number of cities and towns, large numbers of peaceful protesters and rioters gathered to demonstrate against the Gaddafi-led govern-ment's handling of protesters. At the beginning of the protests, protesters and demonstrators threw stones, petrol bombs, and Molotov cocktails—damaging cars and blocking roads. In Zawiya and Zintan, protesters and demonstrators set fire to police stations and security buildings. In Zintan, Benghazi, Derna, and Bayda, protesters and demonstrators set up tents in public spaces. In Tripoli, public television and radio stations were sacked, and security buildings, Revolutionary Committee offices, the Interior Ministry building, and the People's Hall were set ablaze. In the fracas, 38 people, including 10 security personnel, were injured in Benghazi alone.

Police used tear gas and batons, water cannons and rubber bullets to disperse protesters, but by February 16, as protesters began to demand an end to a government that had held sway over Libya for 42 years, live ammunition and heavy weapons, including heavy machine guns and antitank guns, warplanes and helicopter gunships were used against the protesters. From that moment, what began as peaceful protests against the arrest of Terbil metamorphosed into an agitation for a regime change.

As things escalated, many Libyans were arrested across cities and towns. While thousands were arrested during protests, others were picked up in their homes and workplaces. In late January and early February 2011, the mass arrest of real or perceived political opponents of the government was aimed at preempting and forestalling further demonstrations. In the aftermath of February 17, 2011, the mass arrests escalated significantly in Benghazi and Tripoli, Zawiya and Zliten, Khoms and Misurata. In Zawiya and Misurata, the campaign of arrest and detention continued until August 2011 when these areas fell to the rebel forces. However, following their recapture by government forces, arrest and detention began again in earnest.

Witnesses recounted incidences of Gaddafi forces shelling Zawiya, Misurata, and other urban areas with mortars, rockets, and heavy artillery. Such attacks on urban areas only meant mass casualties. While the civil war lasted, print media published and television beamed images of houses with visible remnants of mortars, heavy artillery shells, and rockets—including Grad rockets. In the Nafusa Mountains and Misurata, snipers indiscriminately shot at protesters and demonstrators.

As protests and demonstrations spread from Benghazi and other eastern cities to the western towns and cities of Misurata, Zawiya, Zuwara, Zintan, and Tripoli, the capital, government forces also increased attacks on demonstrators. More and more people were arrested and detained. The Human Rights Watch and media began to report the large-scale use of lethal force on protesters, the disappearances of hundreds of people, the mass killing of antigovernment demonstrators, and other atrocities.

When protests broke out in Tripoli on February 20, Saif Al-Islam, one of Gaddafi's sons, justified the government's arrests and detention as part of efforts at preventing further protests. Among thousands of Libyans arrested were notable politicians and opinion leaders such as Jamal Al-Hajji, who was arrested on February 1, 2011, and Farag Sharany, arrested on February 15, 2011. On February 16, 2011, four brothers—Farag, Al-Mahdi, Sadiq, and Ali Hameid—were also arrested and detained.

Saif al-Islam Gaddafi also warned Libyans that the protests could submerge the country in a civil war. He blamed the protests and demonstration on foreign agitators, especially the United States and its Western allies, and vowed that the government would fight the protesters and demonstrators "to the last bullet." Between February 20 and February 24, 2011, the Gaddafi-led government used excessive force against the protesters. There were reported cases of live ammunition being used to disperse and suppress the protests. The use of excessive force began with Kalashnikov assault rifles and other small arms fire but soon graduated to include heavy machine guns, cluster munitions, anti-aircraft guns, and other heavy weapons. From February 20 onward, Gaddafi forces used anti-aircraft and heavy machine guns against protesters in Zawiya and Misurata, Tripoli and Benghazi, Al-Bayda and Derna, Tobruk and Ajdabiya, among other sites. In these places, large numbers of civilians were killed while tens of thousands were injured.

As the civil war escalated and government forces became more brutal, rumors of different kinds circulated. It was rumored that "death squads," composed of soldiers, mercenaries, and Revolutionary Committee members, were established by Gaddafi himself. Members of these death squads were said to often shoot people who gathered in groups or who tried to assist the wounded or evacuate dead bodies from the streets. It was also rumored that the heads of Gaddafi's military units executed soldiers who refused to fire on protesters. The International Federation for Human Rights claimed that about 130 soldiers were executed for refusing to open fire on protesters and demonstrators.

In a report on February 24, the International Federation for Human Rights maintained that there was no truth to the existence of such death squads and that most of the atrocities allegedly committed by the Gaddafi-led government during the civil war were not true. However, the organization maintained that, while Gaddafi and his men might not have perpetrated such evils, they implemented a scorched-earth strategy and that "it is reasonable to fear that he has, in fact, decided to largely eliminate, wherever he still can, Libyan citizens who stood up against his regime and furthermore, to systematically and indiscriminately repress civilians."[1] According to the International Criminal Court, between February 15 and 25, 2011, government forces killed about 755 Libyans.

The attacks, the court reported, were ordered at the highest levels of government. This report was consistent with Saif al-Islam Gaddafi's speech on February 20, 2011, that "the army from now [sic] will have a key role in imposing security and in returning things to normal at any price." Muammar Gaddafi corroborated his son's declaration on February 23, 2011: "[W]e shall move and [sic] the millions to sanitize Libya an inch at a time, a home at a time, a house at a time, an alley at a time, one by one until the country is rid of the filth and uncleanliness."[2] He concluded by adding that "officers have been deployed to their tribes and their areas to lead these tribes and these areas, secure them, clear them of these rats."[3]

Rather than dousing the protests, these speeches served to escalate things, as demonstrators in Benghazi set up an interim government—the National Transitional Council (NTC)—on February 27. The NTC aimed to coordinate the resistance and to consolidate efforts by rebel forces to change the government of Libya. In addition, it sets itself up as an opposition to the Gaddafi-led government of Libya. Acting as an interim government, the NTC called for a no-fly zone over Libya. In addition, it demanded air strikes against the Jamahiriya. With the protesters' control of Benghazi, the Gaddafi-led government increased its efforts at securing other parts of Libya, while at the same time fighting to regain control of Benghazi.

At this point, what started as peaceful protests had become a full-scale civil war, and former protesters had become rebels, especially in government rhetoric. As the government unleashed the full force of its military on the rebel forces in Benghazi and the surrounding areas, dead bodies piled up on the streets and in the alleys.

In Misurata, Zentan, and Derna, different rebel groups, composed primarily of teachers, students, lawyers, and oil workers, were soon joined by defected police officers and professional soldiers. In both eastern and western Libya, hundreds of Islamists also joined the rebel movement. For example, the so-called February 17 Brigade in Benghazi was a coalition of 12 strong Islamist groups. Others included the Libyan Islamic Fighting Group, Obaida Ibn Jarrah Brigade, and Libya Shield, a group of Islamists based in Misurata and Zaria.

The Gaddafi-led government noted that the rebels were aided by a number of mercenaries from within and outside Africa. In a Libyan television report, a government official reported the arrests and detention of "criminal gangs and mercenaries" from Tunisia, Turkey, and Egypt that were "trained to sow chaos."[4] Dozens of Americans, South Africans and many nationals of other European nations were also arrested, fighting for the rebels. Others included individuals and groups from Nigeria, Niger, Chad, Ghana, and other countries. Libya's Jamahiriya News Agency reported that these men were part of a foreign network trained to scuttle Libya's socioeconomic and political stability by Western nations, especially the United States, Great Britain, and France.

While evidence of any foreign government involvements was rare, it is worth noting that Qatar provided military and economic assistance to the rebels. As published in *The Wall Street Journal* on October 17, 2011, Qatari military advisors, under the direction of Sheikh Hamad bin Jassim al-Thani, the Qatari prime minister, supported the rebels, providing them with "defensive weaponry" that included "tens of millions of US dollars in aid, military training and more than 20,000 tons of weapons."[5] In both spring and summer of 2011 alone, Qatar delivered 18 weapons shipments to rebel forces. NTC-allied officials confirmed to *The Wall Street Journal* that weapons, money, and aid flowed directly to the rebels from Qatar. Ali al-Sallabi, a cleric, was believed to have facilitated this free flow of weapons, aid, and money from Qatar. This flow from Qatar did not stop, even after Gaddafi had been overthrown, as a rebel faction, February 17 Katiba, continued to enjoy dozens of the Qatari shipments of weapons, money, and aid.

Besides provisions of weapons, money, and other aid, Qatar also trained rebel fighters, especially in the Nafusa Mountains. Many were flown to Doha for special training. In the final assault on Bab al-Azizia compound on August 24, 2011, special forces from Qatar fought side by side with the rebels to topple Gaddafi's government. Qatar was the first nation to recognize the NTC as a legitimate government of Libya and to cooperate with it. Russia followed suit in May 2011. China recognized the NTC and met with its representatives in Beijing on June 9, 2011. Many European nations, including the United States, also gave recognition to the NTC and extended aid and military assistance to it.

The use of mercenaries and foreign forces was not only limited to rebel forces alone, as the Gaddafi-led government also employed mercenaries in its regime protection fight. Ali al-Essawi, Libya's ambassador to India, justified government use of mercenaries on two grounds. On the one hand was the fact that Libyan soldiers found it difficult to open fire on fellow Libyans, a situation that served the interests of the rebels. On the other hand, was the defections of military units to the ranks of the rebels. Nouri al Mesmari, Gaddafi's chief of protocol, admitted in an interview with Al Jazeera that mercenaries recruited from Niger, Mali, Chad, and Kenya were among the foreign soldiers fighting the rebels. Many African governments denied this claim, with the African Union chairman, Jean Ping, warning that confusing anyone with black complexion for a mercenary is tantamount to saying that one-third of the population of Libya, which is black, is also mercenaries, a situation that could lead to the persecution of Libyans and immigrant workers from other African countries.

Notwithstanding Ping's warning, evidence abounds to support that Gaddafi recruited about 5,000 mercenaries from Mali, Chad, Sudan, Nigeria, Ghana, and Lebanon. As locals from these countries confirmed, posters and fliers were freely distributed in towns and villages, seeking recruits to fight in Libya, promising to pay $10,000 up front and a final per-day compensation of up to $1,000.

As far as West Africa was concerned, a hotel in Bamako, Mali, served as a recruitment center. As Malian government officials told the BBC, the government found it difficult to stop recruitment from Mali, as many youths found the incentives too appealing. In Ghana, Niger, Chad, and Nigeria, reports showed that recruits were offered $2,500 per day. In addition to these African countries and Malta, EU experts stated that the Gaddafi-led government recruited about 500 European soldiers from different EU countries, especially Serbia and Yugoslavia, at high wages.

Owing to the increasing violence and deaths, immigrant workers and thousands of Libyans fled, as different Western nations and the United States of America issued travel warnings to their nationals. Many foreign citizens in Libya trooped to their embassies, demanding immediate evacuation, as things deteriorated. Protesters, media, and human right groups began to call on the international community to pay close attention to the situation in Libya.

In an apparent attempt to weaken the opposition, Mustafa Abdul Jalil, the former minister of justice, announced that the Gaddafi-led government was prepared for elections. *The Guardian* newspaper later published the government's eight-point plan for Libya on March 29. The plan included a draft national constitution and promised free and fair elections. The NTC rejected the government's plan.

Foreign leaders and human rights organizations across the world condemned the government's handling of the protests and the escalation of violence against protesters and other civilians. Scores of Libyan ambassadors and diplomats resigned their positions, as they could no longer defend the Gaddafi-led government. Libya's ambassadors to the United Nations, Arab League, and European Union as well as those of Australia, Bangladesh, Belgium, France, India, Indonesia, Malaysia, Nigeria, Portugal, Sweden, and the United States resigned from their posts. While many of them did not join the opposition, a large majority denounced the Gaddafi-led government. In a number of Libyan embassies where ambassadors remained in their posts, many hoisted Libya's old national flag, as a sign of support for the uprising.

Within the government, a number of high-level officials also resigned. Among others, Justice Minister Mustafa Abdul Jalil and Interior

Minister Major General Abdul Fatah Younis resigned from the Gaddafi-led government and joined the opposition. Oil Minister Shukri Ghanem and Prosecutor General Abdul-Rahman al-Abbar also resigned and joined the opposition, while Foreign Minister Moussa Koussa fled to the UK after resigning his position. Those who did not resign issued statements condemning the government's handling of protesters.

Besides members of the government and ambassadors, members of the deposed royal family also played roles in the civil war. For instance, the son of the former Crown Prince and grand-nephew of King Idris, Muhammad al-Sanussi, encouraged the demonstrators and protesters in speeches and newspaper reports, describing the slain protesters and demonstrators as heroes and heroines who laid down their lives for the country. In addition, Muhammad, in an interview with Al Jazeera on February 24 pleaded with the international community "to halt all support for the dictator with immediate effect"[6] and for help in removing Gaddafi from power and stopping the ongoing "massacre." He assured the world that the protesters would be "victorious in the end" and, at the European Union Parliament on April 20, called for the imposition of a no-fly zone over Libya as a way to stop the Gaddafi-led government from using aircraft in gunning down protesters and demonstrators. Idris bin Abdullah al-Sanussi, another member of the royal family, met with staffers of the State Department and Congress in Washington, DC. Like Muhammad, Abdullah also pleaded with the international community for help in removing Gaddafi and restoring a democratic government in Libya.

From the military, many senior officials also defected to the opposition. Notable among them were General Abdul Fatah Younis, General al-Barani Ashkal, Major General Suleiman Mahmoud, and Brigadier General Musa'ed. Others included Ghaidan Al Mansouri, Brigadier General Hassan Ibrahim Al Qarawi, Brigadier General Dawood Issa Al Qafsi, and Colonel Nuretin Hurala, the commander of the Benghazi Naval Base. In addition to these, two Libyan Air Force colonels who were ordered to carry out airstrikes against demonstrators and protesters in Benghazi, flew their Mirage F1 fighter jets to Malta, where they sought asylum. These and other professional soldiers who joined the protesters, provided the much-needed military education and training to the protesters and demonstrators.

The establishment of armed opposition groups in different parts of Libya and the formation of a parallel government in Benghazi took the Libyan civil war to another level. Although these groups were composed mainly of Libyans at the beginning, foreigners—some from the United States, Europe, and Africa—later joined them in fighting

Gaddafi. In tandem with these foreigners, rebels picked up arms against the government as the government escalated its attacks on the rebels. As early as February 20, rebel forces overran a number of a military barracks and police stations in Zawiya and Misurata, carting away thousands of arms and ammunitions, including heavy military ordnance.

As noted in the United Nations Commission of Inquiry report, by February 24, 2011, a full-scale armed conflict had begun between government and rebel forces. As rebel forces acquired government arms and other weapons from military barracks and depots, they began to gain control of large areas, beginning with Benghazi. Defected military units aided rebel forces, and, within weeks, the rebels began to expel most of the pro-Gaddafi troops from towns and cities in both eastern and western Libya. By February 25, rebel forces opened the Libyan-Egyptian border, a development that allowed aid and foreign journalists into Libya.

Following the deployment of excessive force in an attempt to suppress the protests, international pressure began to mount on Gaddafi to step down. Consequently, the United Nations Security Council, on February 26, imposed numerous sanctions on the Gaddafi-led government. Included in these sanctions were the freezing of assets belonging to Gaddafi, members of his family, and members of his inner circle. Restrictions were also placed on their travels. Member nations of the United Nations were prohibited from selling arms to Libya. A critical part of the United Nations Security Council's sanctions was the referral of the situation in Libya to the International Criminal Court (ICC) for possible violations of international law and gross human rights abuses, including crimes against humanity.

Like the United Nations, the European Union, Great Britain, United States, and more than 30 other nations also imposed economic, military, diplomatic, consular, and other sanctions on Libya. Libya's total assets amounting to, at least, $30 billion were frozen in the United States alone.

Despite sanctions and resolutions against the Gaddafi-led government of Libya, government forces continued to push eastward, and, in early March, they retook several coastal cities and towns near Benghazi. Following this, a further UN resolution, authorizing member states to establish and enforce a no-fly zone over Libya, was imposed. This new UN resolution mandated member nations to deploy any measure whatsoever to prevent further attacks on civilians.

Concerted foreign intervention in Libya commenced with Canada's deployment of the Royal Canadian Navy frigate HMCS *Charlottetown* to the Mediterranean off the coast of Libya on March 2, 2011. The Royal Canadian Navy did not immediately engage the Gaddafi-led government, as it waited for another 17 days when a multistate coalition, tasked with the implementation of the United Nations Security Council Resolution 1973, intervened on the side of the rebels in Libya.

In addition to the Royal Canadian Air Force, U.S. and British forces fired cruise missiles and engaged in other military operations with their submarines against military establishments and pro-Gaddafi targets within Libya. The French Air Force also undertook sorties across Libya. Other nations that participated in the all-out war against the Gaddafi-led government of Libya were Belgium, Denmark, Italy, Norway, and Spain. Many nations that did not participate in the coalition enforced the no-fly zone and provided military and logistical aid to the rebels.

At the forefront of the effort to rid Libya of Gaddafi was the United States. Gaddafi, in speeches from different hideouts, left no one in doubt that the insurrection against his government was orchestrated by the United States. While there was no iota of truth in such a claim, the United States could not be totally divorced from the rate of change the rebels witnessed, and, without the contributions of the United States and other foreign parties, the rebels would not have defeated the Gaddafi-led government.

Under the auspices of Operation Unified Protector, the North Atlantic Treaty Organization (NATO) spearheaded the arms embargo on Libya on March 23, 2011. NATO's primary mandate was to protect civilians; however, its mission was extended to cover the giving of air support to the rebels, and, in this capacity, NATO prevented Benghazi and other towns and cities in eastern Libya from being reconquered by government forces. NATO coordinated the aerial bombardments on the Gaddafi-led government and implemented the no-fly zone resolution of the UN. The coalition forces, ably led by the United States, coordinated the ground units. France, Qatar, and the United Arab Emirates trained rebel forces and also provided weapons to them. Unlike others, Qatar also deployed hundreds of its own forces on the ground.

With the NATO-led aerial bombardment, the Gaddafi-led government soon found itself incapable of dislodging the rebels, who had been equipped and trained by militaries of Qatar, the United States and other European nations. Within days, the Gaddafi-led government announced a ceasefire. Prior to announcing a ceasefire, the International Criminal Court issued arrest warrants for Gaddafi, Saif al-Islam—Gaddafi's son—and Abdullah Sanussi, the intelligence chief and brother-in-law of Gaddafi on charges of crimes against humanity.

Seeking to end the civil war, the African Union (AU) submitted a proposal for a ceasefire; however, the rebels rejected the proposal on the ground that there was no provision for Gaddafi's removal in it. On August 20, the rebels, aided by a wide reaching NATO bombing campaign, began its final push for the government-held nation's capital, Tripoli. The state house was captured and looted, but Gaddafi escaped.

On September 16, 2011, the United Nations replaced the Gaddafi-led government with the National Transitional Council as the legal representative of Libya in the United Nations. At this point, the question of whether Muammar Gaddafi's 42 years of rule in Libya would end had been settled; the new question was for how long Gaddafi would evade capture. Isolated and ensconced among his ethnic group in Sirte, Gaddafi accused the United States, Great Britain, and other Western nations of plotting his fall in order to gain complete control of Libya's oil wealth.

In strings of cellphone videos on October 20, 2011, Gaddafi's last moments were captured by rebel fighters. He was captured and killed in an open field in Sirte. In one video, the longest serving Libyan leader was seen bleeding on the hood of a truck. He struggled to steady himself, as rebel fighters pushed and pulled him from all sides. In yet another video, he was seen on the ground, as rebel fighters grabbed the hairs on his bloodied head. His trousers were drenched with blood, and bullet holes could be seen on his chest. While the very moment when he was murdered was not shown, later photographs showed his dead body riddled with bullet holes.

Commenting on Gaddafi's death, U.S. President Barack Obama said:

We can definitely say that the Gaddafi regime has come to an end. The dark shadow of tyranny has been lifted, and with this enormous promise the Libyan people now have a great responsibility to build an inclusive and tolerant and democratic Libya that stands as the ultimate rebuke to Gaddafi's dictatorship.[7]

On October 23, 2011, following Gaddafi's death, the National Transitional Council announced the end of his regime and the birth of a new Libya, invariably signaling the official end of the war.

WHY DID THE REVOLUTION HAPPEN?

The Arab Spring, whether in Tunisia or Egypt, was a revolutionary wave of demonstrations and protests that began in Tunisia on December 18, 2010, following Mohamed Bouazizi's self-immolation, and that led to major government changes in Tunisia and Egypt. As this chapter has shown, it also led to a civil war in Libya, which resulted in the death of Gaddafi and the fall of his 42-year-old regime. In other places, especially Syria, Yemen Bahrain, Jordan, Morocco, Algeria, Oman, Iraq, Kuwait, Saudi Arabia, and Sudan, it led to civil uprisings and major protests. In these countries, thousands of ordinary citizens using strikes, demonstrations, marches, and rallies demanded institutional reforms and regime changes. Particularly important was the coordination of the protests and demonstrations through social media.

Anne Applebaum, comparing the Arab Spring with the spate of revolutions in 1848 and 1989 in Europe, argued, "Each revolution must be assessed in its own context, each had a distinctive impact. The revolutions spread from one point to another. The drama of each revolution unfolded separately. Each had its own heroes, its own crisis. Each therefore demands its own narrative."[8] While the heroes and narratives of the Libyan revolution or Arab Spring have been told in the previous section, this section aims at explaining the Arab Spring in Libya within the context of Libyan history.

While not discounting the importance of people's reactions to the police's mishandling of demonstrators and protesters following the arrest of a human rights lawyer in explaining the civil war, this event cannot explain why Libyans picked up arms against the state, ending the life of Gaddafi, Libya's longest serving head of government. At best, it could be argued that the arrest of the human rights lawyer was the immediate cause of the civil war; what, then, were the remote causes of the Libyan Arab Spring?

Although the Libyan revolution shared similar characteristics with its counterparts in Tunisia and Egypt, it differs remarkably from both Tunisian and Egyptian revolutions. Underlying Libya's Arab Spring were the unholy alliances between economic depression and corruption, coupled with the suppression of individual liberties and the violent nature of the government under Gaddafi. As will be noted in Chapter 9, Libya endured a series of sanctions over incidences of terrorism, most especially the various plane hijacking and bombings in different places that were allegedly traced to the Gaddafi-led government of Libya. While the sanctions lasted, Libya was at the threshold of economic collapse. Various United Nations agencies reported incidences of hunger, poor and collapsing socioeconomic infrastructure such as roads, bridges, hospitals, public utilities, housing, transportation, and agriculture, as well as other issues.

Libya was on the edge of economic collapse in 1999; hence, the Gaddafi-led government undertook a rigid economic reform program, which transformed the economy from a socialist, state-planned economy to a capitalist, market-based economy. This economic reform program transformed the vital sectors of the economy, especially in training Libyan youths to find new jobs rather than depending on state-provided jobs, encouraging private sector investments in the economy, and the privatization of public enterprises. This attempt at structurally adjusting Libya's economy was aimed at curbing inflation, reducing the balance of payment deficit, and creating employment and growth. The policy failed to attain any of its goals in Libya due, in part, to the fact that the oil crisis impacted negatively on the government's ability to fund other sectors. Other factors that prevented Libya from achieving structural balance in its economy related to endemic corruption and the easy revenue accruable from oil, which cultivated, among other things, an obtuse fascination with imported goods. The policy failed to stop importation, and the problems associated with irregularity in supply and demand led to price hikes and created balance of payments problems. In addition, government fiscal policy continued to exceed expenditure.

To reduce expenditure, the government stopped subsidizing basic essential commodities, many infrastructural projects were abandoned, taxes were increased on consumer goods, while local and foreign investors were granted taxation exemptions on customs and duties in order to stimulate growth. The outcome of these included economic impoverishment of the masses, mass retrenchment, a staggering rise in food prices, high rates of unemployment, especially among youth below the age of 25 (approximately 65 percent of the total population), a decreasing economic base in the face of an increasing population, structural distortions in the economy, official graft and corruption, and on and on. So, rather than bringing about prosperity, the Structural Adjustment Program (SAP) widened the gaps between the rich and poor in Libya, as it did elsewhere.

As seen in Libya, so it was with other Arab-speaking countries of Africa and the Middle East that adopted the World Bank and International Monetary Fund (IMF) policy of SAP in the 1980s. Economic recession and financial pressures therefore were important factors, if not the main catalysts, that drove the Libyan Arab Spring. This situation was exacerbated by egregious corruption among the ruling elites.

Many of the Libyan youths that protested and demonstrated during the Libyan revolution of 2011 were born and raised during this period in Libyan history. Many were unable to get jobs, even after their university education. They had no decent accommodation, as lack of economic power forced many to live with their parents. Not only were they unable to process the socioeconomic and political situation that Libya found itself, they also had no past to look to for inspiration.

Despite numerous provisions for popular participation in governance in both the constitution and Gaddafi's *Green Book*, Libya (under Gaddafi) was a military dictatorship. The repressive and violent nature of military dictatorship was one of the major factors in the 2011 Libyan Arab Spring. Political apathy was rife in Libya, and, rather than embarking upon mass political literacy, the Gaddafi-led government appointed his henchmen and women into positions. So, while Libya looked like a democratic setup, it was indeed a military autocracy. Political power was shared among Gaddafi's friends and family members. Rather than opening up the political space, Gaddafi cultivated, in government position, many of his friends and family members, members of his ethnic group, and loyalists. This system of absolute rule paved the way for succession within his family and assured a socioeconomic and political system that thrived on ethnic and sectarian sentiments.

To perpetuate the system, Gaddafi routinely use all the instruments of physical violence. Incidences of abductions and disappearances, unwarranted arrests, torture, unfair trials, assassinations, and terrorism were commonplace. Basic and fundamental individual liberties like freedom of speech and freedom of expression, freedom of the press and freedom of organization, freedom of association and access to justice were replaced by political expediency.

The Gaddafi-led government dominated and monopolized the media and was intolerant of opposing views. Public education was also censored, and the free flow of ideas in books, newspapers, and public debates was frowned upon. Libya was a highly authoritarian system where political power resided with Gaddafi and his cronies.

Government agents and secret police routinely harassed journalists, human rights activists, politicians, and trade unionists. Political opponents were sometimes arrested and tried on trumped-up charges and false accusations in order to silence them. Many, including lawyers, journalists, and professors, were under constant surveillance. They were oftentimes blackmailed and sometimes physically abused. In addition to the loss of their jobs, many people were subjected to unfair trials and sentenced to lengthy imprisonments.

The denial of political freedoms and state repression, coupled with the failure of the government to democratize the political space so as to accommodate the youth, were some of the long-term factors in the Libyan Arab Spring. Others included developmental gaps between the various regions and ethnic groups within Libya, as the nation's economic wealth was controlled by a few private individuals who successfully adapted the state for their personal enrichment. These coalesced in a crushing poverty and set the stage for a popular uprising.

Another important factor in understanding why the Libyan Arab Spring occurred was the advent of the new digital age, an age that was characterized by new tools such as Facebook, Twitter, WhatsApp, YouTube, and other social media platforms that allowed for real-time communication among a large number of people. With the reduced cost of mobile telephoning and increasing access to the Internet, information and resources were freely available to young Libyans, and they, in turn, were able to share information and resources in an instant with their friends and peers across the world. This instant, digital communication was beyond the control of the state, and, during the civil war, the government made a series of efforts to censure its use but to no avail.

So when Fathi Terbil was arrested and sympathizers gathered to protest his arrest, images of police brutality against protesters were recorded and broadcast via social media as the events were happening. This was a newer development, a development that the Gaddafi-led government was unprepared for and therefore unable to manage. The ease with which protesters and demonstrators and, later, rebels coordinated large groups of people across widened areas through social media platforms was unprecedented in the history of Libya.

As revolutionary as these new tools were, they were also prone to abuse. For example, many of the horrible images and videos shared among demonstrators and protesters during the Libyan Arab Springs were deliberately doctored. Some were images from the Arab Spring in Tunisia, while others were from Egypt. The unsuspecting demonstrators and protesters were too incensed to know the difference. They just went by these images and videos and vented their anger on the Gaddafi-led government.

Given all this, it can be argued that the arrest of Fathi Terbil by the Gaddafi-led government of Libya was just an incidental factor in the Libyan Arab Spring. The main or the long-term causes of the revolution that swept away Gaddafi and his 42-year-old government included economic deterioration in the face of government corruption, coupled with many years of repressive rule and suppression of individual liberties. This dense landscape of unsavory conditions was exacerbated by the advent of new digital tools that allowed the spread of information, including unfounded rumors and outright falsehood, at the push of a button or a keystroke.

A number of key issues that have come to light following the death of Gaddafi were arrests of real or imagined enemies and the commission of crimes against humanity. Between February and August, tens of thousands of ordinary citizens and suspected government critics, doctors and teachers, international journalists and their informants, members of human right organizations and rebel fighters were arrested by Gaddafi forces across the country. The Gaddafi-led government offered no information on the number of people arrested or where they were detained. None was charged in any court. Following the fall of Gaddafi, all the people arrested and detained during the protests and demonstrations, as well as during the civil war, were released. Many reported incidences of beatings with wooden sticks and plastic pipes, electrocution, and other forms of torture. Many died in custody, while many disappeared without a trace.

In its efforts to defeat the rebels, the Gaddafi-led government launched attacks with mortars and Russian BM-21 "Grad" rockets, mortar-fired cluster munitions, and antivehicle mines fired by Grad rockets in residential areas. In different parts of Libya, especially Ajdabiya, Brega, Misurata, and the western mountains, the government laid tens of thousands of antipersonnel and antivehicle land mines. As the Human Rights Watch noted, the Gaddafi-led government made frequent use of the Brazilian T-AB-1 antipersonnel land mine because of its low metal content, which makes it more difficult to detect and clear.

Hundreds of mass graves have been found since the demise of Gaddafi. About 45 bodies were found in a warehouse in Tripoli, while 34 bodies were exhumed from a mass grave in al-Qawalish. In al-Khoms, 18 bodies were found in a mass grave, while evidence abounds to support an execution of about 10 antigovernment protesters and protesters in Bani Walid.

In areas under National Transition Council (NTC) control, rebel groups were wont to arrest hundreds of people on suspicion of being loyal to Gaddafi. Many of these people were tortured. According to the Human Rights Watch, at least 10 former Gaddafi security officials were killed by rebels in Benghazi and Derna in what appeared to be revenge killings. One other was killed in Baida by a local security group in revenge for supporting Gaddafi.

Many immigrant workers from neighboring African countries experienced violence and arbitrary arrest. Some of these migrants and dark-skinned Libyans were murdered on suspicion of being Gaddafi's mercenaries. It was believed that the death of General Abdul Fatah Younis and his two aides in July was carried out by a commander of one of the opposition forces. In October, rebel forces from Misurata executed 53 Gaddafi supporters in Sirte. As the rebels moved from one part of Libya to another, they left behind trails of revenge killings, looting, arson, and physical violence.

Three days after Gaddafi's death, the bodies of 53 of his supporters were found in front of the Mahari Hotel in Sirte. They were murdered by rebel fighters from Misurata in a revenge killing.

Rebel fighters from Misurata abused and killed their neighbors, the people of Tawergha, accusing them of allying with Gaddafi forces during the siege of Misurata. Over 30,000 people of Tawergha were prevented from returning to their homes after the civil war. Many of these displaced Tawerghans were arrested and tortured in detention. Although many survived their ordeals, a large number lost their lives either from torture or for lack of medical care.

In the western mountains, members of the Mesheshiya ethnic group were abused and killed for their loyalty to Gaddafi. Revenge attacks and killings of populations that were considered Gaddafi loyalists and supporters were common, even after the end of the civil war.

One of the most fundamental drivers of this situation was the presence of a large number of local security forces in Tripoli, Benghazi, and other cities and towns in Libya. Many, if not all, of these local security forces possessed detention facilities where they detained many who were deemed enemies of the revolution and loyal to Gaddafi.

Atrocious activities were not limited to Gaddafi forces and rebel fighters; NATO forces led by the French and British, with the support of the United States, also committed human rights violations. For instance, in early August, the Human Rights Watch investigated four sites in Gaddafi government–held territory of western Libya and found the bodies of 53 civilians killed in NATO bombardments and air strikes. NATO forces also failed to rescue African migrants who were fleeing Libya by sea. In one of the many boats that capsized on the Mediterranean, 63 bodies were recovered. NATO has yet to explain its refusal to protect refugees and the displaced, as well as the high civilian casualties associated with its air strikes.

NOTES

1. James Ohwofasa Akpeninor, *Giant in the Sun: Echoes of Looming Revolution?* (Bloomington, IN: Author House, 2012), 247.

2. International Legal Assistance Consortium, Report of the Independent Civil Society Fact-Finding Mission to Libya, January 2012. Accessed September 14, 2018, at https://reliefweb.int/sites/reliefweb.int/files/resources/Full%20Report_481.pdf

3. Ibid., 21.

4. Ronald Bruce St. John, *Libya: From Colony to Revolution* (Oxford: Oneworld Publications, 2011), 280.

5. Ibid., 286.

6. Marie-Louise Gumuchian, "Gaddafi Nears His End, Exiled Libyan Prince Says," in Reuters, February 22, 2011. Accessed September 14, 2018, at https://www.reuters.com/article/us-libya-protests-prince/gaddafi-nears -his-end-exiled-libyan-prince-says-idUSTRE71L5Y920110222

7. Kareem Fahim, Anthony Shadid, and Rick Gladstone, "Violent End to an Era as Qaddafi Dies in Libya," in *New York Times*, October 21, 2011. Accessed September 14, 2018, at https://www.nytimes.com/2011/10/21 /world/africa/qaddafi-is-killed-as-libyan-forces-take-surt.html

8. Anne Applebaum, "Every Revolution Is Different," February 21, 2011. Accessed September 14, 2018, at http://www.slate.com/articles /news_and_politics/foreigners/2011/02/every_revolution_is_different .html

9

Libyan Civil War, Global Terrorism, and the Rise of the Islamic State

INTRODUCTION

Nine months after the start of the Arab Spring in Libya, Muammar Gaddafi's 42-year government collapsed. With Gaddafi's death, Libyan protesters and demonstrators, rebels, and the international community recorded the first killing of a head of state and government in the Arab Spring uprisings. Prior to his killing, Gaddafi, in a public broadcast, alerted Libyans and the world that al-Qaeda and Islamic State of Iraq and Syria (ISIS) elements had hijacked the uprisings. Al-Qaeda was established by Osama bin Laden, Abdullah Azzam, and many Arab volunteers, as a network of Salafi Islamic groups during the Soviet invasion of Afghanistan in 1988. Al-Qaeda sponsored and carried out the September 11 terrorist attacks that brought down the twin towers of the World Trade Center, killing about 3,000 people in the United States. Al-Qaeda and its affiliates have also carried out series of terrorist attacks in the Middle East, Europe, the United States, Africa, and elsewhere.

ISIS—also known as the Islamic State of Iraq and the Levant (ISIL)— is also a Salafi Islamic group that sacked the Iraqi government and drove its forces out of Western Iraq in 2014. Like al-Qaeda, ISIS and its affiliates have also carried out terrorist attacks in different parts of the world. The United Nations Security Council, the European Union (EU), the North Atlantic Treaty Organization (NATO), the African Union (AU), and many other nations, including the United States, the United Kingdom, Russia, India, among others, designated both al-Qaeda and ISIS as terrorist groups.

When Gaddafi made his broadcast, no one took his claim seriously, as many regarded it as part of his regime-protection strategies. Did Gaddafi have any intelligence to back up his claims? Although the former Libyan ruler was killed without any formal trial or any attempt at extracting information of any kind, events since Gaddafi's death have since shown that elements of al-Qaeda, ISIS, and many other extremist Islamic groups participated in the Libyan revolution. This chapter examines the rise of extremist Islamic groups, including al-Qaeda and ISIS, in the wake of the Libyan revolution.

LIBYAN CIVIL WAR AND THE RISE OF GLOBAL TERRORISM

One month after Gaddafi's death and the liberation of Libya, Mahmoud Jibril and other members of the National Transitional Council proposed the formation of an interim government. As planned, the interim government would, within eight months, organize and supervise the elections into a constitutional assembly and, within one year, organize and supervise elections to the parliament and the presidency.

Winning 26 out of 51 votes, Abdurrahim El-Keib emerged as the prime minister in the interim government, while Osama al-Juwaili was named minister of defense. Other members were Fawzi Abdelali, the minister of the interior; Ashour Bin Hayal, the minister of foreign affairs; Hassan Ziglam, the minister of finance; Ali Hameda Ashour, the minister of justice; and Abdulrahman Ben Yezza, the oil minister. Yousef al-Manqoush was made the head of the Libyan National Army. Many of these men were also heads of militia groups. For example, Osama al-Juwaili was a commander of the military council in Zintan, while Fawzi Abdelali led a militia group from Misurata. Yousef al-Manqoush was one of the military men who defected from the Gaddafi-led government and joined the demonstrators and protesters.

No sooner was the interim government formed than internal crises arose within it. On October 14, 2012, Abdurrahim el-Keib was removed, and Ali Zeidan replaced him as prime minister. Within two weeks of assuming office, Zeidan proposed a new government, composed of individuals from different rebel and militia groups. Notwithstanding these crises, the new administration announced a popular election for July 7, 2012. The General National Congress (GNC), Libya's legislative authority composed of 200 members, took over power from the interim government on August 8, 2012. Of the 200 members of the GNC, 80 were elected through party lists as a way to ensure proportional representation, while the remaining members were individuals from all walks of life.

The interim government formally handed over power to the GNC on August 8, 2012, and Mohammed Ali Salim, the oldest member of the GNC, was made the head of state. The dissolution of the interim government and the handing over of power to the GNC marked the first peaceful transition of power in Libya's history.

The GNC, which was given 18 months to achieve its mandates, was saddled with the responsibility of transitioning post-Gaddafi Libya into a permanent democratic nation. Its responsibilities also included the appointment of a prime minister and a cabinet. Although the GNC was unable to draw up a new constitution for Libya at the end of its 18-month tenure, it organized elections to a newly established House of Representatives—also known as the Council of Deputies.

Although turnout was poor, the election of June 25, 2014, saw the emergence of the Council of Deputies as the legislative assembly for Libya. The Council formed the new government, replacing the GNC on August 4, 2014. While Aguila Saleh Issa emerged as the chairman of the Council, both Imhemed Shaib and Ahmed Huma emerged as deputy presidents of the Council. Abdullah al-Thani was made the prime minister.

Many members of the GNC ran in the election. While some were reelected to the newly established Council of Deputies, others were not. On August 25, 2014, those who were not reelected gathered in Tripoli and formed the National Salvation Government (NSG). These disgruntled former members of the GNC appointed Omar al-Hasi as prime minister. In addition to enjoying the support of Libyans in western Libya, the NSG also enjoyed support of many militias, especially the Libyan Revolutionary Operation Room (LROR) and Central Shield armed groups. The Tripoli-based group, however, did not enjoy the support of the international community.

During the election, voting was disrupted in the Kufra area where the Tebous engaged government forces and in Benghazi where activists sought autonomy for eastern Libya and an election official was killed.

Efforts to disrupt elections by closing five oil terminals at Brega, Ra's Lanuf, and Sidra were curtailed, while in Ajdabiya, local militias killed a profederalism protester who stole a ballot box. In general, voting did not take place in about 6 percent (6,629) of the polling stations. Disruptions, violent protests and killings notwithstanding, about 1.7 million (61.58 percent) registered voters voted across Libya in the elections.

Although the international community and many nations acknowledged the low voter turn-out, they nevertheless accepted and recognized the GNC as the legitimate government of Libya. The NSG, however, rejected the results of the election, claiming low turnout, voter fraud, and the absence of voting in some areas, among other things.

For a fact, only about 61.58 percent of registered voters participated in the election, and in some locations, security concerns prevented voting. The NSG buttressed its position with the fact that Libya's Supreme Constitutional Court ruled that the elections were unconstitutional, calling for the dissolution of the Council of Deputies. The Council of Deputies, however, rejected NSG's claims, citing the fact that the Supreme Court delivered its November 6, 2014, judgment at gunpoint, having been surrounded by armed NSG supporters and militias.

With the Council of Deputies' refusal to dissolve the government, the NSG organized a rival parliament in Tripoli, which proclaimed itself as the new legislative assembly for Libya. The NSG-organized legislative assembly in Tripoli was composed mainly of members of the Justice and Construction Party, an arm of the Muslim Brotherhood.

In this way, two governments emerged in Libya: the Council of Deputies, a democratically elected government, and the Tripoli-based factional government of the GNC. The Council of Deputies enjoyed the support of the international community, United States, Great Britain, Egypt, the United Arab Emirates, and Libyans, especially in the eastern part of the country. In addition, a number of other militia groups, for instance, the Haftar-led Libyan National Army, also supported the Council of Deputies. In turn, the NSG enjoyed the support of Qatar, Sudan, and Turkey, as well as the support of religious extremist groups like the Muslim Brotherhood, an Islamist coalition called the Libya Dawn, and other militia groups. The NSG also had a huge followership in western Libya. Since 2014, there have been incessant conflicts between these two "governments."

Just as intrigues among competing groups and interests emerged at the national level—leading to incessant change of government, local militias, vigilante groups, and Islamic insurgents, including al-Qaeda and ISIS, took over most cities, towns, and villages. Military-grade weapons such as Beretta M9s, M21 sniper rifles, M1918 Browning automatic rifles, M4 carbines, mortars, ammunition boxes, and rocket-propelled grenades, which were stolen from the armories during the revolution, were sold on street corners. In this way, what began as a collective effort to rid Libya of Gaddafi degenerated into sectarian violence and a campaign of lawlessness, as one group fought the other in a bid to control Libya's mineral-rich territories and national government.

While these events were unfolding, African leaders and leaders of governments across the world were expressing serious concerns over the situation in Libya. To this end, the United Nations appointed Bernardino Leon to replace Tarek Mitri as the UN's special representative and head of the United Nations Support Mission in Libya on September 14, 2014. Bernardino Leon, who was later dismissed, proposed a power-sharing formula, which provided for a Government of National Unity and a Presidential Council. Under this proposal, the Presidential Council would be composed of three deputies and two ministers from each of the three regions and would be headed by Fayez al-Sarraj as prime minister. Both the Tobruk-based Council of Deputies' government and the Tripoli-based GNC rejected this proposal. However, after a careful review of the initial proposal, a compromise proposal, supported by the United Nations, was signed by both parties on December 17, 2015.

The signed proposal, popularly known as the Libyan Political Agreement or the Skhirat Agreement, set up a nine-member Presidential Council and a 17-member interim Government of National Accord (GNA). In addition, the signed proposal mandated the existence of a High Council of State, which shall be the sole legislature whose members shall be nominated by the new General National Congress. As a body, the proposed High Council of State shall also serve as an advisory body to the Presidential Council. In addition, general elections were proposed for within two years. It is unfortunate that when talks between the two groups collapsed in Tunis in October 2017, the Shkirat agreement was abandoned.

Given all this, it could be argued that since the killing of Gaddafi, intrigues among competing groups at the national level have led to armed insurgencies in Libya. At the local level, the situation was in no way different, as rebel groups, armed militias, and radical Islamic groups daily engaged one another in their efforts to gain territories, status, and power.

Unfortunately, both the Tobruk-based Council of Deputies and the Tripoli-based GNC depended on these groups for security and police functions. These incessant conflicts and violence, coupled with weapon proliferation, have also affected Libya's neighbors especially Chad, Mali, and Nigeria, where insurgent groups used Libya's military-grade

Table 9.1   Rebel Groups and Militias in the Libyan Revolution, 2011–2018

Libyan Rebel Groups and Militias	Radical Islamist Groups
Libyan Interim Government (Tobruk based)	Islamic State of Iraq and the Levant (2014–2017)
National Forces Alliance	Wilayat Barqa (2014–2017)
Zintan Brigades	Wilayat Tripolitania (2014–2017)
Lightning Bolt Brigade	Wilayat Fezzan (2014–2017)
Qaaqaa Brigade	Shura Council of Benghazi Revolutionaries (2014–2017)
Civic Brigade	Ansar al-Sharia (2014–2017)
Justice and Equality Movement	Libya Shield 1 (2014–2017)
Government of National Accord	February 17th Martyrs Brigade (2014–2017)
Misurata Brigades	Rafallah al-Sahati Brigade (2014–2017)
Petroleum Facilities Guard	Jaysh al-Mujahidin
Abu Saleem Central Security Force	Brega Martyrs Brigade
Tuareg militias	Shura Council of Mujahideen in Derna
Tebou militias	Ansar al-Sharia (Derna)
Fajr Libya militia	Abu Salim Martyrs
Misurata Military Council	Benghazi Defense Brigades
Ministry of Interior	Ajdabiya Shura Council
Al-Bunyan al-Marsous	Al-Qaeda, other Salafist jihadists, and allies
Federal Cyrenaica	Al-Qaeda in the Islamic Maghreb
Mercenaries (allegedly)	
Sabratha Military Council/Sabratha Revolutionary Brigades	
General National Congress and allies	
National Salvation Government (Tripoli based)	
Libya Shield Force	
Western Shield	
Central Shield	
General National Congress and allies	
Libya Revolutionaries Operations Room	

Libyan Rebel Groups and Militias	Radical Islamist Groups
Fajr Libya militia	
Muslim Brotherhood	
Justice and Construction Party	
Awakening	
Brigade al-Marsah	
Brigade Sherikhan	
Union for Homeland	
High Council of Revolution (from December 2016)	
Tripoli Revolutionary Brigade	
Democratic Party	
Amazigh militias	
Mercenaries	

weapons to destabilize these nations. Table 9.1 presents rebel groups, armed militia, and radical Islamic groups that took control and purportedly set up quasi governments in different parts of Libya at different times.

In addition, there were also smaller rival groups. Notable examples include the Islamist Shura Council of Benghazi Revolutionaries, the Tuareg militias of Ghat, local forces in Misurata District, and a host of others in Bani Walid and Tawergha. These armed groups have supported and fought on the sides of either the Council of Deputies or the GNC. Sometimes they also have alternated sides.

AL-QAEDA IN LIBYA

The Al-Jama'a al-Islamiyyah al-Muqatilah bi-Libya, or the Libyan Islamic Fighting Group (LIFG), was founded in Afghanistan in 1995 by Abu Laith Al Libi, a Libyan, and other veterans of the Soviet occupation of Afghanistan. The LIFG participated in the 2011 Libyan Civil War under the name Libyan Islamic Movement. It allied itself with the Libya Shield Force. Its founder, Abd al-Muhsin Al-Libi, was an alleged al-Qaeda organizer who, in 2011, held an important command position in the Libya Shield Force. Abd al-Muhsin Al-Libi and his group were believed to have played a key role in deposing Gaddafi. Since the end of the Gaddafi-led government, Abd al-Muhsin Al-Libi and his forces have allied themselves with the National Transitional Council.

Prior to the Libyan Arab Spring, LIFG denounced the Gaddafi-led government as oppressive, illegitimate, and anti-Muslim. It espoused the establishment of an Islamic state in Libya and attempted to assassinate Gaddafi in February 1996. Although the assassination attempt failed, LIFG continued to engage Libyan security forces and Libyan interests since the 1990s.

Although LIFG denied affiliation with al-Qaeda, hundreds of its members joined and fought on behalf of al-Qaeda in Afghanistan. Many of LIFG high-ranking members were also high-ranking members of al-Qaeda. Notable examples include Abdel-Hakim Belhadj, Atiyah Abd al-Rahman, Abu Yahya al-Libi, Abu Laith al-Libi, Atiyah Abdul-Rahman, Noman Benotman, Mohammed Benhammedi, among others. In a November 2007 audio message, both Ayman al-Zawahiri and Abu Laith al-Libi announced the LIFG's joining of al-Qaeda. Although Benotman denied LIFG's membership of al-Qaeda in a CNN interview, al-Qaeda continued to praise LIFG activities in Libya in ways that suggested that a relationship existed between the two organizations.

One month into the Libyan Arab Spring, members of LIFG in Ajdabiya, placing the group under the leadership of the National Transitional Council, declared support for the uprising against Gaddafi. LIFG later announced a new name, the Libyan Islamic Movement (al-Harakat al-Islamiya al-Libiya). With the successful removal of the Gaddafi-led government, Abdelhakim Belhadj, a leader of LIFG, was appointed as commander of the Tripoli Military Council after the successful defeat of Gaddafi forces in Tripoli.

In addition, Abdel-Hakim al-Hasidi, one of LIFG leaders, declared to an Italian newspaper in September 2011 that LIFG had a link with al-Qaeda. LIFG's denial of links to al-Qaeda stemmed out of a crisis of confidence in al-Qaeda leadership in 1995. Before 1995, Osama bin Laden and members of the LIFG worked closely, having begun together in Afghanistan. Things, however, went awry when Osama bin Laden failed to prevent the Sudanese government's crackdown on Arab jihadists, including the LIFG. The Libyans were expelled from Sudan, a development that soured the relationship between LIFG and Osama bin Laden.

With many of its members returning to Libya, LIFG found itself embroiled in violence with the Gaddafi-led government who did not hesitate to arrest, kill, and jail many LIFG members on suspicion of jihadist activities. In areas like Darna, where the LIFG had more support, the Gaddafi-led government employed thousands of soldiers to crush the LIFG. The Abu Salim Prison massacre of 1996 was the culmination of Gaddafi's brutality against members of the LIFG. In this case, more than 1,000 members of LIFG imprisoned in Abu Salim Prison were murdered in one day.

Some of the survivors of Gaddafi's brutality renounced terrorism, while others became hardened. Noman Benotman belonged in the first category. His renunciation of terrorism explained his open letter of September 10, 2010, where he described himself "as a former comrade-in-arms" who "fought together" and was "ready to die together" with Osama bin Laden "under the banner of Islam" as they "came to the aid of fellow Muslims in Afghanistan."[1]

In the letter, Benotman laid bare the ideological differences between his newfound position on the use of terror and Osama's continued use of terrorism. Among other things, he affirmed Osama bin Laden and al-Qaeda's September 11 suicide bombings in the United States.

Unlike Benotman, many others continued their alliance with Osama bin Laden's al-Qaeda, and it was these elements that inserted Osama bin Laden's al-Qaeda into the Libyan uprising and the subsequent civil wars. Operating under the banner of Al-Qaeda in the Islamic Maghreb (AQIM), al-Qaeda established cells in most Libyan cities and towns. It aimed at the overthrow of the Libyan government and institution of an Islamic state.

More than any other Arab country, Islamic radicalization ran deep in Libya, especially in the impoverished and restive eastern provinces, where socioeconomic and infrastructural development were inadequate before the revolution. These areas provided hordes of recruits for al-Qaeda in Iraq. With the ending of the Iraq war, many of these young men returned to Libya, thereby contributing to the radicalization of youth in the areas. With chaotic leadership at both the national and local levels, following the killing of Gaddafi, areas such as these offered al-Qaeda an ideal environment to recruit, organize, and direct global terrorism.

Acting through remnants of LIFG and the Islamic Emirate of Barqa, cell groups of AQIM first sprang up in Darnah, an impoverished area that had endured many years of neglect. From Darnah, al-Qaeda spread thinly across cities and towns in Libya. Musa Abu Dawud was one of two AQIM terrorists killed in a U.S. drone strike in southwest Libya near the city of Ubari in the Sahara Desert on March 24, 2018. As reported, Dawud trained recruits for operations in Libya. He also supplied critical logistics, including funding and weapons, to AQIM.

ISLAMIC STATE OF IRAQ AND SYRIA (ISIS) IN LIBYA

Following the death of Muammar Gaddafi and the establishment of a new government, a number of rebel fighters joined other militant groups in Syria to fight Bashar al-Assad, the president of Syria. Some of these Libyan elements formed the Battar Brigade. In 2012, Battar Brigade pledged allegiance to ISIS and fought for ISIS in Syria and Iraq.

About 500 members of Battar Brigade, however, returned to Libya in 2014 and formed a new faction—the Islamic Youth Shura Council (IYSC) in Derna. Members of other militias and radical Islamic groups in Libya, especially members of the Derna branch of Ansar al-Sharia, also joined the IYSC. Within months of its establishment, the IYSC assumed control of Derna, killing many people who opposed it, including judges, teachers, and society leaders. Members of the Abu Salim Martyrs Brigade—an affiliate of al-Qaeda—were also killed.

With news of IYSC's activities, especially its control of Derna widely available, the highest command of ISIS sent its leaders to Derna. Leading these delegates were Abu Nabil al Anbari, Abu Habib al-Jazrawi, and Abu al-Baraa el-Azdi. These were known terrorists and acclaimed top-ranking members of ISIS. Abu Nabil al Anbari, for instance, was a senior aide to al-Baghdadi, the leader of ISIS, while Abu al-Baraa el-Azdi was a militant preacher from Syria.

At the city square in Derna on October 5, 2014, members of the IYSC and their allies assembled before these ISIS leaders to pledge allegiance to ISIS. On October 30, 2014, another public parade, involving wide arrays of Libyan youths, rebels, and Islamic radical groups publicly declared allegiance to Abu Bakr al-Baghdadi's ISIS. On both occasions, hundreds of pickup trucks filled with weapon-wielding fighters drove recklessly in Derna, as they celebrated joining ISIS.

In an audio recording that was released on November 13, 2014, al-Baghdadi accepted pledges of these members of IYSC, formally admitting them into ISIS. In the speech, al-Baghdadi announced the presence of ISIS in Fezzan, Cyrenaica, and Tripolitania. He also claimed that members of ISIS were also in al Bayda, Benghazi, Sirte, al-Khums, Jebel Akhdar, and Tripoli.

Besides existing as a stand-alone group, ISIS also affiliated with different al-Qaeda elements in Libya. In Benghazi, Ansar al-Sharia, al-Qaeda in the Islamic Maghreb, and Tarek Ibn Ziyad Brigade went into tactical alliances with ISIS. In March 2015, leaders of the Ansar al-Sharia, most especially Abu Abdullah Al-Libi, declared support for ISIS. Similar developments occurred in Sirte, where Ansar al-Sharia and other radical Islamist groups also joined ISIS. Why were so many Libyan groups and peoples ready to join ISIS and al-Queda? The case of Sirte offers a better perspective into what developed across Libya since the killing of Gaddafi.

While Gaddafi's government lasted, Sirte enjoyed a privileged position—enjoying socioeconomic development, infrastructural development, and other benefits. During the Arab Spring, inhabitants of Sirte were solidly behind Gaddafi and were with him until he was killed.

Following the collapse of Gaddafi's government, many ordinary Libyans and rebel groups considered the inhabitants of Sirte a group of saboteurs. Consequently, Sirte was therefore treated with disdain, and its groups and peoples were not incorporated into the post-Gaddafi government of Libya. This political alienation soon created the enabling environment for different groups within the city to pander to ISIS, as a way of getting political and territorial control in post-Gaddafi's Libya. By 2015, when ISIS announced its presence in Sirte, Ansar al-Sharia had established Sirte as its main enclave. With Ansar al-Sharia itself declaring for ISIS, ISIS began to successfully recruit a huge number of fighters from among disgruntled Libyans, especially former Gaddafi supporters who were alienated from the postwar political order.

By joining ISIS and pledging allegiance to al-Baghdadi, groups from Sirte soon controlled Nofaliya, Harawa, the Ghardabiya Air Base, and the power plants and part of the Great Man-Made River irrigation project.

ISIS made Sirte its base, increasing its state building efforts there and spreading into other areas where it enforced its strict Islamic codes in dress and behavior. Many people in Sirte opposed ISIS's type of Islam and protested. The protests were, however, quenched when ISIS imported fighters from other parts of Libya, including recruits from Chad, Mali, and Sudan.

With the establishment of ISIS in Libya, the country's civil war entered a new phase. Not only did members of ISIS in Libya join other rebels and militia groups in making Libya ungovernable, they also began to export fighters and terrorists into Syria, Turkey, Iraq, Mali, Niger, and Nigeria. As reported in *The Wall Street Journal* in December 2014, so many were recruited from Libya into ISIS and other international terror groups that ISIS leaders in Turkey demanded that their counterparts in Libya should stop sending new recruits their way and that new recruits be used locally in Libya.

In Cyrenaica, Fezzan, Tripoli, Derna, Sirte, al Bayda, Benghazi, al-Khums, Sabratha, and the Libyan capital Tripoli and other cities and towns that came under ISIS's control, buildings bore ISIS insignia and flags, while local radio and television stations transmitted ISIS teachings and sermons. In these cities and towns, billboards were also erected on roads and street corners instructing women on how to dress and conduct themselves in public. One such billboard in Sirte announced the following restrictions on wearing the hijab:

It must be thick and not revealing.
It must be loose (not tight).
It must cover all the body.
It must not be attractive.
It must not resemble the clothes of unbelievers or men.
It must not be decorative and eye-catching.
It must not be perfumed.[2]

ISIS claimed responsibilities for numerous terror attacks in Libya, chiefs among which were nine cases of suicide bombing in Benghazi in November 2014, a twin attack on a Libyan special forces camp in Benghazi on July 23, 2014, an attack on a military checkpoint near Benina Airport on October 2, 2014, and a suicide bombing in Tobruk where one person was killed and 14 wounded. The bombing outside Labraq Air Force Base in Al-Bayda where four people were killed and the bombing near the embassies of Egypt and the UAE in Tripoli on November 13, 2014 were also carried out by Libya's ISIS. Others include the beheading of Mohammed Battu and Sirak Qath, the two human rights activists who were abducted in Derna on November 6, 2014, and the execution of two Tunisian journalists in January 2015. The terror attack on the Corinthia Hotel in Tripoli on January 25, 2015 and a car bomb that killed about 10 people and five foreigners in Tripoli in January were all carried out by Libya's ISIS.

ISIS also carried out attacks on Libya's oil installations. For example, ISIS men opened fire on a French-Libyan oil field on the outskirts of Mabruk on February 3, 2015. In this attack, nine guards were killed. ISIS also murdered 21 Egyptian Christians who were earlier abducted in Sirte. ISIS's attacks in Libya were many. The preceding were just representative examples.

Many communities in Libya made efforts to dislodge ISIS. Owing to its brand of Islam, many Muslims rejected ISIS's teachings, especially on dress, behavior, and punishments such as crucifixions and lashings. Protests against ISIS broke out in Sirte while, in Derna, Benghazi, and Sabratha, infighting within groups pitched ISIS against other militias and rebel groups. In Derna, the Shura Council of Mujahideen and the Libyan Air Force engaged ISIS, and the coalition successfully drove ISIS forces out of their strongholds in Derna.

A destroyed car sits surrounded by building debris in the wake of Egyptian air-strikes in Derna, Libya, on February 16, 2015. The Egyptian warplanes were target-ing members of the Islamic State and the Levant (ISIL) extremist groups. (Bernard Bisson/Sygma via Getty Images)

There were also foreign attacks on ISIS locations and its leaders. For instance, in November 2015, Abu Nabil al Anbari—ISIS's leader in Libya was killed in a U.S. air strike, while the Libyan National Army and French Special Forces dislodged ISIS from its locations in Benghazi. In yet another U.S. air strike, one of ISIS's training camps near Sabratha was destroyed, leading to the death of Noureddine Chouchane, two Serbians, and 40 other ISIS members. Noureddine Chouchane was the leader of ISIS in Tunisia who was linked to the 2015 terrorist attacks in Sousse. After a seven-month-long battle, Libyan forces successfully defeated ISIS in Sirte in December 2016. In January 2017, more than 100 ISIS members were also killed at an ISIS base on the outskirts of Sirte.

THE 2012 BENGHAZI ATTACK

One of the most pernicious attacks carried out by any terrorist group in Libya was Ansar al-Sharia's attack on two U.S. government facilities in Benghazi. Ansar al-Sharia, the mastermind of the attacks, was a radical Islamist group and an affiliate of ISIS. The attacks, which began at 9:40 p.m. on September 11, 2012, resulted in the death of J. Christopher Stevens, the U.S. ambassador to Libya, and Sean Smith, a U.S. foreign service information management officer. Other U.S. officials who were killed in the attacks were Tyrone S. Woods and Glen Doherty—both CIA contractors. No fewer than 10 other U.S. and Libyan officials working in the two facilities sustained different categories of injuries. The number of members of the Ansar al-Sharia who were killed or injured in the attacks may never be known.

Although the relationship between the Gaddafi-led government of Libya and the United States was good before Gaddafi's death, the CIA and a number of other American intelligence and security organizations began to establish a covert presence in Benghazi shortly after the start of the Libyan revolution in February 2011. In addition to implementing the UN measures on Gaddafi, the United States also played roles alongside other nations in the ousting of Gaddafi. After the revolution, the United States continued to remain in Libya, as some of the U.S. Delta Force elite counterterrorist operators worked as analysts, helped the rebels in weapon mop-up, tactical training, and the gathering of intelligence, especially on terrorism in Libya and the North African subregion. The Americans' main concern was the prevention of the transfer of weapons stolen from the Gaddafi-led government arsenal, especially shoulder-fired missiles and chemical weapons, to terrorists.

Despite United States' denial, multiple sources revealed that the Ambassador J. Christopher Stevens–led diplomatic mission in Benghazi was a CIA covert arms-smuggling operation, which aimed at assisting the Syrian rebels in removing Syrian President Bashar al-Assad. As noted in a congressional hearing on the Benghazi attack, the presence of CIA, Joint Special Operations Command (JSOC), and a composite of U.S. Special Operations team in Libya was to ensure that al-Qaeda did not take advantage of the situation in Libya to infiltrate the region. As noted to the House Permanent Select Committee on Intelligence in January 2014: "All CIA activities in Benghazi were legal and authorized. On-the-record testimony establishes that the CIA was not sending weapons . . . from Libya to Syria or facilitating other organizations or states that were transferring weapons from Libya to Syria."[3]

On September 11, 2012, two separate military factions of Ansar al-Sharia opened artillery and mortar fire on the U.S.'s main diplomatic compound and a CIA annex one and half miles away at about 9:40 p.m. Before the attacks, there was no demonstration, no protest, and no provocation of any kind. As claimed after the attack, members of Ansar al-Sharia acted in response to a YouTube video entitled *Innocence of Muslims*, an anti-Islamic video.

It must be noted that, before the attacks in Benghazi, members of a pro–al-Qaeda militia group—The Brigades of the Imprisoned Sheikh Omar Abdul Rahman—had planned a protest to decry the continued imprisonment of Sheik Omar Abdul Rahman in Egypt and called on members across the world to use September 11, 2012 to raise awareness for the release of the blind sheik. Coincidentally, *Innocence of Muslims* was released, a development that spurred protests not only in Cairo but in three other Muslim countries, including Libya.

Given all this, it could be argued that the Benghazi attack was both spontaneous and planned. While members of the Brigades of the Imprisoned Sheikh Omar Abdul Rahman in Libya had planned to demonstrate in support of the release of the blind sheik, the release of the anti-Muslim video—*Innocence of Muslims*—incensed others, especially members of the Ansar al-Sharia who then unleased mortars and artillery fires on the American facilities.

Although there is no evidence linking either al-Qaeda or ISIS to the Benghazi attack, it must be noted that prior to the attacks on September 11, 2012, al-Qaeda leader Ayman al-Zawahiri called on members in Libya to avenge the death of Abu Yahya al-Libi who was killed in a U.S. drone strike in Pakistan by attacking Americans in Libya. A few days after the attacks, al-Qaeda in the Arabian Peninsula noted in a release that the Benghazi attacks were a revenge for the killing of Abu Yahya al-Libi.

As was later discovered, three operatives of the al-Qaeda in the Arabian Peninsula and Mokhtar Belmokhtar, a senior commander in al-Qaeda in the Islamic Maghreb participated in the attacks. Eyewitness accounts of the attacks revealed that rather than responding to Ayman al-Zawahiri's call, members of the Ansar al-Sharia launched the attacks in retaliation for the release of *Innocence of Muslims*.

Whether the attack and similar attacks on U.S. embassies and consulates in three other countries were a spontaneous response to the You-Tube video or were premeditated and carefully planned, it led to the gruesome killing of Ambassador J. Christopher Stevens, Sean Smith, Tyrone S. Woods, and Glen Doherty.

Many Libyans staged public demonstrations condemning the attacks. Ansar al-Sharia's facilities were raided and set ablaze, as Libyans openly declared support for the United States and denounced the activities of Ansar al-Sharia and other militia groups.

International condemnation of the attacks dominated newspaper, radio, and television airtime. Many leaders of Ansar al-Sharia were accused of carrying out the attacks. It was, however, unclear whether either al-Qaeda or ISIS knew anything or contributed in any way to the attacks. The United States nevertheless filed criminal charges against several individuals, including Ansar al-Sharia's leader, Ahmed Abu Khattala. In addition, in January 2014, the U.S. Department of State designated Ansar al-Sharia as a terrorist organization.

Although some were later released for want of evidence to go to trial, the following individuals with ties to both Ansar al-Sharia and al-Qaeda in the Maghreb were arrested in connection with the attacks: Ahmed Abu Khattala (captured in June 2014), Mustafa al-Imam (captured in October 2017), Ali Harzi (a Tunisian), Karim el-Azizi (a Libyan), Faraj al-Shibli (a Libyan), and a host of others.

LIBYAN CIVIL WAR AND TERRORISM IN AFRICA

The Libyan revolution contributed to the dense landscape of terrorism and insurgencies in Africa. When in March 2012, Ansar Dine (AD), a militant Islamist group that seeks to impose strict Sharia law across Mali, claimed control of vast areas of land in Mali's northeastern region, many were not surprised. As detailed in Chapter 8, both the Gaddafi-led government and the rebels who removed Gaddafi from power resorted to the use of mercenaries. Many youths from impoverished areas of Mali, encouraged by the pecuniary gain involved, joined either side in Libya's Arab Spring as mercenaries.

AD's founder, Iyad Ag Ghaly, was a prominent leader in the Tuareg Rebellion that lasted between 1990 and 1995. Iyad's cousin, Hamada Ag Hama, was the leader of Al-Qaeda in the Islamic Maghreb (AQIM). In addition, Omar Ould Hamaha, AD's spokesman, was the military leader of Movement for Oneness and Jihad in West Africa (MOJWA), an AQIM affiliate. Owing to these connections, it was believed that AD also had ties with al-Qaeda.

When AD members overran Mali's northeastern region in March 2012, it paraded more than 100 vehicles, each carrying soldiers and mounted with heavy artillery guns. Following this, it dawned on the world that some of the looted weapons from Libya's arsenal had found their way into West Africa. Many of the arrested members of AD not only confessed to having fought in Libya but also to the fact that Libya was the source of their training, logistics, and weapons.

Another group that benefited from the situation in Libya was Boko Haram, a radical Islamist group based in northeastern Nigeria. Although the precise date of Boko Haram's establishment remains unknown, the group was, however, established by Abubakar Lawan, a computer science graduate, as a nonviolent but puritanical group that aimed to institute Islamic law—the Sharia—in Nigeria. Mohammed Yusuf took control of the group when, in 2002, Lawan left for Saudi Arabia for a master's degree. Since Yusuf's murder in 2009, Abubakar Shekau has been leading the group. Boko Haram carried out terrorist activities of varying magnitude in northern Nigeria, including Abuja, Nigeria's capital, and also in Chad, Niger, and northern Cameroon.

Like Ansar Dine, many members of Boko Haram also confessed to having fought in Libya. Boko Haram was also a beneficiary of Libya's weapons, and, like Ansar Dine, Boko Haram benefited from the training and logistics provided to them by al-Qaeda members in Libya.

NOTES

1. Noman Benotman, "An Open Letter to Osama bin Laden" in *Foreign Policy*, September 10, 2010. Accessed September 14, 2018, at https://foreignpolicy.com/2010/09/10/an-open-letter-to-osama-bin-laden/

2. BBC, "Control and Crucifixions: Life in Libya under IS" in *BBC News*, February 3, 2016. Accessed on September 14, 2018, at https://www.bbc.com/news/world-middle-east-35325072

3. Christopher M. Blanchard, *Libya: Transition and U.S. Policy* (Washington, D.C.: Congressional Research Service, 2018), 11.

10

Libya's Past and Future

Contemporary Libya is certainly a victim of its past. Foreign invasions, conquests, and colonization led to socioeconomic, demographic, and political change. While Phoenician traders inserted the different ethnic groups that formed modern-day Libya into the vortex of global trade, Graeco-Roman rulers and the Vandals brought about serious political change. By the time the Ottomans arrived in Libya, the different ethnic groups along Libya's Mediterranean coast had become a critical part of the Mediterranean trading system. Their counterparts to the south were, in turn, integral to the trans-Saharan trading system.

At that point, not only was Libya on the cusp of socioeconomic and political change, it was also becoming a major player in both Islam and Christianity. The Italian invasion and subsequent colonization radically altered Libya's development. Libyans were faced with the herculean tasks of defending their land from the invading Italians, whose military superiority was not in doubt. Abandoned by the Ottomans and unable to defeat the Italians, the ethnic groups either allied with the invaders or fought them.

Given serious population and economic pressure from Italy, it could be argued that the Italians needed Libya without the Libyans in it. To attain this, the wholesale removal of ethnic groups into concentration camps and landgrabbing followed. Many Italians were resettled in "ready-made" or "off-the-shelf" farms. Schools, which catered mainly to Italians, were built. Libyans were denied access to Western education beyond elementary school and were banned from participation in politics.

As of independence on December 24, 1951, Libya barely had any qualified medical doctors and trained government administrators, professors and engineers, and other key professions. Above all, it was so poor that many, including the United Nations—Libya's trustee—feared for its survival. International aid and rents from hiring out its land to the United States and Great Britain for building military bases remained the only source of national revenue for the newly independent country.

King Idris, the first ruler of independent Libya, banned party politics, as the first set of political parties were ethnically oriented, a development that almost thwarted Idris's nation-building efforts. Although the ban on politics eliminated political bickering, it stymied the emergence of a politically enlightened citizenry. Above all, it prevented the emergence of any credible opposition to the king's reign.

The discovery of crude oil in Libya changed the course of the country's history. Libya transformed overnight from a beggarly nation to one of the richest nations on earth. Under Gaddafi, Libya's oil wealth was used to foster a state-led economic system and to sponsor terrorism. As a military dictatorship, the Gaddafi-led government brooked no opposition. Political opponents were arrested, jailed, an, sometimes killed. Libya's oil wealth masked the political ignorance of its people. After 42 years of Gaddafi's rule, the government burst at the seams, and Gaddafi was removed.

Whether under the Ottomans or Italians, King Idris or Gaddafi, Libyans were denied opportunities for political education. For many, Libya was just a mere geographical expression, as identity politics fostered allegiance to ethnic and/or religious groups, never to the nation.

From Gaddafi's ouster till the last quarter of 2018, Libyans continued to display a general lack of political education and sophistication. Armed militia groups, agitating for narrow ethnic and religious interests, laid waste to the country. Since the establishment of a Government of National Accord (GNA) in January 2016, the government has struggled to consolidate its authority, and the country fractured into two opposing halves—the eastern half versus the western half.

In the east, the House of Representatives (HoR), which is based in Tobruk, aligned with the forces of General Khalifa Belqasim Haftar, the head of the Libyan National Army who, on May 16, 2014, also established

Operation Dignity. Operation Dignity, a few months after its establishment, deployed a combined air and ground assault on Benghazi. As of the writing of this chapter, Operation Dignity controlled most of Libya's oil-rich areas and was notorious for being the biggest single obstacle to peace in Libya. Its leader, Khalifa Haftar, was described as the cause of the crises that is crippling the country.

Haftar's main ambition is to establish himself as the prime minister of Libya. To this end, he refused to support the Government of National Accord (GNA). The UN backed the Tripoli-based GNA, while the Tobruk-based HoR depended on General Haftar and an array of powerful armed groups across the country. Since August 2018, members of the Seventh Brigade have been fighting the Tripoli Revolutionaries' Brigades and the Nawasi Brigade, two of Tripoli's largest factions. Unlike Tripoli Revolutionaries' Brigades, the Seventh Brigade is based in the outskirts of Tripoli. The group, like others in small towns and villages across Libya, noticed the successes of militia groups within the capital, especially the wealth, power, and ostentatious life being led by rebel commanders in the cities and towns and marched on Tripoli. Those who remained in small villages and towns turned the roads and city streets into battlegrounds, as they engaged in lawlessness and fought rival groups in pitched battles, leaving behind bodies.

The firing of rockets randomly into densely populated areas has become commonplace in contemporary Libya. Hence, in the first week of September 2018, the Presidential Council declared a state of emergency due to the growing violence, insecurity, and lawlessness in Tripoli. Public safety for public and private possessions, vital institutions and the security of lives of civilians are some of the major current concerns of the GNA.

Besides his supporters in eastern Libya, General Haftar also enjoyed the support of the United Arab Emirates, Egypt, and Russia. In March 2015, the HoR, Libya's elected legislative body, appointed Haftar as the commander of the Armed Forces.

While dealing with the HoR and Haftar in the east, the GNA also faced intense resistance from the General National Congress (GNC) in the west. Incessant fighting between government forces and Haftar's men have become widespread since the beginning of 2018. As of the beginning of September, the situation has become so bad that heads of government in the United States, Great Britain, France, Germany, and others across Africa have raised serious concerns about Libya's survival as a nation.

Despite international efforts to rid Libya of remnants of ISIS and al-Qaeda, contemporary Libya is now a net supplier of terror recruits. As

Libyan National Army Field Marshal Khalifa Haftar (second from left), flanked by Libya's parliament speaker Aguila Saleh Issa (second from right), looks on during an International Congress on Libya at the Elysee Palace in Paris, France, on May 29, 2018. (ETIENNE LAURENT/AFP/Getty Images)

many Libyan officials noted, over 500 ISIS and al-Qaeda cells currently abound in Libya. It is believed that ISIS's Desert Brigade and Office of Borders and Immigration are now domiciled in Libya.[1] While the first is composed of capable leaders and planners who could plan and execute acts of terrorism, the other is responsible for external operations, logistics, and recruitment.

Like politicians and armed militias, these radical Islamic groups were also interested in controlling Libya's oil wealth. For ISIS and al-Qaeda, controlling Libya's oil wealth would avail them the much needed financial power and staging post for their activities. Given that both groups have lost territories in Iraq, Afghanistan, Syria, and other places due to the intensification of the U.S.-led global fight against terrorism, ensuring that Libya knows no peace serves these groups' interests.

Currently, there is no denying the fact that the Libyan state is gradually disappearing, as it has become hard to say who controls the state between elected government officials and armed militia groups. State institutions have all disappeared. How long will Libya remain this way?

In the bids to find a lasting solution to the Libyan situation, the United Nations, like the African Union, has presided over many agreements and cease-fires, none of which has, so far, produced any lasting peace. Given this bleak outlook on Libya's current situation, does the country stand a chance to evolve into a truly democratic nation?

While not discountenancing the importance of current efforts to cultivate militia groups and their leaders, the path to lasting peace in Libya lies with building the country's institutions. For instance, as long as armed militias perform police functions, peace will continue to elude Libya. The international community therefore needs to do more in helping Libya to revamp its institutions. In the same vein, for as long as ethnic consciousness overrides national identity, the journey to lasting peace in Libya will remain elusive. While a government of national unity is a good starting point, the road to any lasting peace in Libya is a confederation, where various ethnic groups could develop at their own pace.

NOTE

1. Frederic Wehrey, "When the Islamic State Came to Libya" in *The Atlantic*, February 10, 2018. Accessed on September 14, 2018, at https://www.theatlantic.com/international/archive/2018/02/isis-libya-hiftar-al-qaeda-syria/552419/

Notable People in the History of Libya

Abdelbaset Ali Mohmed al-Megrahi—a Libyan Arab Airlines head of security and director of the Centre for Strategic Studies in Tripoli, who was tried and jailed by a panel of three Scottish judges for the bombing of Pan Am Flight 103 over Lockerbie, Scotland, on December 21, 1988. The justices, who sat a special court at Camp Zeist, the Netherlands, found al-Megrahi guilty and sentenced him to life imprisonment. Lamin Khalifah Fhimah, al-Megrahi's coaccused, was found not guilty and was subsequently acquitted.

Abdel Salam Jallud—Libya's prime minister and second-in-command to Muammar Gaddafi between July 16, 1972, and March 2, 1977. Between 1970 and 1972, he was the also minister of finance. As deputy chairman of the Revolutionary Command Council, Jallud supervised the oil sector, bringing up innovative measures to ensure Libya's control of its oil wealth. When Libya's Arab spring broke out in 2011, Jallud defected, hastening the collapse of Gaddafi's 42-year rule.

Abdullahi Ibn Saad—the Arab leader who marched on Tripoli in 647 BCE with an army of 40,000 Arabs. He conquered the Byzantines and took Tripoli and other towns in western Libya, including Sufetula, a city 150 miles south of Carthage.

Adrian Pelt—a Dutch journalist, international civil servant, and diplomat who was elected as under-secretary-general of the United Nations Organization in 1946. He supervised the drafting of Libya's first constitution and also the country's independence.

Ahmad Karamanli—a Turkish warrior and founder of the Karamanli dynasty who ruled Tripolitania between 1711 and 1745 under the title of Pasha of Tripolitania. Ahmad was reputed for his intelligence and bravery. He murdered the Ottoman governor of Tripolitania and established himself as the Pasha of Tripolitania. Ahmad employed corsairs who extracted tributes from ships plying the Mediterranean shipping routes. After gaining control of Tripoli, he extended his control to Fezzan and Cyrenaica. He died in 1745.

Amr Ibn al-'As—a contemporary of Prophet Muhammad and an Arab military commander who led the Muslim conquest of Egypt in 640. In 642 BCE, he led Arab horsemen into Cyrenaica and instituted Islam after conquering the city.

Anthony Gauci—the proprietor of Mary's House, a clothing retailer on Tower Road, Sliema, Malta. He claimed to have sold clothes and an umbrella to Abdelbaset al-Megrahi and was the only witness who tied the Lockerbie Bombing to al-Megrahi and Libya. Gauci died at the age of 75 on October 29, 2016, in Malta.

Fathi Terbil—a human rights activist and lawyer who represented relatives of over 1,000 prisoners killed by Libyan security forces in Abu Salim Prison in 1996. His arrest in February 2011 sparked a violent demonstration in Benghazi and precipitated the Libyan Arab Spring that brought an end to Gaddafi's 42-year rule in Libya. Following Gaddafi's ouster, Fathi was appointed as a Youth Representative in the National Transitional Council (NTC).

Idris Sanussi—a political and religious leader who was originally Emir of Cyrenaica and, in 1951, became King of Libya. He was deposed in 1969. When his cousin, Ahmed Sharif al-Sanussi abdicated and fled to Egypt, Idris became the leader of the Sanussi Order. He died in Cairo, Egypt, on May 25, 1983 at the age of 94.

Italo Balbo—an Italian governor-general of Libya and commander-in-chief of Italian North Africa. He merged Tripolitania, Cyrenaica, and Fezzan into one nation, Libya. He was killed when Italian anti-aircraft guns accidentally shot down his plane was over Tobruk.

Khalifa Belqasim Haftar—a field marshal in the Libyan Army and leader of the Libyan National Army, a militia group involved in the ongoing Second Libyan Civil War. His forces, which were loyal to the Libyan House of Representatives, controlled Libya's main oil-rich areas and remain instrumental in the dense landscape of violence and war in Tripoli since the beginning of 2018.

Majid Giaka—a former guard at the Libyan Arab Airlines and member of the Libyan intelligence service who defected and became a CIA asset in August 1988. Giaka claimed that his bosses at the Libyan Arab Airlines, Abdelbaset al-Megrahi and Lamin Khalifah Fhimah, were members of the Libyan secret service. His testimony, which the Scottish Criminal Cases Review Commission called into question in June 2007, led to the conviction of Abdelbaset al-Megrahi over the Pan Am Flight 103 bombing.

Mohammad Abulas'as El-Alem—the mufti of Tripolitania between 1945 and 1951. He was one of the signatories to Libya's Independence Constitution. Following independence, he was elected president of the Libyan National Assembly.

Muammar al-Gaddafi—leader of the Free Officers Movement who deposed King Idris in 1969. He was a revolutionary leader, politician, and political theorist who ruled Libya for 42 years. Between 1969 and 1977, he was the chairman of Libya's Revolutionary Command Council and president of the Libyan Arab Republic. Between 1977 and 2011, he was the head of the Great Socialist People's Libyan Arab Jamahiriya. He authored *The Green Book*, a political and philosophical treatise containing his ideologies for governance in the Third World. He was killed on October 20, 2012, after NATO bombers and rebel militia from Misrata attacked Sirte.

Omar al-Mukhtar Muhammad bin Farhat al-Manifi—the national hero and symbol of anticolonial resistance in Libya. Also known as The Lion of the Desert, Omar led the Sanussi movement in Cyrenaica against European colonization, especially the Italians in Libya, the French in

Chad, and the British in Egypt. After many attempts, he was captured by the Italians in Al-Mukhtar near Solonta and was hanged in 1931.

Sayyid Ahmad Sharif al-Sanussi—the founder and supreme leader of the Sanussi Order. His daughter, Fatimah el-Sharif, was the queen consort of King Idris I of Libya.

Glossary

African Union (AU)
A continental body of African states and successor of the Organization of African Unity (OAU).

Amir
A leader of the faithful or a head of an independent Muslim community.

Aouzou Strip
A territory in northern Chad, paralleling Libya's southern border and believed to be rich in valuable minerals. It was occupied by Libya in 1973 and annexed in the following year. It is believed to be rich in uranium.

Arab Socialist Union (ASU)
A mass organization that was created in 1971 to provide a framework for popular participation and representation within the political system. It was reorganized in 1975 to incorporate local-level institutions such as the Basic People's Congresses (BPCs) and Municipal People's Congresses (MPCs).

Ba'ath
Another name for the Arab Socialist Resurrection Party, a pan-Arab party that Michel Aflaq and Salah ad Din al Bitar founded in Damascus by in the 1940s.

Ba'athist
A member of the Ba'ath party.

Baladiyat
An administrative unit in Libya.

Bani
Arabic for an ethnic group, a people, or a nation.

Caliph
Literally, a successor to the Prophet Muhammad or a spiritual and temporal leader of the Islamic community.

Cultural Revolution
Proclaimed on April 15, 1973, it was one of the major government policies under Gaddafi, which aimed at preventing the erosion of Libya's Arab and Islamic heritage by foreign cultural influence.

Cyrenaica
One of the largest historic regions in eastern Libya. It derives its name from the ancient Greek city-state, Cyrene, which is called Barqu in Arabic.

Dey
A junior officer commanding a company of janissaries. From 1611, it was used to describe the head of government in Tripolitania.

Divan
A council of senior military officers during the Ottoman period.

Fezzan
One of Libya's three historic regions, located in the southwest.

Free Officers Movement
A secret organization of junior Libyan army officers and enlisted men who carried out the September 1, 1969, coup against King Idris. Colonel Gaddafi was the founder and head of this organization.

Front de Liberation Nationale du Tchad (Front for the National Liberation of Chad) (FROLINAT)
A Muslim insurgent movement in Chad supported by Libya.

General People's Committee
Formerly the Council of Ministers. It later became the name of the cabinet in March 1977.

General People's Congress
Established under Colonel Gaddafi, a body that performed both the executive and legislative functions of government. It became the formal supreme organ of government in March 1977.

The Green Book
An ideological testament that contains Gaddafi's political, economic, and social thought, as well as revolutionary precepts of Arab socialism. The first volume was published in 1976 and the second in 1978.

Ibn
Literally "son of." It is used as a prefix or as part of a proper name to indicate patrilineal descent.

Imam
Generally, an Islamic leader and a recognized authority on Islamic theology and law. He also leads prayer sessions at a mosque.

Jamahiriya
An Arabic word that literally describes a state of the masses, people's authority, or people's power. Gaddafi officially declared Libya the Socialist People's Libyan Arab Jamahiriya on March 2, 1977.

Libyan Dinar (LD)
A unit of currency that, on September 1, 1971, replaced the Libyan pound that was in use before independence. The Libyan dinar is divided into 1,000 dirhams.

Nasserism
The teachings of Gamal Abdel Nasser, a former Egyptian leader who espoused the belief in pan-Arabism.

Organization of Arab Petroleum Exporting Countries (OAPEC)
A body that coordinates petroleum policies of major oil-producing Arab states such as Algeria, Bahrain, Egypt, Iraq, Kuwait, Libya, Qatar, Saudi Arabia, Syria, and the United Arab Emirates.

Organization of Petroleum Exporting Countries (OPEC)
An organization that coordinates petroleum policies of 13 major oil-producing countries. Members include Algeria, Ecuador, Gabon, Indonesia, Iran, Iraq, Kuwait, Libya, Nigeria, Qatar, Saudi Arabia, the United Arab Emirates, and Venezuela.

Pasha
A regent, representing the sultan in Tripolitania. It also describes an Ottoman provincial governor or military commander.

Qadi
A judge of a Sharia court.

Quran
The holy book of Islam.

Revolutionary Command Council (RCC)
The supreme organ of the Gaddafi-led revolutionary government, established in September 1969 and dissolved in 1977.

Revolutionary Committees
Established in November 1977 to supervise the Basic People's Congresses and to fight bureaucracy. Over the years, it becomes the unofficial spy organization, members of which were devoted to Gaddafi and his teachings.

Sharia
Islamic law, both civil and criminal, based on the Quran and the hadith. Other sources include the consensus of Islamic belief, consensus of the authorities on a legal question, and analogy or elaboration of the intent of law by Islamic scholars and imams.

Shia
Also called Shiite, one of two main divisions of Islam. As an Arabic word, it means a party, for instance Shiat Ali (Party of Ali). Adherents, who are referred to as Shias or Shiites, believed that the Quran is open to interpretation and elaboration by inspired imams.

Sunni
One of two main divisions of Islam. The Sunni consider themselves the orthodox adherents of the *sunna*, adherence to Islam as practiced by the Prophet Muhammad. Adherents believe that the Quran is not subject to interpretation or elaboration.

Third International Theory
The major tenet of Gaddafi's revolutionary ideology, which offers alternative political, economic, and social ideologies to the Third World countries on governance. Also known as the Third Universal Theory and the Third Theory.

Tripolitania
One of Libya's three historic regions, located in the northwest. It derived its name from Tripolis, which means the "Three Cities." It is the most populous city in Libya.

Wali
A governor general of an administrative division during Ottoman rule.

Zawiya
(plural, *zawaayaa*) A lodge containing a mosque, a school, and quarters.

Bibliographic Essay

Until recently, the literature on Libya has been dominated by non-Libyan and non-African authors. This phenomenon, which cannot be dissociated from Gaddafi's iron hold on intellectual freedom during his 42-year rule, created a general tendency among authors to regard the history of Libya as history of foreigners and conquerors. Two major authors dominated the field on Libyan history—Ronald Bruce St. John and Dirk Vandewalle.

For a general history, the most popular works are Ronald Bruce St. John's *Historical Dictionary of Libya* (Scarecrow Press, 2006) and *Libya: From Colony to Revolution* (Oneworld Publications, 2012). Like St. John's two volumes, Dirk Vandewalle's *A History of Modern Libya* (Cambridge, 2nd ed., 2012) presents the history of Libya in a fashion in no way different from how Hugh Trevor-Roper described the history of Africa in 1965, as only the history of the Europeans in Africa." Both authors, idiosyncratic in their various approaches, presented Libya's (early) history as the history of foreign invaders, traders, and conquerors. No attempt was made to credit the indigenous people of Libya with any development, any ingenuity, and therefore any history. In their discussions of foreign invasions into Libya, the literature was replete with accounts of Phoenician traders, Greek invaders, the Ottomans, and Italian colonizers. Little or no effort was made to explore Libyans' contributions to their own history. Where mentions were made, Libyans were either described as rebels or as ethnic warlords. Libyans anticolonial struggles were not seen as nationalistic, and Libyans fighters were not seen as freedom fighters. Indigenous efforts at preserving ethnonational identity were lumped with religious affinity and explained away as resulting from pan-Islamic and pan-Arab sentiments.

As a result of this approach to Libyan history, no clear-cut distinction existed in the literature on Libya's preinvasion and precolonial peoples and societies. Who were the native inhabitants of the areas now known as Libya? What were their histories? Neither of these authors provided any clue whatsoever about the pre-European and pre-Arab ethnic composition of Libya. Their histories, as far as some of these authors were concerned, were unimportant. Unlike Ronald Bruce St. John and Dirk Vandewalle, J. A. Ilevbare, in his *Carthage, Rome and the Berbers* (Ibadan University Press, 1980), discussed the ethnonational history of Carthage and Libya's Berber populations, noting their political, economic, and social structure before and after contacts with the Greeks. John Wright, in *A History of Libya* (Columbia University Press, 2012), briefly discussed the pre-European and pre-Arab indigenous population of Libya under the general heading of "The Hunter-Artists." He was about the only non-African author who made any effort to recognize that the history of Libya cannot begin with the history of outsiders, no matter how great the contributions of these outsiders might be. Like Ronald Bruce St. John and Dirk Vandewalle, John Wright also devoted considerable attention to the exploitation of foreign invaders and traders in Libya, and the contributions of Libya's indigenous people were either glibly recognized or treated as a footnote to the history of outsiders in Libya.

Another important work on Libyan history is John Oakes's *Libya: The History of Gaddafi's Pariah State* (History Press, 2011). Oakes's discussion on the indigenous population was limited to the Garamantes, and, like other authors, considerable attention was placed on foreign invasions and conquests. While Oakes tied the Ottoman invasion of Libya to the trans-Saharan slave trade, he lumped Libyans efforts at rejecting Italian colonization with Islam. Like others, Oakes also described Libyans' anticolonial struggles in clearly biased terms— describing Libyans as "Desert rats," Desert foxes," and the like. However, unlike others, Oakes's main concern was to project Gaddafi as a dictator and Libya as a pariah state. Oakes, like others, placed considerable emphasis on Gaddafi's involvement with the Irish Republican Army, the Palestine Liberation Organization, the various bombings, plane hijackings, and weapons of mass destruction.

In Ruth First's *Libya: The Elusive Revolution* (Penguin, 1974), the causes and consequences of Gaddafi's 1969 revolution that ousted King Idris's monarchy were discussed. This book provides a wealth of information on the religious, economic, and social underpinnings of Libyan politics, its oil revenues, and the pursuit of Arab unity. Only Ronald Bruce St. John's *Libya: From Colony to Revolution* (Oneworld Publications, 2012) comes close to First in his elaborate discussion of Libya's oil wealth and fascination with pan-Arabism.

Although different authors have presented Gaddafi's views on politics and power, to gain a more nuanced understanding of Gaddafi's political thoughts, his book, *The Green Book* (Hades, 2017), contains Gaddafi's raw thoughts on the nexus between democracy and the authority of the people, solutions to Third World socioeconomic problems, and his most famous Third Universal Theory. Just as Ronald Bruce St. John's *Libya: From Colony to Revolution* (Oneworld Publications, 2012) and Dirk Vandewalle's *A History of Modern Libya* (Cambridge, 2nd ed., 2012) are essential reading in understanding the history of foreign invaders and conquerors in Libya, Gaddafi's *Green Book* is a *sine qua non* to any work on the political and economic history of Libya under Gaddafi.

Anyone interested in the international dimension to Libya's recent history, especially the role of the United States, will find Geoff Simons's two books on Libya useful. For instance, in *Libya: The Struggle for Survival* (Palgrave Macmillan, 1996), Simons presented a detailed account of how the West, particularly the United States, responded to Libya's involvement in the bombing of the Pan Am airliner over Lockerbie in 1988. The author emphasized that the U.S. response was predicated on its ambition to become a sole military superpower in the "New World Order." Simons argued that by targeting Libya and manipulating the United Nations to impose sanctions on Libya, the United States revealed its hegemonic objective and its distaste for international law in combating global terrorism. The author situated his arguments within the rubric of Libya's colonial past, its oil wealth, and its impact on the United States.

Similar arguments could be found in his *Libya and the West: From Independence to Lockerbie* (I. B. Tauris, 2004), where Simons traced the history of Libya from 1969 when Colonel Muammar Gaddafi took over after a successful coup d'état. The author emphasized Gaddafi's penchant for breaking preexisting bilateral agreements and his eventual building of an authoritarian state that became increasingly isolated by the United States and its allies in the West. The book also details Libya's sponsorship of terrorism. As the author argued, the 21st century offered Libya an opportunity to retrace its steps, especially in the face of the U.S. penchant for influencing the United Nations against nations that were considered unfriendly to the United States.

Anna Baldinetti, in *The Origins of the Libyan Nation: Colonial Legacy, Exile and the Emergence of a New Nation-State* (Routledge, 2014), addressed the emergence of the Libyan nation and rise of nationalism among Libyan exiles in the Mediterranean region. In addition to tracing the root of Libya's nationalism to the colonial period, the book also explained Libyan nationalism as a product of pan-Arabism. On Libya's and Gaddafi's roles in international terrorism, the various works previously mentioned dedicated either a chapter or section of a chapter to discussing this. The only book-length text on Gaddafi and international terrorism is Abdelbaset al-Megrahi and John Ashton's *Megrahi: You Are My Jury: The Lockerbie Evidence* (Birlinn, 2012), which chronicled al-Megrahi's firsthand account of the investigation, findings, judgments, and critiques of the Lockerbie bombing trials. In this book, the authors argued that Abdelbaset al-Megrahi was not only innocent of the charges but was also a victim of dirty international politics between the West and Gaddafi. The book compiled the flaws in the investigation and the follies in the judicial process that led to Megrahi's conviction. Megrahi's account established his innocence and exonerated Libya and Muammar Gaddafi from the bombing of the Pan Am airplane over Lockerbie, Scotland.

In general, most of the literature on Libya presents Gaddafi as a tyrant and a dictator. Luis Martinez, in *The Libyan Paradox* (Columbia University Press, 2007), abandoned this familiar and well beaten path and explained Libya and Gaddafi's post-2003 reforms and abandonment of confrontation toward America and Europe as deriving from the United States' militant attitude in the wake of 9/11 and the invasion of Iraq in March 2003. Gaddafi's sudden abandonment of nuclear weapons, the opening up of Libya's economy to the West, and his general change of tactics in relating with the West were discussed in the book. As the author argued, for Gaddafi to maintain a hold on his country in the face of increasing U.S. meddling in the affairs of other nations, Libya needed to evolve into what the author called an "authoritarian liberal state." Many readers would find this book controversial.

In *The 2011 Libyan Uprisings and the Struggle for the Post-Qadhafi Future* (Palgrave Macmillan, 2013), Jason Pack edited nine chapter essays that focused primarily on the 2011 Libyan Uprisings in a thematic fashion. The volume investigated how preexisting social, regional, ethnic, and religious dissections influenced the trajectory of the 2011 Libyan Uprisings and the implications of these for post-Gaddafi Libya. Unlike other books, this is one of a few works in the literature that are devoted entirely to the Libyan Arab Spring.

Another important work on the Libyan Uprising is Lindsey Hilsum's *Sandstorm: Libya in the Time of Revolution* (Faber & Faber, 2012). This book compiled the personal stories of six Libyans as the uprising unfolded. It is one of a handful of works that adopted a *longue durée* approach to explaining the uprising. The book situated the uprising within the context of Libya's colonial history, monarchy, and dictatorship. The book also revealed the Gaddafi family's excesses and the efforts of many Libyan diasporas who returned home at the wake of the revolution to provide different services that helped in bringing Gaddafi's 42-year rule to an end. Like Hilsum, Alex Crawford also presented personal accounts from Libya's uprising of 2011 in *Colonel Gaddafi's Hat* (Collins, 2012). In this book, Crawford shared his experiences as a journalist who accompanied the rebel army as they captured the Green Square, Tripoli. Combining personal accounts of Libyans during the revolution, Crawford's book presented gripping detail not only about victory but also about the chaos that has since enveloped Libya.

Additional Resources

Adler-Nissen, Rebecca, and Vincent Pouliot. "Power in Practice: Negotiating the International Intervention in Libya" in *European Journal of International Relations*, Vol. 20, No. 4 (2014), 889–911.

Akande, Dapo. "The Effect of Security Council Resolutions and Domestic Proceedings on State Obligations to Cooperate with the ICC" in *Journal of International Criminal Justice*, Vol. 10, No. 2 (2012), 299–324.

Akpeninor, James Ohwofasa. *Giant in the Sun: Echoes of Looming Revolution?* Bloomington, IN: Author House, 2012.

Anderson, Lisa. "Nineteenth-Century Reform in Ottoman Libya" in *International Journal of Middle East Studies*, Vol. 16, No. 3 (August 1984), 325–348.

Applebaum, Anne. "Every Revolution Is Different" in *Slate Magazine*, 2011, accessed September 14, 2018, at http://www.slate.com/articles /news_and_politics/foreigners/2011/02/every_revolution_is_dif ferent.html

BBC. "Control and Crucifixions: Life in Libya under IS" in *BBC News*, 2016, accessed September 14, 2018, at https://www.bbc.com/news /world-middle-east-35325072

Bearman, Jonathan. *Qadhafi's Libya*. London: Zed Books, 1986.

Benotman, Noman. "An Open Letter to Osama bin Laden" in *Foreign Policy*, 2010, accessed September 14, 2018, at https://foreignpolicy .com/2010/09/10/an-open-letter-to-osama-bin-laden/

Blanchard, Christopher M. *Libya: Transition and U.S. Policy*. New York: Congressional Research Service, 2018.

Bloxham, Donald, and A. Dirk Moses. *The Oxford Handbook of Genocide Studies*. Oxford: Oxford University Press, 2010.

Bodansky, Yossef. *Target America & the West: Terrorism Today*. New York: S.P.I. Books, 1993.

Brett, M., and E. Fentress. *The Berbers*. Oxford: Blackwell, 1998.

Burr, J. Millard, and Robert O. Collins. *Darfur: The Long Road to Disaster*. Princeton, NJ: Markus Wiener Publishers, 2006.

Cardoza, Anthony L. *Benito Mussolini: The First Fascist*. London and New York: Pearson Longman, 2006.

Chapin Metz, Hellen. *Libya: A Country Study*. Washington, DC: GPO for the Library of Congress, 1987.

Chorin, Ethan. *Exit the Colonel: The Hidden History of the Libyan Revolution*. New York: Public Affairs, 2012.

Cordesman, Anthony H. *A Tragedy of Arms—Military and Security Developments in the Maghreb*. Westport, CT: Greenwood Publishing Group, 2001.

Crawford, Alex. *Colonel Gaddafi's Hat*. London: Collins, 2012.

Davis, Robert C. *Christian Slaves, Muslim Masters: White Slavery in the Mediterranean, the Barbary Coast, and Italy, 1500–1800*. London: Palgrave Macmillan, 2003.

Diamond, Jared. *Guns, Germs, and Steel*. New York: Norton Press, 1999.

Duggan, Christopher. *The Force of Destiny: A History of Italy since 1796*. New York: Houghton Mifflin, 2007.

Ebner, Michael R., and Geoff Simons. *Ordinary Violence in Mussolini's Italy*. New York: Cambridge University Press, 2011.

Ehret, Christopher. *The Civilizations of Africa*. Charlottesville: University Press of Virginia, 2002.

Fahim, Kareem, Anthony Shadid, and Rick Gladstone. "Violent End to an Era as Qaddafi Dies in Libya" in *New York Times*, 2011, accessed September 14, 2018, at https://www.nytimes.com/2011/10/21/world/africa/qaddafi-is-killed-as-libyan-forces-take-surt.html

Falola, Toyin, Morgan Jason, and Oyeniyi A. Bukola. *Culture and Customs of Libya*. Santa Barbara, CA: ABC-CLIO, 2012.

Gibbon, Edward. *The History of the Decline and Fall of the Roman Empire*. London: John Murray, 1862.

Gumuchian, Marie-Louise. "Gaddafi Nears His End, Exiled Libyan Prince Says" in *Reuters Africa*, 2011, accessed September 14, 2018, at https://af.reuters.com/article/libyaNews/idAFLDE71L28Q20110222

Heywood, Linda, Allison Blakely, and Charles Stith (eds.). *African Americans in U.S. Foreign Policy: From the Era of Frederick Douglass to the Age of Obama*. Chicago: University of Illinois Press, 2015.

Hourani, Albert. *A History of the Arab Peoples*. London: Faber & Faber, 2002.

International Law Commission. *The Obligation to Extradite or Prosecute: Final Report of the International Law Commission*. New York: United Nations, 2014.

International Legal Assistance Consortium. Report of the Independent Civil Society Fact-Finding Mission to Libya, 2012, accessed September 14, 2018, at https://reliefweb.int/sites/reliefweb.int/files /resources/Full%20Report_481.pdf

Islamic Revival. "Was Britain behind Gaddafi's Coup in 1969?" in *Khilafah Magazine*, 2011, accessed on September 14, 2018, at http:// islamicsystem.blogspot.com/2011/02/was-britain-behind-gadaffis -coup-in.html

Mann, Michael. *The Dark Side of Democracy: Explaining Ethnic Cleansing* (2nd ed.). Cambridge: Cambridge University Press, 2006.

Metz, Helen Chapin. *Libya: A Country Study—Education*. Washington, DC: Library of Congress, 1987.

Morayef, Heba. *Truth and Justice Can't Wait—Human Rights Developments in Libya amid Institutional Obstacles*. New York: Human Rights Watch, 2009.

Naylor, Phillip Chiviges. *North Africa: A History from Antiquity to the Present*. Austin: University of Texas Press, 2009.

Nelson, Harold D., and Richard F. Nyrop. *Libya: A Country Study*. Library of Congress Country Studies. Washington, DC: United States Government Printing Office, 1987.

Oliver, Roland. *The African Experience: From Olduvai Gorge to the 21st Century* (Series: History of Civilization). London: Phoenix Press, 1999.

Pack, Jason (ed.). *The 2011 Libyan Uprisings and the Struggle for the Post-Qadhafi Future*. London: Palgrave Macmillan, 2013.

Pappe, Ilan. *The Modern Middle East*. Abingdon, UK: Routledge, 2005.

Polidori, R., A. Di Vita, G. Di Vita-Evrard, and L. Bacchielli. *Libya: The Lost Cities of the Roman Empire*. Cologne: Konemann Verlagsgesellschaft mbH, 1999.

Rabinovich, Abraham. *The Yom Kippur War: The Epic Encounter That Transformed the Middle East*. New York: Schocken Books, 2004.

Redford, Donald B. *Egypt, Canaan, and Israel in Ancient Times*. Princeton, NJ: University Press, 1992.

Rogan, Eugene. *The Arabs: A History*. New York: Basic Books, 2012.

Sarti, Roland. *The Ax within: Italian Fascism in Action*. New York: Modern Viewpoints, 1974.

Seale, Patrick. *Abu Nidal: A Gun for Hire*. New York: Hutchinson, 1992.

Smeaton Munro, Ion. *Through Fascism to World Power: A History of the Revolution in Italy*. Manchester, UK: Ayer Publishing, 1971.

Smith, Brent L. *Terrorism in America: Pipe Bombs and Pipe Dreams.* New York: SUNY Press, 1994.

Stegemann, Bernd, and Detlef Vogel. *Germany and the Second World War: The Mediterranean, South-East Europe, and North Africa, 1939–1941.* Oxford: Oxford University Press, 1995.

St. John, Ronald Bruce. *Libya—Continuity and Change.* New York: Routledge, 2011.

Stokke, Hugo, Astri Suhrke, and Arne Tostensen. *Human Rights in Developing Countries: Yearbook 1997.* The Hague: Kluwer International, 1997.

Taylor, Blaine. *Fascist Eagle: Italy's Air Marshal Italo Balbo.* Missoula, MT: Pictorial Histories Publishing Company, 1996.

Uhlig, Siegbert, Maria Bulakh, Denis Nosnitsin, and Thomas Rave. *Proceedings of the XVth International Conference of Ethiopian Studies.* Wiesbaden: Harrassowitz Verlag, 2006.

Wehrey, Frederic. "When the Islamic State Came to Libya" in *The Atlantic,* 2018, accessed on September 14, 2018, at https://www.theatlantic.com/international/archive/2018/02/isis-libya-hiftar-al-qaeda-syria/552419/

Whittaker, David J. *The Terrorism Reader.* New York: Routledge, 2012.

Wright, John L. *Nations of the Modern World: Libya.* London: Ernest Benn, 1969.

Index

Note: Italicized page numbers indicate illustrations; page numbers followed by *t* indicate tables.

About the Author

BUKOLA A. OYENIYI, a Fellow of the New Europe College, is a social historian of Africa. He holds a doctorate degree from Universiteit Leiden, the Netherlands, and teaches African history at Missouri State University, Springfield. Dr. Oyeniyi has authored a number of books, contributed chapters to edited volumes, and published articles in peer-reviewed journals. Samples of his published works include *Dress in the Making of African Identity: A Social and Cultural History of the Yoruba People* (Cambria Press, 2015); *Nigeria: Africa in Focus* (coauthored with Toyin Falola) (ABC-CLIO, 2015), and *Culture and Customs of Libya* (coauthored with Toyin Falola and Jason Morgan) (Greenwood, 2012).

Sample journal essays include "'Leave No One to Tell the Tales': The Role of Pain and Recollection in Post-Conflict Reconciliation in Africa" in *African Peacebuilding Network, Social Science Research Council, Working Paper* No. 10, 2017; "One Voice, Multiple Tongues: Dialoguing with Boko Haram," *Democracy and Security* Vol. 10, No. 1, 2014; "Poverty Alleviation and Empowerment of Small-Scale Industries in Nigeria: The Case of Tie and Dye Makers Association," *African Journal of History and Culture*, Vol. 5. No. 6, 2013; "The Greed-Grievance Debate and the Ife-Modakeke Conflicts," *Social History*, Vol. 35, No. 3, August 2010; and "Dress in Nigeria's Nationalist Discourse," *Identity, Culture and Politics: An Afro-Asian Dialogue*, Vol. 12, No. 1, July 2011.

Titles in the Greenwood Histories of the Modern Nations
Frank W. Thackeray and John E. Findling, Series Editors

The History of Sweden
Byron J. Nordstrom

The History of Syria
John A. Shoup

The History of Thailand
Patit Paban Mishra

The History of Turkey, Second
Edition
Douglas A. Howard

The History of Ukraine
Paul Kubicek

The History of Venezuela, Second
Edition
H. Micheal Tarver

The History of Vietnam
Justin Corfield